How to
Find Heaven

How to Find Heaven:

Your Guide to the Afterlife

by THERESA CHEUNG

SIMON &
SCHUSTER

London · New York · Sydney · Toronto · New Delhi

A CBS COMPANY

First published in Great Britain by Simon & Schuster UK Ltd, 2015
A CBS COMPANY

1 3 5 7 9 10 8 6 4 2

Simon & Schuster UK Ltd
1st Floor
222 Gray's Inn Road
London WC1X 8HB

www.simonandschuster.co.uk

Simon & Schuster Australia,
Sydney

Simon & Schuster India,
New Delhi

A CIP catalogue record for this book is available from the British Library

Paperback ISBN: 978-1-4711-4284-0
eBook ISBN: 978-1-4711-4285-7

Typeset in the UK by Hewer Text UK Ltd, Edinburgh
Printed in the UK by CPI Group (UK) Ltd, Croydon CR0 4YY

Contents

Acknowledgements   vii

INTRODUCTION: Where is heaven?   1

CHAPTER 1: Seeker of the truth   11

CHAPTER 2: Select a route   52

CHAPTER 3: Taking the road less travelled   124

CHAPTER 4: Fast track to heaven   208

CHAPTER 5: Lighting the way   275

AFTERWORD: You have reached your destination!   321

Calling all truth-seekers   323
Final word   325

Acknowledgements

I had a burning desire to write *How to Find Heaven*, but having a burning desire to write does not necessarily mean you will find a publisher willing to support and work with you, especially in today's unforgiving economic climate. I am incredibly grateful, therefore, to my wonderful editor, Kerri Sharp, for her belief and trust in me, and to my lovely agent, Clare Hulton, for her support. I would also like to express my appreciation to everyone at Simon & Schuster involved in making this book happen. Every book I write feels like a little miracle and, when you consider all the challenges and potential pitfalls along the way from idea stage to finished product available in bookstores and online, it really is.

As always, heartfelt thanks to all the sensitive, inspiring people who contributed their fascinating stories to this book. I want you to know you are making a very real difference by sharing your words and your spirits, and are bringing comfort and hope or a sense of possibility to those who read them and need to hear what you have to say. I would also like to thank anyone who has ever got in touch with me over the years via my angeltalk710@aol.com email and/or via my website www.theresacheung.com, or, more recently, through my Facebook and Twitter pages. You may not know it but you are a constant source of insight, inspiration and encouragement to me as we all work together to spread the life-changing message that heaven is real.

My sincerest gratitude goes to Kim Nash, a remarkable lady with a passion for books www.kimthebookworm.co.uk and, as good fortune would have it, the afterlife. Kim's insight, hard work, brilliance and support on my social media sites is changing and inspiring the lives of my readers every day. Kim, you are a star. Thank you.

And finally, a massive thank you to loved ones, family and friends for their patience, understanding and love as I went into self-imposed exile to complete this book. I focused my energy so intensely on the writing that I was probably really difficult to reach and communicate with on many occasions and I do hope you will understand and forgive me . . . and read the book!

Surely it is not wrong for us to think and talk about heaven. I like to find out all I can about it. I expect to live there through all eternity. If I were going to dwell in any place in this country, if I were going to make it my home, I would inquire about its climate, about the neighbours I would have – about everything, in fact, that I could learn concerning it. If soon you were going to emigrate, that is the way you would feel. Well, we are all going to emigrate in a very little while. We are going to spend eternity in another world . . . Is it not natural that we should look and listen and try to find out who is already there and what is the route to take?

Dwight L. Moody

You grow to heaven. You don't go to heaven.

Edgar Cayce

There is nothing impossible to him who will try.

Alexander the Great

Where is heaven?

*Our lives begin to end the day we become silent about things
that matter.*

Martin Luther King

- You are a spiritual being having a human experience, not a
  human being having a spiritual experience.

- Heaven is a reality and can be found right here, right now,
  on earth as well as in the next life.

I'm not asking you to agree with these two statements. I
would just like you to ponder them as you read the pages that
follow. Then at the end of the book feel free to get in touch
and let me know if what you have read has compelled you to
agree or disagree. I would love to hear from you, as reading
your reactions to what I say, as well as your insights, stories
and experiences, is what I enjoy most about being a spiritual

writer. (Details about how to contact me if you feel inspired can be found on page 321.)

I truly believe that the more people like us think and talk about heaven, the more real and the closer to earth it becomes. In the decades I have been writing about heaven my aim has always been to encourage more talk about what really matters in life. To keep the debate about the big questions – Why are we here? Is there an afterlife? What is the meaning of my life? Where is heaven? How can I find it? – alive and current and, most important of all, relevant to the world as it is today, *not* as it was two thousand years ago.

I'm not asking you to agree with me; all I am asking is that you open your mind to the very real possibility that the afterlife exists – and can be found not just 'out there' in some higher realm of existence, but also all around and within you at any moment. My effort is to help clear away the doubts, fears and other rubbish that can pollute your heart and close your mind to an eternal realm of infinite possibilities. If I can provide you with a clean slate my work is done, because I know that an uncluttered and curious mind has a magic and power all of its own. The seed has been sown. The spirit within you has awakened and will immediately seek out and attract to you what is mysterious, magical and not of this world. Exciting times lie ahead . . .

About this book

According to recent polls, as many as two-thirds of us believe in the promise of heaven, or an afterlife. But what exactly is heaven and how can you find it? Why, in an increasingly secular world with religion steadily on the decline, is belief in heaven increasing? Is there proof that heaven exists? Is it possible to talk to departed loved ones? In short, is it possible to find heaven on earth?

In this book my aim is to answer as many of these questions as possible and, by so doing, bring the age-old search for the meaning of life bang up to date. Drawing on all the knowledge and experience I've gained over the last thirty years researching and writing extensively about religion, spirituality and the para-normal, I will share what I have discovered about recognising the presence of heaven and departed loved ones in everyday life.

As I worked on this project I was fully, deeply aware of the conflicted world we live in today. You just need to read newspapers or go online to be reminded constantly of the intolerable and often senseless suffering, violence, poverty, injustice, cruelty and despair that seem to be everywhere. Some of this suffering is down to natural disasters or accidents, but an ever-increasing number are caused by our inability to relate to each other in a humane way, most especially when there are religious, economic or political differences.

Many times in my writing career I've banged my head and my keyboard in frustration at the sorry state of the world. Many times I've felt despondent and wondered if I am fighting a losing battle. A sense of futility would overcome me. How, for example, can you tell the family of a murdered loved one that heaven exists? How can you tell an innocent child who has lost everyone they love and everything they know to a brutal war they don't understand that there is beauty, wisdom and magic in the world? How can you convince people who have suffered unimaginable cruelty, injustice, pain and loss that love is stronger than death and is all that really matters in this life and the next?

How indeed.

And who am I to be writing a book like this? Am I truly the right person to put forward the case for heaven when I clearly see how the harsh injustices of life point to the contrary?

Often – sometimes because life dealt me or those I care about a blow and sometimes for no reason at all – I've lost conviction and suffered incredible and extreme doubt. It even happened again when I was working on my first draft of this book.

My closest and oldest friend – a lovely person with the kindest and most honest heart – had devoted the last ten years of her life to starting her own photography business, alongside caring for her sick mother and her family. In the male-dominated photography world her task was not easy, and she encountered many frustrations in her struggle to build up a client base, but finally in the last few years exciting jobs and contracts were coming her way. And then one day she came back from a walk in the park with her children to find that thieves had broken into her house and stolen all her electronic and photographic equipment. The shock and sense of violation that someone had been in her home – even her children's rooms – was unbearable to her. She also knew that she would not be able to fulfil work waiting to be delivered, clients would be disappointed; and, in her line of work where there is so much competition, that was a disaster. In less than an hour these thieves had destroyed years of honest hard work. Where is the justice in that?

I spoke to my friend soon after the burglary and her normally strong, warm voice sounded weak and thin. I instinctively knew that if ever there was a moment for me to offer spiritual support now was it, and I tried to tell her that things happen for a reason and she should feel sorry for the people who had committed the crime and so on, but my words felt hollow. Even I didn't believe them at the time. I was angry and upset for her, so I stopped talking about there being a purpose and offered her my practical support and help instead.

That was not an isolated incident. Throughout my life, on the numerous occasions when I've faced horrific setbacks or lost someone I love, I've felt confused and angry and despairing. These should have been the moments when my belief in spirit should have given me the greatest strength, but it didn't. Many times I've sincerely doubted that heaven exists. Many times I've looked up to the skies and seen only darkness and emptiness, and not light or possibility. I truly admire people who have rock-solid faith during times of hardship and injustice – but will openly admit I am not one of them. I was named after an incredible woman – Mother Teresa – but I lack her courage, her humility, her selflessness and her deep faith. I have been a coward frequently in my life. I often get puffed up in my own self-importance. I try not to be selfish but I know I am, and my natural instinct is to doubt – not just the existence of heaven, but even myself and my credentials to talk and write about heaven. Mother Teresa I most certainly am not!

So you see, writing this book has been an almighty struggle – and I've been plagued with self-doubt. But rightly so, as I believe it to be perhaps the most important and honest spiritual book

I've ever written – and if you are familiar with me as an author, you will know that I've written a fair few books and been honest in all of them. Originally, *How to Find Heaven* was intended to be a *How to . . .* companion volume to *How to See Your Angels*, where I would answer questions about the afterlife and offer practical and straightforward advice on how to see the spirits of departed loved ones and communicate with them, but it turned into far more than that. Writing it became a truly cathartic experience and in the process I found what I believe to be my own path to heaven. It is my sincere hope that as you read it, you will be inspired to rediscover the true meaning of your life.

That's why I decided to start the book with my own spiritual journey and chapter 1 is personal. I want you to get to know who I am. I want you to see that I'm not a saint or a mystic or a psychic – contrary to what you may read about me in the press. I am an ordinary woman with flaws and many, many of them. I will discuss some of the roads to heaven I've travelled down in my life, and how each one frustrated and disappointed me in some way until I had one of those 'aha' moments when all the scattered pieces of my life suddenly formed a bigger picture.

Chapter 2 will take you on a guided tour of some very well-travelled routes to heaven, bliss, salvation, the afterlife, spirit or whatever word you want to use. I will discuss the world's major religions – Christianity, Buddhism, Hinduism, Islam, Judaism among others – and the directives they give about finding heaven. I'll also take a look at lesser-known paths, such as scientology and even the atheist movement. You'll see that each religion or movement presents convincing, powerful and often profound routes to fulfilment, and you may find that you want to travel down one of these roads. However, there are also strong arguments against following any group or movement and I will offer those too so you can see both sides – and decide for yourself.

Chapter 3 moves beyond religion and takes you down a road that is less travelled – and often travelled alone rather than in a group. It discusses the current increase in belief in the world of spirit and an individual relationship with the divine, and how modern science, the internet and religious extremism and disillusionment have all contributed to this phenomenon. It also answers in clear and simple language the most frequently asked questions about the afterlife, and offers direct 'proof' of the existence of heaven with true accounts of lives transformed by glimpses of heaven on earth.

Chapters 4 and 5 show that heaven isn't just 'out there'; it can also be discovered within. Indeed, the journey within is the fastest route to heaven on earth and this section will help you discover heaven from the inside out. There will also be advice on spiritual awakening, or knowing when the time is right for you to find your own path to heaven, as well as how to actually see, hear or sense spirit and departed loved ones yourself. The book concludes with some divine insights that you can dip into anytime you need help, guidance, healing and reassurance that heaven is real and you can find your unique path to it, right here, right now.

Throughout, my aim is to present the search for bliss like the search for hidden treasure – easier to discover if you have the right map or route guidance. However, these directions will not be written in stone and they will not point to one specific path or route. That would be taking away your freedom of choice and your ability to think for yourself and grow spiritually.

In other words, what you read will not be instructions or commandments but rather suggestions or guidelines to help you find your own way to heaven. I will always encourage you to look deep within, listen to your heart and trust it to find your path. This book is about many things but above all it is about *you* and your completely unique spiritual journey.

Sprinkled like stardust in the book you'll also find a handful of stories from ordinary people who suddenly had an extraordinary experience they could not explain and which transformed their lives forever. I included them because I didn't want you to make the mistake of thinking that only special, spiritually or psychically gifted people are able to find or see heaven. Their stories will show that anyone, whatever age they are and whatever their background or culture or education, can journey to the other side.

As I repeatedly say in all my books there is nothing special about me. I am an ordinary fortysomething mother of two – my son is sixteen and my daughter fifteen – and although incredible, astonishing things have happened to me in my life and I long for them to continue to happen, as nothing would give me more inspiration – I am not a psychic, a medium, a mystic or a guru. I do know, however, that we are all born with the map to heaven encoded within our heart, but as we grow up we lose our sense of direction and need to rediscover the secret route we once knew but have somehow forgotten along the way.

And finally, please don't feel despondent if you don't think you have ever had anything magical or extraordinary occur in your life. I simply included these stories because I hoped they would encourage you to keep an open mind – because a closed mind, a mind that does not ask 'what if' or what 'could be', will almost certainly block your path to spiritual growth.

A closed mind cannot grow or change. An open mind, on the other hand, is a transformative mind that can cross the bridge between this life and the next, where time does not exist and life does not end in death. An open mind will also help you to see the world around you in a different, more magical way – because when you start to see the world in this way, start to think that anything is possible and nothing is ever what it seems, including yourself, I promise you that heaven will seek you out. You will see signposts put in your path and hear the messages being conveyed to you, just like the people in the stories. You may also start to look back on your life and see how, in hindsight, the hand of heaven has always been there, gently shaping your life in mysterious ways without you even realising it.

Heaven is shaping your life now – as you read this book.

I sincerely hope that anyone who longs for spiritual guidance (with or without religion) will find this book a source of nourishment and inspiration. Think of it as your guide to heaven, pointing the way and providing direction, a reminder of the constant presence of the divine in your life from cradle to beyond the grave. Use it for strength, guidance and encouragement whenever, during periods of darkness and doubt, you feel in need of comfort, hope and love; whenever you long for a sense of closeness with departed loved ones; whenever you need reminding that heaven exists and you can find it anytime you want, right here and right *now*.

And so, if you are ready to open your mind, eyes, ears and hearts so that you can begin the most important journey you will ever take in this life – your journey to heaven – read on . . .

Heaven is not the end – it is only the beginning.
David Brandt Berg

CHAPTER ONE

Seeker of the truth

What you know you can't explain, but you feel it. You've felt it your entire life, that there's something wrong with the world. You don't know what it is, but it's there, like a splinter in your mind, driving you mad.

Morpheus, *The Matrix*

The search for heaven, understanding the meaning and purpose of my life, has always been my driving force. I would not have it any other way. Life without that search would feel utterly meaningless and mundane. I suspect you feel the same way. I know you are a fellow seeker of the truth. How do I know?

I know because you are holding this book in your hand and your spiritual hunger drew you to it because of its title – even if you picked it up in a moment of idle curiosity or because you wanted to find ways to disagree. You were meant to read it, as nothing in our lives is truly random.

Think about how you came across this book. Perhaps your spirit sought it out directly because you have read my books or other books of this nature before? Perhaps you came across it by chance? Did a friend lend it to you? Did it catch your eye in a library, bookstore or waiting room, or did you just find it lying there? I have had so many incredible letters and emails from people all over the world who have told me about the remarkable coincidences that drew them to one of my books and made them feel as if they were meant to read it. But however you came across it, the fact that you are reading it right now tells me that searching for heaven – or, if you don't like using the term heaven, a sense of meaning and magic, or infinite happiness and possibility – is the driving force of your life.

I'm also guessing that, like me, you will have already tried to find your heaven in a number of different ways. Maybe some of these ways gave you more hope than others, or perhaps none gave you hope or reason to trust in something higher at all and you are disillusioned. Either way I know that you, like me, still long to find heaven on earth.

It might help at this stage if I share with you some of the spiritual paths that I've experimented with or been strongly influenced by in my life. I hope that sharing some of my experiences will help you to take a look back on your life and reflect on the motivations for all the life choices you have made. I'm convinced that if you do, you will realise that everything you have ever done – even if there was no obvious spiritual dimension to it – has consciously or unconsciously been for the same simple and obvious reason – you thought it would make you feel happy or fulfilled in some way. In other words, you thought it would bring you closer to a state of bliss, closer to glimpsing the possibility of heaven on earth.

Wasted

As I approach the big Five-O, I often reflect on my life so far and can't help but smile and think of that famous quote from Oscar Wilde: 'Youth is wasted on the young.' I look at photographs of myself aged sixteen and see an intense, slender and, if I can say so myself, rather lovely, earnest-looking young girl. But then I go back in time and place myself in the body and mind of that young girl, and she is deeply unhappy and full of self-loathing for her body. She has one obsessive thought running through her mind over and over again: I need to be slimmer. If I am slimmer, I will feel happier, cleaner, purer – closer to spirit, closer to heaven.

Anorexia is a body-, mind- and spirit-crushing condition. Many people think it's about conforming to the waif-like model ideal circulated in the media. For me, it wasn't just about social expectations and I can see in hindsight that there were other motivations. The first was about taking control. I guess at the time there were a lot of things going on in my life – my mother's depression and then cancer diagnosis, my father's disability and mildly autistic traits, our unconventional, poverty-stricken lifestyle as a family of travelling spiritualists, to name just a few – that felt out of my control. My body was, however, something I could control, so control it I did and to an obsessive degree.

The second reason was my complete lack of self-confidence. I had no idea who I was or who I wanted to be. I did believe in a world of spirit because that is what I had been taught to believe from as young as I can remember, but I also felt a complete disappointment as I'd never had any direct proof of heaven myself. Talk of seeing spirits was a totally natural thing in a family like mine but I clearly had not inherited the gift. I had inherited a curious mind and a passion for learning about the paranormal but I couldn't actually see, hear or sense spirit. I longed to see dead people like the little boy in the movie *The Sixth Sense*, or to have the power to read minds, but I saw nothing – absolutely nothing. I knew a lot about the paranormal but didn't experience it.

In other words, I could talk the talk but I couldn't walk the walk. Deep down, this made me feel like a failure. I was born into a family of spiritualists but, without inheriting the sight, what was my identity? Who was I? I was a spiritualist who couldn't see spirit.

I probably wasn't fully aware of it at the time but there may have been a spiritual dimension to my eating disorder. Feelings of disconnection from my body also triggered my condition. I wanted to feel free, to become so light I could float rather than walk. It's hard to explain but my body felt heavy and dirty, as if flesh weighed me down. I wanted to feel pure and cleansed and airborne – like spirit. Fasting is a common practice in many religions and if you have ever gone on a fast you will know that for brief periods of time abstinence from food can make you feel cleansed, energised and renewed. Instead of food, I devoured books about great saints and mystics who had fasted for forty days and forty nights (impossible and very unhealthy) and recklessly thought I had to follow suit. I can see now that I was in some way searching for heaven by trying to become as close to resembling spirit as possible. I was misguided and foolhardly but, at the time, thought I was on the right path. It is only now I can see that I was on a path to nowhere but an unhappy life or an early grave.

Mercifully, I was able to pull through my eating disorder without being admitted to hospital. Heaven intervened. However, because my 'healing' wasn't dramatic but, as you will see below, could also be explained psychologically or as a co-incidence, I didn't recognise it for the miracle that it was at the time. Only now, as I reflect on a significant turning point in my young life, when darkness turned to light, can I see that divine forces were at work.

I remember the day clearly when anorexia began to lose its control over me. It was in the middle of summer and I woke with foul pains in my head. For five long days I had abstained from any food or drink apart from apples and black coffee. The destructive and overwhelming voice of anorexia switched on the moment I opened my eyes, as it had done relentlessly for the previous three years. Anorexia would tell me to do something and I would have to listen. It didn't matter what it was that I had to do, anorexia was going to provide the solution – or so I thought. This particular morning it told me to keep going with my apples and black coffee routine, but to no longer eat the skins of the apples.

Painfully, I pushed myself into a sitting position and swung my legs over the side of the bed. My hip bones felt sharp and tight and this comforted me. I noticed immediately that for some inexplicable reason the curtains were not drawn and the window was wide open. This was highly unusual as I suffered from hay fever and always closed my windows and curtains at night and often during the day – the obsessive-compulsive voice in my head would never let me forget to do that. I wondered if my mother had perhaps come in during the night and opened the window, but then I remembered that she was away, staying with friends. It was just me in the house.

Wearily, I dragged myself towards the window to shut it and pull the curtains across. Sunlight hit my eyes directly and I squinted. I tried to draw the curtains but just couldn't! My arms would not move. It was like someone stronger than me was standing in front of me and pinning my arms to the sides of my body, gently but firmly. I relaxed, took a deep breath and tried again. The same thing happened. I could not move my arms. I tried to go back to my bed but my feet wouldn't move either. I could not move an inch. It felt like something was forcing me to stand still and face the sunlight.

Time stood still, so I am not sure how long I was frozen to the spot but am guessing around twenty minutes to half an hour. For the first ten minutes I struggled a lot, but then when I realised this was useless I stopped fighting and just stood there, letting the sunshine pour itself all over me. Then, as the warmth wrapped itself around my body, a sudden, sharp clarity came to me. I realised in that moment that if I continued my extreme behaviour anorexia would eventually kill me. I didn't want to die and the instant I made the decision to live I was able to move again. My arms were no longer trapped and my feet could move. Something had let me go!

My recovery was gradual but steady from that day onwards. Standing there in the sunlight I had chosen life and not death. It took a while, but eventually mealtimes were no longer a battleground. My mum said that she thought a spirit had drawn my curtains back, opened my window and wrapped its arms around me, but although I wanted to believe it, I couldn't quite. My doubting mind told me that I had simply forgotten to draw the curtains the night before and that food deprivation had made me too weak to lift my arms. My anxiety and fear told me that I wasn't special or psychic enough for something miraculous like that to happen to me.

However, even though doubt and lack of self-belief still plagued me, something happened that day to clear my mind. There wasn't room for the voice of anorexia in my head any more. I started taking better care of myself and gave myself permission to eat. There was a huge amount of work to do in terms of building my self-awareness and self-esteem, but in hindsight I see that day as the moment my spiritual journey began in earnest. My mum, who saw spirits and spoke to spirits all her life, told me that when I was ready to open my heart and my life to heaven it would appear. I doubted her. I wanted to believe her so much but I doubted her.

Born again

With my insatiable hunger for spiritual understanding it is hardly surprising that as I approached my twenties I was drawn to religion. The natural choice for me was Christianity, as it is what I had been taught at school. I was convinced I would find all the answers I needed there. My spiritualist family was not Christian and I was not baptised, but this did not bother me in the slightest. Perhaps this was my destiny and the reason I had not inherited the gift of seeing spirits like my mother and grandmother had? Perhaps this was where I truly belonged? Perhaps Christ was calling me? To have a faith so strong, proof was not needed. Perhaps this was my destiny.

Also, the Church can be wonderfully welcoming to any that come with a humble and earnest desire to learn and join in. Indeed, feeling a bit of an outsider in my own family, and in life generally, suddenly I belonged somewhere. My peer group tended to be interested in dating, parties, pop music and fashion but none of that had any appeal to me at all. I was always hunting for something deeper. I wanted to learn and grow spiritually, and to live a life that had meaning, deep, spiritual meaning.

For two years I devoured every book I could on Christianity, went to church religiously (forgive the pun) and was baptised and confirmed. I devoted hours of my time to charity work and good causes. I attended classes and went on a week's retreat of complete silence. That was a sensational experience. To escape the incessant and unnecessary chatter that goes on and be able to focus only on what is deep and meaningful in beautiful silence is pure bliss.

The Christian message of a loving God sacrificing his only son to wash away our sins so we could start a new life in Christ was beautiful and simple but powerful, and made complete sense to me. The people I met were warm and supportive; I felt like I belonged to a family at last, so for a while I was convinced this was my answer – the eternal answer. I even had vague fantasies about becoming the first female priest for the Church of England or joining a nunnery.

Eternity may have been a bit of an ambitious prediction – I was a committed Christian for just two years. And the reason for my fall from grace was further study. When I was nineteen, to the astonishment and shock of everyone, including myself, I was offered a place at King's College, Cambridge to read Theology and English. To say it was a surprise is an understatement, as I left school at sixteen with very poor grades.

To this day I don't know what possessed me to apply to Cambridge University of all places. I was born into poverty and nobody in my family had any academic aspirations for me. I had been in the bottom sets for most subjects at school and hated everything about the place. Teachers had clearly written me off. However, when I started to study for my A levels – religious studies, English and history – by myself at home (combining it with paid work in a care home) I discovered a thirst for knowledge that I did not realise I had, and this evidentially showed in the top grades I managed to achieve. In a moment of recklessness I applied to Cambridge, believing that the only realistic chance I stood of being accepted was at my other choice universities. Incredibly, it was only Cambridge that offered me an interview. All the other universities rejected me because home study was extremely unconventional at the time and gathering proper academic references virtually impossible. In the end, one of my referees was my mother's therapist! But it didn't seem to faze Cambridge, as they looked at who I was, invited me for an interview and must have liked what they heard because they offered me an unconditional place.

To be offered a place at Cambridge having come from an underprivileged background like mine was mind-blowing. To this day I am eternally grateful for their willingness to take a risk and give an outsider like me, someone who had dropped out of the school system, a chance to prove myself. I went to Cambridge fired up with feelings of gratitude and excitement and eager to learn everything!

It is often said that the more you learn the more you realise how little you actually know, and this was certainly true of my time at Cambridge. And the first casualty of my increasing knowledge base was my Christian faith. Instead of feeling like the answer to all my questions, or the destination of my search for heaven, my Christian belief began to feel restrictive.

You see, at Cambridge I also studied in great depth the other major religions of the world – Buddhism, Hinduism, Judaism, Islam and so on – and, as I researched them, I found profundity and power in each. The idea of committing myself exclusively to one religion seemed limiting. I can understand, and I certainly cannot condemn, anyone who commits themselves to one religion as long as that faith brings them happiness and encourages them to be respectful and kind to others. However, for me personally, I found that as I studied each religion I lost myself in the profound beauty of that particular faith. I believed and saw glimpses of heaven in each one. I could see myself following the rules, and beliefs, of all. I saw them all as paths to bliss and therefore could not commit myself exclusively to one faith in particular.

So, Christianity wasn't my calling after all . . .

Eternal student

Liberated from adherence to one religion, I went full circle in my spiritual journey and returned to the path my mother had set me on as I was growing up. She always told me that religion and spirituality were not one and the same. Although religion could be a valid and worthy path to heaven, it was not the only path to heaven and certainly not an essential requirement for finding heaven. In other words, you do not need to be religious to be spiritual.

At its best, religion is designed to be a source of spiritual comfort and moral guidance. It can also provide a caring family of like-minded people who help others in need. We all need to feel we belong and at times the power of a group speaks louder than the power of an individual. But religion can also be the cause of war, discrimination, suffering and pain – all of which are a world away from spiritual tenets of compassion, love, comfort and kindness.

Religion is defined by teaching and tradition. Spirituality, on the other hand, emanates from an inner search, the quest to find your own truth. While religion tends to have an 'us' and 'them' mentality, spirituality sees all people as equal. We are all spiritual beings whose purpose is to discover our own heaven. From my study of religion, it was obvious to me that Jesus wasn't a Christian and Buddha wasn't a Buddhist. These great and inspiring men didn't set out to create a religion; they just encouraged others to look deep within themselves for answers. They saw that eternal truth is always there, but often hidden because our minds are polluted by prejudice, fear, guilt, doubt.

I still recall this eureka moment of understanding, and it had strong echoes of my earlier experience at the window when I saw the light and my eating disorder lost its control over me. I was gathering notes for an essay and poring over the Old Testament book of Job, wondering why on earth a loving God would inflict such pain on someone who had done nothing but have complete trust and faith. The library was very dark and musty but then a shaft of light came in from the window and hit me square between the eyes. For a moment I was dazzled and couldn't see my work, so I closed my eyes.

I can't explain it but when I opened my eyes I felt completely energised, as if I had swallowed a piece of heaven. I realised in that moment that I wouldn't find eternity in old books or ancient traditions or even religions. Heaven wasn't something that was out there, to be witnessed only after death. Heaven was right here. Heaven was the spirit within me and all around me. It was not so much a place but a system of energies that sustains and nourishes us in both this life and the next.

After that lightbulb moment I became, in my typically eager fashion, an obsessive seeker of spiritual truth and awakening. First, I strived to connect with my higher self through dream interpretation and meditation. Then I explored every area of spiritual and esoteric growth that I could discover. I studied the dreaming mind in depth, hunting for hidden messages and clues to greater self-awareness and connection to spirit. As I researched I discovered that when we dream we melt into a land of symbolism, which is the hidden language of spirit. Not only can dreams give us clues to issues in our waking lives, but they are also a place where past, present and future collide and where we can catch a glimpse of deceased family members. Dream interpretation can help bring the workings of heaven into our consciousness.

Meditation is a wonderful tool that can help us to become aware of the endless possibilities heaven or spirit can bring, but this was an area of spiritual development at which I failed woefully. I found it impossible to meditate, unable to clear my mind and frequently falling asleep.

I had more success with my study of the esoteric arts. Blessed with a photographic memory, I mastered the basics of astrology, tarot, numerology, I Ching and colour therapy, and even found I could earn a bit of money doing private and public readings. I also attended countless séances and psychic development courses, hoping that finally the veil between this life and the next would be lifted and I would actually see spirit at long last.

Although I may have had sudden bursts of inspiration now and again which filled me with a sense of awe – and delving into the psychic arts was exciting and, dare I say it, fun – to be honest I didn't really make as much progress as I would have liked. It seemed that the more knowledge I gathered and the harder I tried to find heaven, the less I saw. It was so frustrating. I longed for heaven so much. I had an encyclopaedic knowledge of matters spiritual, but no personal proof to point me in the right direction and give me the absolute conviction I craved.

And then my mother died . . . and heaven seemed further away than ever before. If ever there was a time for spirit to reveal itself to me, surely that had to be the moment? Surely my mum, who believed so passionately in life after death, would find a way to reach out to me? I expected a sign from her. I longed for a sign from her – but I didn't get one.

All I got was silence.

Black hole

The more I begged, the more I looked for signs, the more I pleaded, the louder the silence became. And the louder the silence, the more life started to spin around me. Strange impulses I didn't understand began to take over. I would find myself laughing when people cried and crying when they laughed. I would forget what day or even month it was, or even on one occasion where I lived. Each day became harder and harder to navigate, as bit by bit my life just stopped making sense.

Again with the benefit of hindsight what I was experiencing was the acute pain and confusion of grief, but I didn't accept that at the time. I truly thought I should have been able to cope better than most with the death of a loved one because of my belief in life after death. However, my belief didn't seem to offer any comfort at all. Often, I would find myself overcome with a desperate need to see or touch something that had belonged to my mum, like her spectacles or her favourite pen. I was terrified that I might forget what she looked like, so I carried a picture of her everywhere and would obsessively check it was still in my pocket or purse every few minutes. I needed to know that she had been real. I would stare at the few precious possessions I had left of her and grief would rip my heart apart.

Like a hammer hitting a bruise, the fact that I would never see or touch her again in this life was excruciatingly painful. I was never going to be able to talk to her or hear her cry or laugh again. My spiritualist friends told me that she was alive in spirit, but I didn't want to hear about spirit. I wanted to hear about the here and right now. I was going to have to carry on without her and I didn't know how. I would cry for hours at a time, and then when I was exhausted and thought there were no more tears left, the pain and tears would hit me again. And all the while in my heart I would still beg for some sign from my mother to ease my suffering. There was some weird logic to it all. It was almost as if the more I suffered and the more I cried, the more I felt I deserved a sign. Surely my mum would take pity on me? All I wanted was something small to reassure me that she was close by and watching over me from the other side. All I got was quiet and emptiness. All I heard was the beating of my own heart.

Living in a state of grief, confusion, longing and exhaustion eventually took its toll and, before I could do anything to stop it, full-blown depression took over. Depression, for those who have not experienced it, is like your heart and your mind are breaking and all the goodness has been sucked out of you. For me, it was like living in a fog all the time – there was no colour in the world around me. Even when I was with people I felt alone. I lost my ability to connect with any of the things that used to make me feel good about myself and life. I was stuck in a meaningless, dark void or pit of despair. My face began to tell the story of my inner world. I would look in the mirror and see a corpse, because I could not muster the energy to move any facial muscles. My eyes were dead, like pools of vacant darkness. I would wonder how I existed from day to day. So, as well as grieving the death of my mother, I now grieved the loss of someone else close to me – myself.

In short, depression is like a thief: it takes everything away from you that has meaning and leaves only sadness and emptiness in its place. It is a black hole that sucks up all your life force so there is nothing left. I was the living dead and felt like my spirit was rotting away. I didn't have any joy, energy or desire, and sometimes when I woke up in the morning I wished I'd died in my sleep. I did somehow carry on with my work as a teacher and writer, as the routine probably kept me from losing it altogether, and when I was with people I hid my pain as best I could. I was a bit like a robot, but there were many times when I could not even face that routine and I would call in sick and spend days on end curled in a ball in my bed.

I stumbled through this excuse for an existence for close to a year. I did want to get better but just couldn't, I didn't know how to, and because I was too ashamed to tell anyone my sense of isolation was extreme.

Lights in the darkness

And then, like the appearance of a rainbow after a storm, I had a visitation from my mother, not in spirit form but in my dreams. Nothing dramatic or sensational happened in my dream. My mother simply came into my room and started tidying it as she used to when I was a teenager. I saw her pick up some discarded clothes from the floor and place them on a chair. I saw her put bags and books away in my cupboard. I tried to call out to my mum but she didn't seem to see me. I noticed that she looked radiant and full of life and so unlike the fragile person cancer had reduced her to in the last year of her life. The dream felt so real that, when I woke up, for a few wonderful minutes I was convinced that I would hear Mum calling me down for a cup of tea like she used to.

Of course, I never heard Mum call my name but I do believe I had felt her spirit reach out to me. It had been more than a dream – I just knew that instinctively. It gave me great comfort and was the first of many reassuring dreams, sudden hunches and coincidences that brought tiny rays of comfort back into my life. I may not have realised it fully then but each one gave me a burst of energy and the strength to do something life-enhancing for myself – even if it was relatively trivial like going for a walk or booking an appointment at the hairdresser's. At the time I put my gradual improvement in mood down to the passage of time, but again I was wrong, as dreams, along with coincidences and sparks of intuition, are often the first and gentlest arrows point-ing the way to heaven. This is because they are the form of communication least likely to cause alarm or concern. I was in such a fragile emotional state I simply would not have been able to cope with anything more intense.

So, to recap, in the years following my mother's death I went from complete despair and doubt that the afterlife existed, to tentative optimism based on dreams and coincidences and other subtle signs that felt like they were heaven-inspired.

The problem was that each experience, as life-enhancing as it was at the time, never seemed quite enough. It did not take long for the voices of doubt in my head to question and second-guess everything again. I was so ready to believe in heaven, so longing to see it in the world around me, but, like a distant peak, the closer I thought I was getting, the further away it seemed to be. Dreams were not nearly enough for me. I wanted to see and hear my mother with my eyes open not closed. I needed some real proof, not something that psychologists could explain away as the product of a grieving mind trying to find relief from the pain of losing someone. So my search for heaven began once again. This time, though, instead of looking in books or in the clouds for answers, I searched for heaven in human form.

Connecting

Somewhere deep down I always knew that the answer to all my questions had something to do with feelings of love, so not surprisingly after my mother's death I looked for a sense of completion in my relationships. I craved connection – the idea of a soulmate to complete me, a spiritual union. Perhaps this was my path to heaven?

My heart was broken many times, and I wish that in my day there had been a self-help book like *The Rules* telling me how not to scare the life out of a man or become the living embodiment of Glenn Close in *Fatal Attraction*! However, when I look back now, as painful and humiliating as every break-up was, each one showed me two very important things. First, that my heart was open and ready to love; and second, that I needed to love myself before I could love someone else fully.

One incident stands out. I was on a tube train one day, trying not to cry and resisting an irrational and dangerous urge to end all my pain and torment by harming myself in some way. The reason I was tearful and anxious was that I had just sunk to a new low both emotionally and physically, when I'd found myself kneeling on the patio and shouting through the letterbox of my boyfriend's flat – or, to be correct, I should say ex-boyfriend.

My boyfriend had been the centre of my world for the last two years. I thought he was my soulmate and we were destined for each other. I didn't think I could live without him and I didn't think he could live without me. But clearly he could live without me because he had walked away from me and towards another woman. I had heard her voice in the flat as I shouted through the letterbox, begging my boyfriend to take me back. I warned you I'd sunk to a new low!

My ex never answered the door that day and it is hardly surprising. When we'd first met, though, it had all been so different. He'd done all the chasing and would not take no for an answer. I was swept off my feet and, as lovers do, we were inseparable, talking for hours about anything and everything. Being in love is intoxicating, almost like a drug, and for a while at least I thought I had found heaven. I was in love and heaven was gazing into his eyes.

It wasn't long before my whole life was wrapped around my boyfriend. My identity merged into his and making him happy was all I cared about. He was my life and I thought this was going to last for life. It lasted around two years, but in those two years I lived my life around my boyfriend's every mood and whim – even if that whim was to be abusive emotionally and physically towards me. When it happened I should have left but I wanted to help him. I wanted to show him that I loved the bad and the good in him. I thought my love for him would transform him. I became attuned to his every need, constantly trying to prove my love to him. I wanted to be everything to him – to make myself needed and indispensable.

This wasn't the first relationship that was defined by my eagerness to please and tendency to put the needs of others before my own. More often than not my identity was defined by what others thought of me. If my friends were bored, it was because I was boring. If my peers didn't have time for me, it was because I didn't matter. If my boyfriend appreciated me, I felt good about myself. If I couldn't match someone's need or mood, I was terrified they wouldn't like me, and not being liked felt like a living death. I was making my life impossible, because the harder I tried to win someone's respect, friendship or love, the more I lost touch with who I was or what my needs were and the deeper my feelings of doubt became.

Rewinding to the tube train and my realisation that I had become little more than a stalker . . . When my boyfriend didn't answer the door I hid for over two hours close to his dustbins, and then followed him and his new girlfriend as he took her to exactly the same place for coffee he'd once taken me. I watched him laugh in the same way he used to laugh when he was with me. I saw him order the same drink. It was the most exquisite torture to watch, but I couldn't tear myself away. Finally, fatigue took over and I had to make my way home. I had given everything to this relationship but it had not been good enough. Being attuned to the needs of others was the only way I knew how to be with people. I was dependent on their approval, but even giving everything I had wasn't enough for them to stay with me. Perhaps I just wasn't worth staying with?

Clearly heaven thought I was worth something because as I sat there on the tube, eyes red and full of tears, I got exactly the advice I needed at exactly the right time. Call it coincidence but for me that day it felt like the voice of heaven. The lady asked me if I was okay. I nodded but she could see I was lying. She said she would hazard a guess, based on her experience as a mother with daughters and granddaughters, that I was crying over a guy. She told me what she always told them and that was not to go crying over someone who isn't going to cry over you. I deserved better than that.

As she spoke those words I felt a subtle ripple of power pass though me, as if my spirit was forcing me to listen and take notice. I had this quiet feeling of comfort and calm, the sense that I was destined to hear this lady's advice, because it suddenly became clear to me in a way it never had before that I was crying over someone who didn't feel the same way about me. I had given the relationship everything but he had not committed himself in the same way. Why was I crying over someone who didn't want to make an effort for me?

Crying wasn't going to change anything. I couldn't change how my ex felt about me, but I could change how I felt about myself. I did deserve better. The spirit within me deserved better. Looking to a relationship to create good feelings about myself was making me lose all sense of purpose and clarity. It was making me forget that I had a piece of heaven inside me, and I needed to connect with that for comfort, inspiration and guidance.

Over the years I had been conditioned to believe that a good or spiritual person is a selfless person, but again in my eagerness to find heaven I had gone overboard. I needed to learn that being good or spiritual is not the same as always putting the needs of others before your own. Of course, we can all bring heaven closer to earth if we reach out to others in times of need and help ease their burdens if we can, but it is also important to honour and respect the spark of divinity that lives inside each one of us. Slowly but gradually I began to remind myself that my life had value. I didn't need the approval of others or their acceptance. I wasn't being selfish if I disagreed or said no from time to time; I was paying attention to what boosted rather than drained me. I was becoming a person of spirit. In short, seeking feelings of comfort and love from the inside out rather than the outside in.

Destiny calling

And when I started to respect myself more and look inside myself for feelings of approval, love and comfort my life changed for the better, especially when it came to affairs of the heart. When I wasn't looking for love it found me. I met the gentlest, kindest, loveliest man, got married and had two children. For a good few years I thought that having a family was as close to finding heaven as was possible on earth.

Becoming a wife and then a mother to two young children is an all-consuming experience. There were moments of pure bliss and contentment, but there were also moments of exhaustion and frustration, just as there are with all wonderful things in life. I loved my family and being with them made me believe heaven was real but – as was so often the case with me – it wasn't enough. I needed more to fulfil me, and I thought that 'more' was to return to work and my lifelong passion – researching and writing about the paranormal.

Curiously, considering how disappointed I was with my apparent inability to see spirits, my fascination for the spirit world didn't disappear as I got older and 'wiser'. Instead, it became stronger and more powerful. If I couldn't find heaven myself then I would find people who did and try to learn from and be inspired by them. So I began to gather together stories from people all over the world who believed they had glimpsed heaven. I researched, interviewed, edited and turned these stories into features and eventually into books.

Over the next ten years I followed my passion and was fortunate enough to be successful at it and have two *Sunday Times* top ten bestsellers. Reading the stories sent to me by people from all around the globe felt like a divine calling. Perhaps it was my destiny to remind people that heaven existed, even if I didn't have any rock-solid proof myself. My calling was to believe without absolute proof – as that is the very definition of faith. This was what I was meant to do, as every letter or email I got seemed to bring a little piece of heaven closer to earth.

And the more I began to understand that often in this life we get what we need and not necessarily what we want, the more heaven began to appear all around me. I even had a number of extraordinary experiences – one of which may well have saved my life. I've told the story many times in my previous books but, in a nutshell, I was at a busy junction intending to turn left but the voice of my mother called to me and told me to turn right. It was incredible. I didn't see my mother but I felt as though she had entered my being, and the hands on my steering wheel turned right against my intention to turn left. I heard her speak to me, I actually heard her. I later discovered that if I'd taken the left turn, I would almost certainly have been involved in a motorway pile-up involving two trucks I had been trailing and the two cars immediately behind them. The crash killed three people – one of whom would have been me had the voice of my mother not saved me that day.

This was a huge turning point for me spiritually and it had taken me more than three long decades of doubt to get there, but I moved forward from that point with renewed faith and optimism. I began to understand that heaven had been revealing itself to me all my life through dreams, coincidences and flashes of intuition, but I didn't recognise them for what they were at the time. The crisis of faith triggered by my mother's death had opened my eyes and renewed my conviction.

So, for the next few years of my life I lost myself in the joys of family and buried myself in my other passion – writing about the world of spirit. I finally thought I had found happiness and, when I gave radio interviews about my books and the spiritual life, I didn't feel a fraud talking about my belief in the world of spirit. But then, about four years ago, I realised that my contentment, my happiness and my belief that heaven exists and can be found on earth, wasn't real at all.

Erosion

It is ironic that it was to be one of my readers who almost completely destroyed me. Ironic because until that point it had been my readers and their inspiring stories and insights that had always strengthened my conviction during moments of doubt. This time, however, one reader decided to launch a systematic campaign against me. I won't go into the details but all I can say is that for close to two years I was hounded by one individual. For the life of me I can't understand why, but obsess he did. And the vitriol, which didn't have any basis in fact or truth, was incredibly hurtful.

At first I simply ignored the negativity, which is what my publishers also advised me to do as they were aware of the situation but were powerless to stop it. But gradually, as weeks turned into months and then years and he wouldn't go away, he began to get to me. I used to love going online to gather information but I became nervous of the internet, fearful he might have said something vile. I used to joyfully open emails or letters from my readers, eager to hear what they had to say so that I could respond with gratitude, but I started to worry that the next email or letter might be from him or someone like him. I stopped wanting to communicate with my readers. It's not that I can't take criticism or frank discussion of what I write about – in fact, as you'll have seen at the beginning of this book, I welcome that. I don't expect or even want everyone to like or agree with what I do. However, when the attacks become unpleasant, and are based on untruths which you know you shouldn't dignify with a reply because it would just fan the flames, the poison can begin to eat away at your spirit.

Hounded for my belief in spirit, I started to lose confidence in myself again. It was a gradual process but slowly everything I had built up began to erode. Perhaps this guy was right and I was deluded or getting the facts wrong? Perhaps I didn't know what I was talking about? Perhaps I shouldn't be talking about anything I wasn't one hundred per cent sure of?

All my doubts came back. I lost my faith, but if it had been real in the first place I would not have lost it. I was struck by panic and fear, and made the decision to stop writing. Emails and letters came in but I left them unanswered. In the process, I gave up a part of myself. Frightened of being hurt again, I decided to hide to protect myself from the pain. And because I made this decision out of fear, fear began to take over my life. I became a virtual recluse – terrified of even opening my door to the postman.

Perhaps I was all wrong? My readers deserved better than someone weak and fearful like me. I was too full of doubt to be a worthy mouthpiece for the existence of heaven on earth. I had been given subtle signs of the afterlife that should have convinced me, but even they were not enough. I started to think that even if I had a full-blown vision of my mum, sooner or later doubt would always come back and I would put it down to hallucination.

What was wrong with me?

I had tried in every way I knew to find heaven. I had not just been a seeker of the truth. I had been an obsessive seeker of the truth and now heaven seemed further away than ever before. If you've ever watched the movie *Amadeus*, I felt a bit like the character Salieri, who had dedicated his life to music but in return for this sacrifice did not receive from God the genius to match his passion. Mozart, however, had none of Salieri's dedication but effortlessly produced music that sounded like the voice of heaven. Salieri's frustration that he cannot produce immortal music like Mozart eventually drives him mad with grief and bitterness. Was I heading the same way? I had given everything to my quest for heaven but in return I was rewarded with only doubts and uncertainty.

I hated myself for not being able to fully believe. I loathed the way I always doubted everything I had experienced myself. Sure, I had many blissful moments in my life when doubt had temporarily disappeared, usually following a remarkable coincidence or a profound dream or a burst of insight, but these moments had always been temporary. The effect would wear off and I would be hungry again for more proof, more evidence that heaven can be found on earth. I didn't want glimpses of heaven – I wanted to actually see it.

My depression returned. It was darker and more terrible than ever before because I could not explain it away with grief over my mother's death or a relationship breaking up, or postnatal depression. This time I was simply depressed. The trolling had just been the trigger. I know it wasn't the cause. I was in a deep, dark pit of despair and there seemed to be no way out.

And then, just as I was about to settle into a life of quiet desperation and disillusionment, everything changed. And, as is so often the case, it changed in the most ordinary but extraordinary way.

Doubtful

Although I was in a very uncertain, dangerous place I tried to hide my anxiety as best I could from my children because I did not want them to believe that adult life was all about tears, doubts and pain. I may not have felt good about myself but I so wanted them to live a life of joy, conviction and passion. So for them I pretended to be content and serene – not easy, but I hope I convinced them. (One day when they perhaps read this book they will discover the truth, but I trust then they will be old enough to understand.)

I was talking to my children about history in connection with some homework they were doing on the Middle Ages. We spoke about what a difficult and often ignorant time it was, and how the prevalent belief back then was that the earth was flat, but thankfully in time people began to question and doubt and this changed everything. I heard myself saying to my children, 'So you see, doubt can be very good. Without doubt we would still be in the dark ages. If people didn't question accepted belief there would be no progress in the world. That's why I want you both to always doubt and question, always be curious, always make your own minds up.'

I went on to tell them something I had read about the terrible tragedy of 9/11 and the Twin Towers. After the first plane had struck the first tower, people in the second tower were naturally shocked and terrified. The instinctive reaction of many was to leave and go home but a large number of them were stopped from doing so by voices of authority instructing them to return calmly to their desks. The perfectly understandable argument was that they should not add to the chaos outside. Nobody, of course, could have predicted that another plane was on its way to strike the second tower. Many people followed the advice given and returned to their desks – and their deaths. Some, however, doubted the wisdom of what they had been told and didn't feel comfortable carrying on as normal when there was tragedy unfolding so close by. These people decided to get out and that decision saved their lives.

What would you have done in that situation? Of course, you have the benefit of hindsight but you need to pretend you don't know what happened to those who went back to their desks. Give yourself a few minutes now to pause and think, because the answer you come up with will give you a great deal of information about yourself – useful, profound information that may just transform your life.

I often wondered what I would have done. Would I have followed my instinct to leave or listened to the advice given by officials and stayed? I like to think that I would have left, but a part of me acknowledges that, on the spur of the moment when I was afraid and uncertain, I might well have let the voices of authority resolve my dilemma and make my decision for me. It is always much easier to let someone else make a decision for you, especially when times are uncertain, rather than think for yourself.

So, perhaps my doubting nature when it came to matters spiritual or profound wasn't a curse at all but a blessing, because it was urging me to constantly question my beliefs and discover who I was in the process. Without change, my spiritual development would stagnate. There would be no learning, no experience and no growth. Within our growing is a miracle.

My thinking in all the decades that I'd been seeking proof for the existence of heaven had always been that the essential ingredient for a spiritual life was absolute faith – a life without doubt. All the religions tell us that doubt is the enemy. Faith is the answer. And in my previous books, even though I always distinguished between religion and spirituality, I had still unconsciously carried forward the message of the overwhelming importance of faith. I had encouraged my readers to simply believe even when there was no proof. This isn't necessarily wrong, but if you have a questioning mind and struggle with the concept of blind faith, as I so often do, it can make you feel like a failure when you desperately want to believe but just can't.

In a lightbulb miracle moment everything became transparent. Doubt has incredible power. If you think about it, doubt is behind everything great that has ever been achieved in the world. Scientists and innovators, whose discoveries have improved the lives of countless people, always start from a position of doubt. Religion, on the other hand, is built on faith and although this faith has done a great deal of good in the world it has also led to conflict and suffering.

Perhaps, then, my life of constant doubt and searching was not wrong after all but a crucial part of my ongoing spiritual journey. Perhaps people who doubt and question have a deep connection with the world of spirit. Perhaps my destiny was to doubt. So many times in my life I had felt that something was wrong with me because of my doubts. Even though I had written countless books on the afterlife, had experiences myself and read thousands of amazing stories from people all over the world, sometimes I still seriously doubted if heaven was real. Time and time again I would come to the conclusion that something was wrong with me. I wasn't trying hard enough. I wasn't studying enough. Whatever it was, it was my fault. I would do everything I could think of to move away from that period of doubt because doubt was the enemy. To have faith in heaven was not to doubt, right?

I could not have been more wrong.

A life without doubt is a comfortable and secure life, but what if comfortable and secure wasn't what was right for me? What if comfortable and secure actually prevented my spiritual growth? What if I needed doubt to grow closer to heaven?

Perhaps doubt wasn't necessarily a sign of weakness but of strength?

Doubt is a painful and troubling state I tried to escape from because it crushes your idea about heaven – the idea about heaven that makes you feel as if you have all the answers. Heaven becomes what you believe it to be. Doubt distances you from that belief but that does not mean heaven is far away. Doubt means your current idea about heaven is dying and evolving. So doubt is not something that should be shunned; it should be embraced. It is a sign that you are transforming, growing and discovering who you truly are. It is a sign of spiritual awakening.

It is hard to see doubt in this way when you feel your life is collapsing around you and you lose faith in everything you thought was real, but heaven is using doubt to encourage you to look deeper inside yourself. Heaven wants you to doubt because heaven wants you to grow. Your crisis of faith is to help move you further on your journey towards heaven.

Letting go

The experience of deep doubt is often called the 'dark night of the soul', when someone feels that heaven is impossible to find and may not even exist at all – this is when despair moves in. Despair is frightening because it can feel like you have no control and no clarity, but to grow spiritually you need to learn to let go of the desire to control and learn to trust instead.

If you have ever done one of those exercises where you fall backwards and have to believe that the person behind you will catch you, that is the kind of trust I'm talking about here – trust that comes out of emptiness and surrendering the desire to control. In other words, heaven will always evade you if you don't go through periods of doubt and even darkness. If your faith excludes doubt then your belief becomes like a hobby, something comfortable and easily controlled and unchanging. Doubt is heaven's way of ensuring that you don't ever stop growing spiritually and discovering what is divine within and around you.

Doubt didn't make me a failure spiritually. It made me a seeker of the truth – my own personal truth. I needed to continue doubting because eventually, one day, doubt would lead to me discovering something on my own. I needed to doubt until there was no doubt left and I found my own path to heaven.

I'm aware this sounds very complicated, but it really is so simple – as most great truths are. All those years of seeking the truth and what I'd actually been doing was copying or following a spiritual path that worked for other people but which wasn't necessarily right for me. My mind believed in something but my heart didn't trust it. Each one of us is completely unique and trying to copy someone else is a way of avoiding being yourself.

If I wanted to know who I was, if I wanted to find my proof of heaven, I needed to be myself. I needed to let go of intellectual ideas of what heaven was and how to see it. I needed to let go of the need for certainty. I needed to trust what was intrinsic to me. I needed to understand that believing and following was about my thoughts – my head – but trusting was about my feelings – my heart. So instead of trying to fit myself into some existing system of belief or longing for direct proof of heaven through a supernatural experience or sighting of departed loved ones, or trying to find bliss through family or work, I needed to listen to my own heart and my own dreams about heaven. I needed to trust myself. I needed to love rather than hate my doubting mind – because it was a part of me. I needed to trust not my head but my heart.

I started by becoming conscious of whenever I felt happy, loving and kind, and the more I noticed these blissful things about myself, the more I began to identify with them. I learned what brought heaven closer to me and what pushed it away. I started to make the discovery of heaven within me the purpose of my life. And the more I identified with the heavenly, loving and compassionate part of me, the more real heaven felt. Heaven was no longer something 'out there' but something right here inside me. It was who I really was and always had been. And the more I accepted the heavenly part of myself, the more I began to be aware of little miracles happening all around me and to sense the unbreakable connection between this world and the next. I didn't need to search for heaven because heaven was finding me.

So, it has taken me nearly five decades to finally understand that the journey to heaven is one that each person must navigate for themselves – and certainly for me, doubt is and always will be an essential part of that journey. Perhaps your chosen path will be to follow a religion, or perhaps you will find your connection to heaven through dedicated study, meaningful work, artistic endeavour, innovation, invention, cooperation, good deeds, or through family and loved ones. Perhaps you will be among the few whose belief is rock solid because you have had an encounter with a departed loved one, or had a supernatural experience of some sort, and this has changed your life forever. Or perhaps you will find heaven through gentle signs and coincidences that give you the strength you need to believe at just the right time. Or perhaps you will simply tune in to the feelings of love and goodness and truth that exist within your heart, and these will be your inspiration and your strength.

However, whichever path you choose, the absolutely crucial first step is to allow yourself to question and doubt what you think you should believe. Keep doing that until there is no room for doubt left in your heart. Don't shut down any opportunity to discover if you are on the right path and don't feel guilty about changing path or direction if your heart tells you to. To be a real seeker of the truth the only essential requirement is that you keep an open mind, because it is only when your mind and heart are open that the voice of heaven can speak to you and directions will come to you as sweetly as music.

I thought that my curious mind was the enemy blocking my spiritual progress, but all along it was my need to know and my crisis of faith that were pointing me in the right direction. This is not to say that you need to experience depths of despair and self-doubt to find your heaven. Some people are blessed with natural gifts of understanding and resilience that grow stronger not weaker with a crisis, but for me the only way to learn was to reach rock bottom. I had thought doubt and the despair that resulted were my enemies, and the way to get back on track was to dispel doubt, but heaven had other plans for me. It was complete transformation or nothing. I needed to doubt everything so that if I made the decision to trust, it was my decision. I needed to stop trying to imitate or please others, or look outside myself for answers. I needed to find them within myself. I needed to confront the darkness, confusion and pain of my soul and discover meaning for myself.

And in the depths of my despair I did find a new meaning. Like a full moon that illuminates a dark night, I realised that heaven had been all around and all within me all my life – I just hadn't seen or understood it. And the reason I had not had the vision was rigid thinking. All the rules and requirements I had in my head didn't leave any room for heaven to let itself into my heart. I thought all I needed to do was learn the correct techniques, follow the right rules, join the right movement and then I would glimpse the other side. I did not understand that spiritual growth is about the growth of the whole person, and this is a lifelong process of learning to listen to the voice of heaven speak within your heart. It is about learning to love yourself unconditionally, however many flaws you may think you have; and about letting go not of doubt but of fear – fear of not belonging, of being called weird, of not impressing and, above all, fear of what your intuition, dreams and heart might be telling you.

Accept

Until I was able to love the part of myself that doubted, I would never be able to grow spiritually. I needed to trust my instincts and let them guide me through this life and the next – to understand that a doubting mind was not an unheavenly mind and that, as long as I kept my heart open to the possibility of miracles, heaven would find a way to speak to me.

Once you can accept and love yourself and your perceived weaknesses in the same way – in other words, start to believe in yourself regardless of the criticism of others and to embrace your weaknesses for the spiritual lessons they teach you – you will find that your life transforms in countless ways. You will feel more alert and alive because spirit has stirred within you. You will radiate joy and contentment. Fitting in won't be your priority any more because you are finding your own path, making your own choices, finding your own route to heaven.

If you choose the comfortable path, the convenient one everybody before you has gone down, which makes you think you are doing the right thing because everyone else is doing it, your spirit will always feel unsatisfied. There will always be a vague feeling of unease and discontent that you can't quite pinpoint. However, when spirit fully awakens within you that unease will be gone because you will be finding out your own truth.

Once you get in touch with your inner truth – trust yourself – you will start to find heaven everywhere within and around you. On extremely rare occasions you may glimpse spirits of loved ones who have passed to the other side, but heaven is far more likely to manifest itself to you through your dreams, coincidences or flashes of intuition or subtle signs, such as the appearance of a white feather. Heaven can also be found in animals or children, or through a mysterious scent or gust of air, or a hug from a loved one, or a piece of memorable music or the words in a book, or in the kindness of other people who are consciously or unconsciously guided by the spirit inside of them.

And this is just the beginning – the possibilities for heaven to reveal itself to you in this life and the next are endless . . .

You don't go to heaven, you grow to heaven

> But I tell you – and you may mark my words – you will come someday to a craggy pass in the channel, where the whole of life's stream will be broken up into whirl and tumult, foam and noise: either you will be dashed to atoms on crag points, or lifted up and borne on by some master-wave into a calmer current – as I am now.
>
> Mr Rochester, *Jane Eyre*

As well as learning to embrace all aspects of myself, including my doubting nature, I also had to overcome another belief that was stopping me dead in my tracks: that if I knew I was on the right path to heaven my life would suddenly become much easier. I would no longer have any problems and all would be sweetness and light. However, one thing I have discovered over the years is that this is almost certainly not the case. I have learned through time and life experience that you don't go to heaven, you grow to heaven, and sometimes growth can be challenging, painful and frightening.

Right now, as I write this book, the year 2014 is drawing to a close. Tensions in the Middle East and Eastern Europe are at boiling point and the future feels uncertain. When innocent air travellers lost their lives in a misdirected missile attack over Ukraine, my email was swamped with questions from readers asking one simple question: 'Why?' If heaven exists, why is there so much brutality and injustice and unkindness in the world? Why did these people have to die in such a brutal and senseless way?

I'll be honest with you – I don't know why. I could tell you that there is goodness and love in this world and the next, and the more of us who choose to follow the path of light rather than the path of darkness the stronger this love and goodness will become, so that one day perhaps it will eclipse the darkness altogether. Even as I write these words, though, I know they are a tepid and inadequate response to the presence of pain and suffering. All I can say is that just as each one of us needs to accept that we are not perfect and that we have flaws, so too do we have to accept that this life – as magical and as beautiful as it can sometimes be – also has a terrible, dark side. Sometimes for reasons we will never understand in this life, the world is cruel and intolerable things happen to innocent people.

Perhaps in the next life we will understand, but in this life we can't see the bigger picture. I often compare it to the reverse side of a tapestry – all messy ends and false starts – but if you turn the tapestry over everything makes perfect sense and a picture or pattern emerges. In other words, trying to explain the spiritual in human terms and the reason why things happen isn't possible in this life. All we can do is seek out what is heavenly in ourselves and others, and let our inner light guide us through this life and into the next. All we can do is trust that goodness will prevail – because trusting in the existence of heaven, especially when life is full of challenges and obstacles and you are full of doubts and fears, is the only way you can be sure you are walking on the right path.

I sincerely hope that by being honest about the many doubts I have experienced in my life, and continue to experience, I will help you to understand me better. I hope that it also explains why, after writing dozens of books and encyclopaedias about matters spiritual, I had a burning passion to write this book. In all the years I have been an author I have never stopped wondering how many other people there are out there who, like me, long to know what their destiny and purpose is, who long to find heaven but whose vision and progress are clouded by doubt when they don't feel they are getting anywhere. I wanted to show that all this doubt, longing and uncertainty are not signs of despair and distance from heaven but calling cards from heaven – you may not realise it at the time but heaven is drawing you closer.

More than meets the eye

I hope the words I write here will offer reassurance and be a source of inspiration and guidance. I want you to refer to them over and over again when you are going through challenging times, experiencing the pain of loss or grief, or at any time you find that doubts and fears stop you in your tracks and you find yourself wondering why on earth you can't find heaven. I want you to understand that what you are experiencing is not darkness and confusion but the signs of spiritual awakening. (On page 209 I'll discuss in greater detail what these signs are so that you can recognise them for yourself.)

This book is dedicated to everyone who knows deep inside their hearts that there has to be something more to this life than meets the eye. It is for all those who have a passion for spiritual development and perhaps an urge to help and inspire others, but simply don't know where to start. It is for everyone who sincerely believed they were on the right road but then felt doubtful and disillusioned.

Above all, I want it to be read by anyone who needs to be reassured that doubt and insecurity are not a sign of weakness but a mark of spiritual strength. It is the divine spark inside them, urging them to reassess and redirect their energy towards a higher and greater purpose. It is the voice of heaven reminding them of the importance of struggle and constant transformation for spiritual growth. It is heaven calling their name.

This astonishingly beautiful quote says it far better than I can:

A pearl is a beautiful thing that is produced by an injured life. It is the tear from the injury of the oyster. The treasure of our being in this world is also produced by an injured life. If we had not been wounded, if we had not been injured, then we will not produce the pearl.

Stephan Hoeller

CHAPTER TWO

Select a route

*If I ever reach heaven I expect to find three wonders there:
first, to meet some I had not thought to see there; second, to
miss some I had expected to see there; and third, the greatest
wonder of all, to find myself there.*

Confucius

This chapter will explore a range of perspectives about
heaven taken from believers and non-believers alike. As you
read, I hope you will see that all these perspectives have something deep and compelling to offer; and if one belief system or
approach in particular speaks to you – and does no harm to
anyone else – there is absolutely no reason why it can't be your
route to heaven.

The promise of heaven

Although the word heaven can be used to refer to the skies above and endless planets, stars and galaxies of the universe, many of us think of it as a transcendent place where God, or the gods, and angels reside and where our spirits go after death. It is also defined as a state or feeling of supreme bliss, joy, contentment, paradise that can be experienced within as well as visualised. However, as this book attempts to show, heaven is undefinable in human terms because it is not of this world and, in addition, it will be experienced by each person in a totally unique way.

Despite variations in narratives about heaven among different religions, the belief that there is an afterlife of some sort remains. Heaven is a spiritual place or dimension where there is only peace and tranquillity and no more pain or suffering. There is eternal joy, and the possibility of uniting with departed loved ones exists. It is a place where our spirits return home and where there are only positive things and no negatives.

Sounds truly blissful!

From the point of view of a sceptic, or non-believer, the problem with all this is that there is no proof whatsoever for the existence of heaven. It is all based on belief. Indeed, for many religious people there is no need for proof because faith is all they need to sustain and inspire them. Scientists have studied people who believe in heaven and come to the conclusion that their conviction may be down to a personality trait encoded in our genes – this gene has even been given a name: 'the God gene'. This particular gene has been isolated and studied and been shown to control certain chemicals in the brain, and these chemicals affect the way we view the world around us. Studies have also shown that during intense prayer or meditation, changes take place in the brain and the parts that monitor sense of space and time become less active. So that uplifting feeling of losing yourself is attributed to God.

And while scientists are busy proving that belief in heaven is a purely physiological phenomenon, humanists and atheists take this to its logical conclusion in their assertion that heaven is a myth – it does not exist. If you are an atheist, you don't think your spirit will live on after your death and your priority is to make this life as fulfilling and rewarding as you can because it is the only one you are going to get.

Everyone is entitled to their view and I respect the opinions of scientists, atheists and sceptics as much as I respect the opinions of Christians, Hindus, Buddhists, Muslims and those of every other religion. However, opinions are just that – opinions and not facts. Sceptics are quick to point out that there is no absolute proof for the existence of heaven and it is all a question of belief, but, to turn things on their head, there is also absolutely no proof that heaven does *not* exist. Nobody can be one hundred per cent sure what happens when we die, until they die. Atheists have closed their minds to the idea of an afterlife, but what if they are wrong?

And as far as the atheist's assertion that there is no proof that heaven exists goes, there are a vast number of people who would strongly disagree, and chief among them are those who have glimpsed the other side through near-death experiences, or NDEs.

Crossing over

Millions of people all over the world claim to have had near-death experiences that gave them a glimpse of the afterlife. It is unlikely there will ever be solid scientific proof of life after death, but these accounts from people who have actually been on the brink of death and returned to tell their stories do give us something that comes extremely close. These voyagers to frontiers unknown report astonishing glimpses of a world beyond, a world that shimmers with light, magic and love.

Near-death experiences offer perhaps the best proof we have of life after death. In most cases these experiences happen when a person's life hangs in the balance or their hearts stop temporarily. The experience is surprisingly common and, in the overwhelming majority of cases, those who have experienced them are left with a new-found sense of wonder. Indeed, in some cases, like Elizabeth's below, the experience is so enchanting that all fear of death is gone.

Lightning speed

In 1991 I died in a car crash. I remember chatting with my friend in the back seat one moment and then seeing the fear in her eyes the next as a car crashed into the side of us.

The next thing I can remember is travelling at lightning speed and being dazzled by a golden light. It felt like one of those fun rides you go on at a theme park – not the ones that make you want to throw up – the ones that make you giggle. It took a while for my eyes to adjust and the travelling sensation to stop and then I found myself in a golden room. In this golden room I 'remembered' everything about my life and felt every emotion I have ever felt. I also felt the impact that my life had had on others, both the good and the bad. I felt the pain I had caused my mum when I ran away from home, the anger I had caused my sister when I stole her shoes and clothes. I felt everything. After I had 'remembered' my life, my next instinct was to laugh. I laughed because I felt light, free and happy. I was also laughing at myself and all the times in my life I had got worked up about things that don't really matter.

Then someone came to meet me. It was my aunt. She'd always been a bit of a rebel and as I was growing up she was the only one I really felt understood me. I missed her wisdom terribly when she died. My aunt took me by the hand and we both laughed and danced with happiness. The feeling of elation was so incredible.

Suddenly, I was looking down at two cars mangled together. Traffic was backed up on both sides of the road and there was a great deal of confusion. I saw two men rush towards the scene with green outfits and white cases. I saw them lift my head and shine lights into my eyes. My friend in the car was standing on the side of the road, sobbing, and her mum, who was also sobbing, was being carried away on a stretcher. That was when I remembered my accident, and as I did I started to melt back into my body. I remember wanting to make a difference with my life and focus more on my life purpose. I also remember not wanting to leave my aunt, but feeling reassured that I would see her again soon – as spiritual time is measured very differently from physical time.

I was halfway back into my body when I stopped and tried to pull back towards my aunt, who was still hovering by my side. I looked over at my sobbing friend. As soon as the question of my death, and how the trauma of it would impact her life, formed in my mind I was back in my body. I opened my eyes and instantly recognised the two paramedics I had already seen. Later in the ambulance, I told them about my experience on the Other Side, which I now know is called a near-death experience. They didn't seem surprised at all as I guess they probably hear about it all the time in their job.

My experience has taught me that everything we do in this life is 'remembered' in the next, and that if we knowingly cause others pain and upset we will relive that when we pass on. It also taught me that my life has a purpose and that I should not worry so much about things that really don't matter. Twenty-five years later there isn't a day that goes by that I don't draw strength, hope and inspiration from my experience, because I know that death isn't an ending but a wonderful new beginning, where there is love and laughter. Do I fear death? Not in the slightest. On the day I 'died' I never felt so alive.

Some people argue that such experiences are dreams or hallucinations, but to those who've had them they are so much more than a dream. They are a spiritual awakening. Many lose their fear of death and are left with a life-changing sense of awe and wonder and absolute trust in the existence of heaven.

Experts have, of course, tried to explain near-death experiences from a psychological, physical or religious standpoint, but to date no medical, scientific or psychological rationale has convincingly explained how, for example, people of different ages and from different cultures typically report very similar experiences involving a tunnel of light and meetings with departed loved ones. It is wonderful that scientists are actually investigating the phenomenon of NDEs and taking them seriously, but it would be even more wonderful if they could keep their minds open to the very real possibility that one way to explain them is that they actually happened.

So if heaven could be real, the next question is how to find it. Let's take a look at some paths to heaven that have been well travelled over the centuries and also some newer routes.

Finding heaven

You'll find major world religions listed below as well as some less well-known ones. There is also introductory information about belief systems that aren't religions as such but have their own ideas about finding fulfilment and meaning in life. Don't let the brevity of my descriptions deceive you, because each of the paths listed below is far more complex and profound than stated here. But if I tried to do full justice to them all, this book would be ridiculously huge, and extend to several volumes! I have tried simply to give you the bare basics – and if you want to take a deeper look at any path because it speaks to your spirit and you feel it might be the right path for you, I urge you to do some research of your own.

I also strongly urge you not to skip this brief A to Z section. You may believe that you know all there is to know about most religions but I can assure you that what you read here will give you pause for thought. I've studied religion in great depth and thought I knew all this, but – as you'll see at the end of this section when I talk about the path I was most drawn to – in compiling the A to Z I realised just how limited my knowledge actually was!

Please forgive me too if all known paths are not included here, as I'm sure I've missed out a great deal – again word count made it impossible for me to cover everything. I just hope that what I have detailed below gives you a stimulating and thought-provoking insight/introduction to the many paths to heaven you can choose from.

Roads to Heaven – A to Z

Atheism

It seems ironic to start this A to Z to heaven with a philosophy about life that doesn't actually believe in the existence of an afterlife, but if you study the movement in greater detail you will find that such a generalisation isn't entirely accurate.

So what do atheists believe?

This isn't easy to say because they do not abide by a particular set of beliefs or follow certain traditions or rituals, so you can't really explain atheism in the same way as you could a religious movement. Often, atheists are defined by their disbelief in a God or higher power that created us and influences our lives, but this does not do them justice because they do have their own beliefs and morality – but ones formed independently of belief in God. However, as atheists don't have a standard to judge themselves by, and there is nothing to limit their ideas and theories about morality, avoiding generalisations is not easy.

As far as moral standards are concerned – again, this is generalising – atheists draw on the values of a wide range of different thinkers, leaders, mystics, writers and religious figures. It is wrong to say that atheists completely reject the Bible or other holy books and teachings. In fact, many regard the moral arguments and advice in the Bible, or any other important religious book, as an inspiring standard to live by. Atheists tend to value logic and facts above conviction and belief, and the concrete above the abstract, i.e. material reality above spirit.

Although there are exceptions, the great majority of atheists are united in their belief that religion injures society more than it heals it. There is no concentrated campaign to abolish religion – as atheists respect the right of each individual to find their own path to fulfilment – but generally they do believe that the world would be a happier, more peaceful and better educated place if people were not religious.

Many atheists do not believe in an afterlife. When you die you crumble to dust and cease to exist. However, once again generalisations can't and shouldn't be made, as some atheists don't deny altogether the existence of an afterlife. Instead, they try to define it using scientific methods, such as quantum mechanics.

Quantum physics revolutionised science by assigning as much importance to the observer as to his or her observations. It gave reasons to suppose that this life may be more than just a complex arrangement of physical matter brought about by chance. It provides a more optimistic view by suggesting a complex arrangement of physical matter consisting of dynamic packages of unpredictable energy, or an interconnectedness or wholeness to the universe reminiscent of the teachings of many mystics. In itself, it does not postulate the existence of an afterlife but it does provide a mechanism by which mind can affect matter – as is the case in extrasensory perception – and a mechanism in which non-physical entities such as the spirits of departed loved ones could exist by slightly shifting the probability distribution associated with individual quantum events. In short, from a logical or rational perspective heaven can't exist, but from a quantum perspective it is something humans have yet to understand well enough.

So, within atheism there is still room for belief in some kind of heaven – even if it's not the kind of heaven most of us are used to dreaming about.

Bahá'í

The Bahá'í faith was founded by Bahá'u'lláh in Iran in 1863, so it is one of the world's younger religions. According to Bahá'í, humans do not need to be saved from evil or their sinful nature but from false ideas about the world and their purpose in it. For this reason God sent a number of messengers or prophets to enlighten people: Abraham, Krishna, Moses, Buddha, Zoroaster, Jesus, Muhammad, Bahá'u'lláh and so on. All these prophets uttered divine truth and revealed the nature and will of God to their world in a way that the specific culture they were speaking to would understand. After death a person's soul continues its spiritual journey until it eventually finds union with God.

According to Bahá'u'lláh, each one of us has a soul and this soul animates our physical bodies. The soul is also the focal point of love and compassion, faith and courage, and it does not die but endures forever. When the human body dies, the soul is released and continues its journey through the spirit world, which is not a remote or removed place but a timeless extension of our own world.

Although the nature of the soul after death can't be known and the afterlife remains a mystery, Bahá'u'lláh likened death to the process of birth – there will be pain and fear as in the pains of labour, but then there will be great joy. He explains: 'The world beyond is as different from this world as this world is different from that of the child while still in the womb of its mother.'

The womb comparison neatly summarises the Bahá'í view of life on earth. In much the same way as the womb is a vital place for our earliest physical growth and development, this life is the matrix for the development of our souls. Indeed, our earthly existence is a kind of dress rehearsal or training ground where we can learn, develop and fine-tune spiritual qualities needed for the next life.

In a more abstract sense, heaven is also seen as a state of being close to God; and hell a state of remoteness from God. Failure to develop spiritually distances us from God in this life and the next, and places us in a hell-like state. The key to spiritual growth, which ensures our safe passage to heaven in this life and the next, is to follow the path revealed to us by God's messengers.

Buddhism

Buddhism has an entirely different concept of heaven from many other religions. It is not so much a place but a state of being – a state of supreme bliss and enlightenment. There is also no God in Buddhism as the ultimate spiritual authority or source of guidance. The path to enlightenment is therefore very much up to the individual and depends on their desire for spiritual growth.

Reincarnation – the idea that we are reborn in any number of possible forms – is an important element in Buddhism. The primary aim of a Buddhist is to break free from the cycle of rebirth and reach the final level of enlightenment called nirvana, which is a transcendental, blissful, spiritual state of ultimate happiness. There is no individual existence in nirvana but a unity with the cosmos. The quality of a person's next life is very much determined by past-life experiences, and a person's last thought at the moment of death is crucial. If that thought is a meritorious one then any future existence will be positive, but that life is also temporary and when it is over a new life begins, determined by another defining karmic energy. This cycle of death and rebirth continues endlessly until a state of 'right view' is achieved, along with a dedicated resolve to follow the Noble Path which ultimately leads to nirvana.

Nirvana is the final state the soul reaches as it reincarnates through different lifetimes. These lifetimes are visualised as a chain of lamps being lit until the final lamp goes out and nirvana has been achieved. Nirvana means 'extinguishing' or 'going out'. The Ferris wheel of reincarnation is kept alive by our desires and craving, but when we are able to eliminate all desires it is possible to escape the cycle of rebirth. A person who has extinguished all desire is said to be liberated or a saint and has reached a state of nirvana.

Just as Christianity started with Christ, Buddhism started with the first Buddha. The name buddha is actually a title meaning 'one who is awake', in the sense that they have woken up to the real meaning of life. Born as Siddhārtha Gautama in Nepal around 2,500 years ago, Buddha did not claim to be a son of God or a prophet. He was simply a human being who discovered the secret of becoming enlightened – which means understanding life in the deepest way possible.

What makes Buddhism distinctive from Christianity and Hinduism is the notion that people do not have eternal souls. Instead, they are a transitory collection of habits, memories and desires which delude one into thinking that they consist of an individual self. This false self can reincarnate in body after body but, together with the corporeal body in which it reincarnates, is the source of all suffering. The goal is to find release, and for Buddhists this means letting go of the false sense of self so that the bundle of memories and impulses is extinguished and there is nothing left to reincarnate or experience pain. The individual dissolves into nothingness and is liberated.

According to Buddhism, neither heaven nor hell is a final destination for the soul because both are otherworldly realms from which a soul can be reborn. In other words, they are temporary states – stepping stones on the path to nirvana. For example, in hell a person is not condemned to eternal damnation for human weakness and does not have to suffer there forever, as merit or karma acquired previously can help him or her work upwards. Also, the Buddhist concept of heaven and hell is not just outside this world but within this world itself. This quote sums things up well:

The wise man makes his own heaven while the foolish man creates his own hell here and hereafter.

In other words, hell is wherever there is suffering in this life and the next, and heaven is wherever there is joy or happiness. In this life, humans will experience both suffering and joy so that they realise the full nature of existence. In the otherworldly realms of heaven and hell, however, there is only ever joy in the case of heaven or suffering in the case of hell, but whether the soul is in heaven or hell it does not have to stay there forever and can still be reborn. Buddhists believe that all people, however wicked their life has been, have the potential to attain enlightenment or nirvana, and they have multiple lifetimes to reach this ultimate spiritual goal.

Christianity

The Christian faith has no suggestion of reincarnation. Heaven is a place beyond death where there is no more sadness, suffering and pain. It is a beautiful experience where the departed can enjoy the presence of a loving creator God and the love of each other.

In contrast to Buddhist belief, Christians are not guaranteed a place in heaven. We are born sinners and the only way for us to be cleansed of our sins and be worthy of a place in heaven is to rely on God's grace. God took pity on us and over two thousand years ago sent his only son, Jesus Christ, to be a sacrifice for our sins. If we believe in Christ and the sacrifice he made for us, and subsequently live a good Christian life, we are eligible for entry to the kingdom of heaven when we die. Christians are confident that the death and resurrection of Christ took place for every single man and woman on the planet, and everyone can be welcomed into his presence and be forgiven for their sins in this life and the next because God's love for us, made manifest in Jesus Christ the Lord, conquers all.

Christianity has three major branches – Orthodox, Roman Catholic and Protestant – which have distinct views of the afterlife. Orthodox Christians believe the souls of the righteous go to heaven after death, but this is only a temporary place until the final judgement, when

Christians are given a new spiritual body and get to spend eternity with God in paradise. Being in the presence of God will be torture for unbelievers and they will get to spend eternity in hell.

The Roman Catholic Church believes in an eternal afterlife. They also believe that the pope is God's representative on earth. According to Pope John Paul II, head of the Catholic Church from 1978 until his death in 2005, heaven, hell and purgatory (see below) are not actual places but states of being of the soul. Those souls that have received grace through the rituals of baptism and Eucharist will spend eternity in God's presence, while those that have not will spend eternity separated from God.

Some Orthodox Christians and Roman Catholics believe in a place known as purgatory – a kind of transitory state between life on earth and eternal life in heaven. It is where human souls can be purified and justice done for a lifetime of wrongdoing, but time spent there can be shortened by the prayers of those alive on earth. Catholic theology also teaches that sinners can confess their sins to priests and these sins can then be forgiven. It does not matter how terrible the sin. If the sinner truly repents he or she will be forgiven.

Most Protestants believe that heaven and hell are actual places of either eternal bliss for those who have received God's grace through faith in Jesus Christ or eternal torment. Some interpret the Bible's vivid descriptions of heaven and hell literally, while others interpret them metaphorically.

In general, most Christians aren't entirely sure what will happen to their souls when they die, but belief that death is not the end is a defining feature. Believers are comforted by the thought that after death they will meet God. God is just and no one will suffer a fate they do not deserve. They also know that God is love and nothing in this life or the next can separate them from the eternal love of God, which manifested itself on earth in Jesus Christ the Lord.

The various subdivisions or denominations within Christianity have differences that are defined by issues such as doctrine, Church authority, the role of priests and clergy, the nature of Jesus, the authority of the pope and so on. All denominations recognise each other as Christians and acknowledge the divinity of Jesus. There is also the common belief that death is not the end and those who have led a Christian life will go to heaven.

The largest Christian denomination is the Catholic Church, which recognises the pope in Rome as God's anointed spiritual leader. This is followed by the Protestant Church, which does not recognise the authority of the pope, and then the Orthodox Church, which represents Eastern practices. After that there are a number of smaller denominations such as Baptists, Quakers, Methodists, Jehovah's Witnesses, Mormons and Church of the Latter-day Saints, to name but a few. Each of these denominations has its own distinctive beliefs and practices and, in some instances, sacred texts, but they all regard themselves as true Christians, and the majority tenet among them is that belief in Christ is the only way to obtain eternal life. There are also some non-denominational Christians who don't follow any branch of Christianity at all.

Confucianism

Confucianism, which began in China in the fifth century BC but is currently enjoying a revival, can be regarded as both a religion and a philosophical movement. Most of its focus is on teaching followers how to live a moral life in the here and now. The afterlife is unknowable, so effort should be made to make this life the very best that it can be.

Confucius did not set out to start a religion. He urged those he taught to seek inspiration and truth from the past, most especially from respect for ancestors. What a person does in this life is considered vastly more important than thoughts of a future heaven. Living life in a way that honours one's ancestors and makes one worthy of being honoured by future descendants is key. Therefore, the most significant way in which thinking about the afterlife influences Confucian beliefs and practice is the follower's responsibility both to their ancestors and descendants.

By leading a moral and sincere life, a Confucian sees salvation both in the here and now – in the sense of attaining the Confucian goals of membership in a community (starting with family) as well as individual engagement with ultimate meaning or supreme power (*Tian*) – and in eternal life – in the sense of becoming a model or example for the generations that follow.

When Confucians talk about heaven they do not have in mind a realm of eternal bliss and reward for those who believe or lead a moral life. Heaven is simply a name for the most elevated spiritual state. Although there are differing views within Confucianism, it is clear that Confucius himself did believe in some sort of spiritual survival, and in the immortal spirits of ancestors who have died. However, he was of the conviction that as we know so little about this life, why waste our energy trying to understand an afterlife we know even less about? When one of his disciples asked him about death he replied: 'We haven't yet finished studying life to delve into the question of death.'

Eckankar

Founded in 1965 by spiritual master Paul Twitchell – although followers accept the existence of many spiritual masters throughout history – Eckankar means 'co-worker with God'. It is a 'religion of light' that believes each human soul is an eternal fragment of God and that God loves the soul that is on a journey back to God.

Belief in reincarnation features strongly. The soul passes into a new human or animal body after death. Life is a series of experiences, all of which teach important lessons. There are also consequences for our decisions and actions, and lessons will carry on across lifetimes as the soul continues to reincarnate and gain understanding, thereby realising his or her own true inner divinity. Past-life studies feature strongly in Eckankar religion.

The divine spirit of God which flows through all living things is known as ECK and is thought to be the bridge between human souls and God. Light and sound are twin aspects of ECK and it is awareness of ECK that brings spiritual enlightenment. ECK masters are said to be mouthpieces of the divine spirit and they can guide people through past-life regressions, dreams, soul travel, meditations and other spiritual development techniques. Past ECK masters include Socrates, Plato, Jesus, Moses, Martin Luther, Michelangelo, Mozart, Einstein and so on, who all allegedly made astral journeys for their discoveries.

The soul is a part of God and wants to remember and understand that part of its nature, making learning and self-development the primary goal of Eckankar. To understand God one must also understand the self, as they belong to each other. In other words, according to Eckankar belief there is a fragment of heaven within each one of us, and we need to rediscover and reconnect with that to discover heaven.

Through multiple lifetimes spiritual lessons are learned until we are finally ready to reunite with God and become a part of God again. All of us are on a journey back to God. Dying is called translating and there are different levels of heaven and the astral plane.

Gnosticism

This is an age-old spiritual path currently enjoying a revival. It focuses on the acquisition of gnosis, which is individual direct knowledge of the divine. Gnostic beliefs are many and varied but some common themes can be found. I'll do my best to paraphrase them but, as with all the belief systems in this chapter, words will never be enough and I can only scratch the surface. If you want to know more, I urge you to do your own research and study – indeed, for gnostics immersing yourself in study and amassing facts are key.

Gnostics believe that there is a transcendental spiritual unity and force but that our universe was not created by this unity. It was created by spiritual beings with inferior powers, who desire to separate humans from unity (God). Each human being possesses a spark of the ultimate divine unity inside them but the outside aspect is the creation of inferior creatures. Because of this, the spark of transcendental awareness within us is trapped and stupefied by the forces of materiality and the mind. However, the ultimate unity has not abandoned the slumbering sparks within us and is constantly making an effort to awaken them and liberate us. Through gnosis – the acquisition of spiritual knowledge – the divine essence can rouse within us.

Gnosis is not something that can be acquired by belief or good deeds or by the performance of rituals, traditions and practices. From prehistory, messengers of light have been sent from the ultimate unity to help promote gnosis in the souls of humans. The greatest of all these messengers in our matrix was the word of God manifest in Jesus Christ – a teacher who also imparted mysteries (sacraments) to his apostles and their successors. By practising these sacraments and striving for the salvation of gnosis, it is possible for humans to liberate themselves from material restraints. The goal of liberation is freedom from bodily existence and a return to the ultimate unity (God).

If this all starts sounding complicated, you may want to watch the famous *Matrix* movies, which draw a lot on gnostic myth and belief. If, like me, you enjoyed the trilogy immensely but didn't quite understand what on earth was going on, here is a quick recap: To return to the light (heaven) the gnostic must recognise the evil, deception and unreality of the material world and distance himself from it. The only way to do this is to awaken the divine element within him by cultivating it with gnosis, or hidden knowledge. This knowledge is the key to salvation, liberation and unity with God.

Hare Krishna

This is a relatively new religious movement, established in America in 1965 and with foundations in Hinduism. Followers of Hare Krishna believe in one all-powerful being – Krishna, the supreme personality or godhead – and their goal is Krishna consciousness. Krishna has many names and is the same divinity that Muslims call Allah and Christians call God.

The Hindu text Bhagavad-Gita, the Song of the Lord, written around 250 BC is the most important sacred text. The Gita narrates the story of the warrior Arjuna and his encounter with Krishna, and is regarded as literal truth.

Followers of Hare Krishna believe that each one of us is an eternal servant of Krishna; but in this life our souls have forgotten that and, instead of devoting ourselves to Krishna, we devote ourselves to our own pleasure. This will cause unhappiness because the material world is not our real home. We belong to the spiritual world, the kingdom of Krishna is our real home. The aim of our material life is to reconnect with Krishna and one way to do this is to recite the holy names of God in the chant below. This is because it is thought that Krishna is present in the sound vibration of his name.

Hare Krishna, Hare Krishna, Krishna Krishna, Hare Hare
Hare Rama, Hare Rama, Rama Rama, Hare Hare

Asceticism, celibacy, vegetarianism, avoidance of drugs and alcohol, meditating, evangelism and congregational worship are other paths to Krishna consciousness.

As far as belief in the afterlife is concerned, the eternal soul does not die. Krishnas believe we are eternal, the soul never dies and can reincarnate countless times. Our destiny in the next life will be determined by what we are thinking at the time of death. Hell is for those who have lived a sinful life. Those who have been good go to heaven and those who have lived in Krishna consciousness reconnect with Krishna and see and hear Krishna. This is the highest perfection.

Hinduism

This religion has a lot in common with Buddhism but there are also important differences. Salvation (moksha) is achieved when a person has been liberated from the cycle of reincarnation and returns to God.

The Upanishads, the ancient set of Hindu religious texts, teach that there is an unchanging part of the self which is called the atman, or deep self. This part of a person is identical to Brahma, or the unchanging god who has never been trapped in the unhappy cycle of life, death and rebirth (samsara) and who transcends all the other gods and goddesses in Hinduism.

There are countless different gods in Hinduism and a number of different opinions about the nature of salvation. Some schools of thought believe that a soul always keeps its individuality when it becomes one with God, whereas another suggests that salvation is about getting rid of the false self and merging with God so that individual identity becomes indistinguishable from God. What unites all the various schools of thought, however, is the samsaric cycle of the law, or karma.

Put simply, karma is like a natural law which ensures that every good or bad deed or desire eventually returns to a person in this life or a future one in the form of reward or punishment equivalent to the original deed or desire. It is the necessity of reaping karma that compels people to reincarnate over many lifetimes. And if a person dies before they reap the effects of their karma, they will do so in their next life. Coming back in another lifetime allows karma to reward or punish by means of the circumstances into which a person is born. For example, someone who was a murderer may return as a victim, or someone who was generous may be born into a prosperous family and so on.

Liberation from the unending cycle of death and rebirth is called moksha and in Hinduism it represents the ultimate aim of life. Liberation is attained by erasing the bad karma earned by evil actions and desires, and there are several ways of achieving this, from selfless devotion to a particular god or appeasing the gods by the proper performance of rituals, to highly disciplined yoga techniques and acquiring knowledge into the hidden nature of reality.

In Hinduism, heaven and hell are not final resting places but the experience of the passage between death and new life, as there is always the possibility of rebirth if there is still karma to reap. A Hindu also experiences both heaven and hell in this life: if we are good we are in heaven and if we are bad we are in hell.

Although there are differences, moksha, or unity with the godhead, could be said to have the most similarities with the familiar concept of heaven as a state of eternal bliss and peace. But what happens when a soul finally breaks free from the unhappy cycle of rebirth and attains moksha? The Upanishads teach that the individual atman merges with the cosmic Brahma. The metaphor of a drop of water losing identity when it's dropped into and becomes part of the ocean is often given. However, this famous image isn't strictly correct as according to Upanishadic thinking the atman has never been separate from the Brahma, so the sense of individual identity is an illusion.

Moksha is, therefore, a simple waking up from a dream of being separate. It is becoming aware of the divinity within you and all around you.

Humanism

This is not a religion but a belief that this life is all that there is. The universe is a natural phenomenon and there is no magic or paranormal side to it. Humanity and reason are therefore guiding moral principles to live by, and human welfare, empathy and happiness should be at the centre of any ethical considerations.

As far as the afterlife is concerned, humanists do not believe it exists. They also don't believe there is any purpose to the universe or destiny for the human race or individual lives. Humans should give their lives meaning by finding happiness in the here and now and being kind and helpful to others.

The Humanist Manifesto 2000 reads:

> . . . *naturalists maintain that there is insufficient scientific evidence for spiritual interpretations of reality and the postulation of occult causes. Classical transcendentalist doctrines no doubt expressed the passionate existential yearnings of human beings wishing to overcome death. The scientific theory of evolution, however, provides a more parsimonious account of human origins and is based upon evidence drawn from a wide range of sciences.*

Perhaps the main reason for humanists to discount the possibility of an afterlife is that they firmly believe that humans should concentrate on what is happening in their lives and in the world right now. They believe that the idea of bad deeds or good actions being punished or rewarded in some otherworldly realm stops us creating justice in the present; stops us striving for a better life.

Having said all this, a humanist might not completely discount the idea of an afterlife, because although there is no direct evidence for it they do acknowledge that humans have much to learn. There is strong evidence against it; its existence is therefore rather unlikely; and at any rate it just isn't relevant to the much more important issues facing us today in the world we know exists – that, in a nutshell, is the humanist perspective on an afterlife.

Islam

The word Islam means 'submission to the will of God' (the Arabic word for God is Allah) and followers of Islam are called Muslims. There is only one God in Islam and, according to Muslims, he sent a number of prophets to teach them how to live according to his law, which is recorded in their holy books, the Koran and Sunnah. Jesus and Moses were prophets but the final and most significant one was Muhammad.

To Muslims, Islam is more than a religion. It is a way of life. There are five pillars of faith in Islam: declaration of faith, praying five times a day, giving money to charity, fasting and pilgrimage to Mecca. The path to God is to follow as closely as possible the moral codes and religious precepts of sharia and Sunni law, because following the prophet Muhammad's example is the best way to connect with the divine. To outsiders it can seem uncompromising and intolerant – and extremists have sadly encouraged that view – but the Muslim who truly understands the teachings of his religion and follows in the footsteps of his prophet is refined, gentle, truthful, likeable, tolerant and kind to all people, including non-Muslims.

If you are a Muslim death is regarded as the end of physical life and the beginning of a spiritual rest period before the destruction of the world on the Day of Resurrection, when Allah will raise all people, including the bodies of the dead, to be judged on their deeds in life. During this period of soul slumber the deceased remain in their graves awaiting final judgement, but the good may glimpse visions of heaven and the bad may see visions of hell. After judgement, those who are good will go to eternal paradise and those who are bad to eternal hell. Paradise is described as a place of physical and spiritual pleasure, with food and drink, beautiful gardens and grand mansions and virgin companions. There is no sickness, pain, sadness or death. Hell, on the other hand, is a crater of intense suffering and pain.

The prophet Muhammad said that everyone will see God on the Day of Resurrection, as easily as one can see the sun when there are no clouds. According to some Muslim commentators, Allah can show mercy and rescue a soul from hell if enough punishment has been given. Likewise, in paradise there is opportunity for further advancement:

> *Life after death is actually the starting-point of further progress for man. Those in paradise are advancing to higher and higher stages in knowledge and perfection of faith. Hell is meant to purify those in it of the effects of their bad deeds, and so make them fit for further advancement. Its punishment is, therefore, not everlasting.*
>
> Muslim.org, an Ahmadiyya website

Muslims believe that salvation and entry to paradise on the Day of Judgement will come only to those who recognise and worship Allah, and who perform more good deeds than bad ones in their lives. Imitating the prophet Muhammad will also help, as will reciting prayers, fasting, going on pilgrimages and doing good works. Dying in service to Allah (martyrdom) is believed to send a worshipper straight to paradise.

It is important to point out that there are subdivisions within the Muslim faith and the most significant are Shia and Sunni. Both Shia and Sunni Muslims share the same fundamental beliefs and practices of Islam and their differences were originally more political than spiritual. However, over the centuries these political differences have led to a number of divergent ideologies and practices which have gone on to develop a spiritual significance.

The differences date back to the death of Muhammad and who should succeed him as leader of the Muslim faith. Sunni Muslims believed that the new leader should be someone who was best suited to the demands of the job. In Arabic, the word Sunni means 'one who follows the traditions of the prophet'. Abu Bakr, a close friend of Muhammad, was elected caliph of the Islamic nation. Shia Muslims, however, believe that after Muhammad's death leadership should have passed directly to his cousin/son-in-law, Ali ibn Abi Talib. Therefore Shia Muslims (the word Shia in Arabic means a group of supportive people) have throughout the centuries refused to recognise the authority of elected Muslim leaders, preferring instead to follow a line of imams who they believe have been appointed by God or the prophet Muhammad.

This division has led to a number of differing religious practices and opinions between the groups, but it is important to remember that Shia and Sunni Muslims share the same Islamic faith and belief in eternal paradise. Their divergence is not unlike the major schism that took place within the Christian faith between Roman Catholic and Protestant (see Christianity).

Jainism

The origins of Jainism date back to sixth-century India and also have their roots in Hinduism, but there are differences between the two religions.

There is no creator God in Jainism. Salvation is achieved by the individual taking charge of his or her own destiny. Jainists believe the universe consists of three realms – the heavens, earth and the hells. There are seven heavenly realms and the highest realm is for liberated souls, hence the well-known phrase 'I'm in seventh heaven'. The soul in every human is eternal and therefore has the potential for divinity, and the purpose of human life is to achieve eternal liberation (moksha) through the acquisition of infinite perception, bliss and power. This may take several lifetimes to achieve.

Belief in reincarnation and resulting karma features strongly in this religion. Whereas in Hinduism and Buddhism karma is the natural moral law of the universe – and whether karma is good or bad is offered as explanation for why some of us are born healthier, wealthier and luckier than others – in Jainism there are two different kinds of karma. One is destructive and only affects the soul, and the other is non-destructive and only affects the body. Within both types there are also several categories of karma and different ways to be released from them. The only way to shed all karma is to be released from them all.

To be cleansed from karma a person must have the right knowledge and belief, and also act in the right manner. Depending on the spiritual development of an individual, death in Jainist belief can mean being reborn in another human life or joining liberated souls in heaven. It can also mean being punished in one of the hells. Such punishment, however, is not eternal, as once punished enough a soul can be reborn into another human life.

Jediism

The Jedi were first mentioned in the 1977 classic movie *Star Wars*, and featured in all the sequels. George Lucas – the creator of *Star Wars* – researched Taoism and Buddhism and a number of other belief systems for his conception of the Jedi. Thanks largely to the massive popularity of the movies and the existence of the internet allowing online communication, followers of the Jedi religion have increased significantly over the years.

The existence of the Force – an impersonal energy that permeates everything in the universe – is crucial for all Jedi beliefs. In some ways it is similar to the Christian belief in the Holy Spirit or the Chinese qi. The biggest problem for Jediism to be taken seriously as a religion is that it originated from a work of fiction – but followers might argue that sacred stories in the Bible, such as the Garden of Eden, are also works of fiction.

The Jedi code is as follows:

> *There is no emotion, there is peace.*
> *There is no ignorance, there is knowledge.*
> *There is no passion, there is serenity.*
> *There is no death, there is the Force.*

The Jedi believe that mental training can help them become spiritually aware of and in touch with the living force flowing through and around us. Maintaining a clear mind that focuses on the present is the way to ease stress. Becoming mindful of their thoughts and focusing on the positive is healthy for mind, body and spirit. The Jedi also listen to their intuition and trust and use their feelings. If they focus on negative feelings that can take them to the dark side, such as anger, hate and fear, they must meditate on the Jedi code and purge these emotions.

Being warriors of peace, the Jedi believe that conflicts can be resolved through understanding and harmony. They will only use the power of the Force for what is positive, peaceful and just. Love and compassion are central and a person must love themselves as well as others. In this way, the positive energy of the Force is harnessed. They also believe that nothing in life is random and that every living thing has a purpose. Understanding that purpose – even when things appear to be negative – comes from a deep awareness and appreciation of the Force. As far as the afterlife is concerned, the Jedi do not believe in death but in eternal life. The soul and spirit continue in the nether-world of the Living Force.

Judaism

Jews believe in one single creator God and it is possible for each Jew to have a personal and individual relationship with Him. Anyone who is born to a Jewish mother is a Jew and, according to Jewish teachings, God appointed Jews to be his chosen people to set an example of spirituality and moral behaviour in the world. Someone who is not born a Jew can convert to Judaism, but it is fairly difficult to do.

Like Islam, Judaism is more than a religion. It is a way of life and everything a Jew does can be considered an act of worship. Jews believe a person should be judged by the way they live their faith and by their contribution to the holiness of their community and the world. Repentance, good deeds and a devoted life are the keys to salvation.

From Judaism's perspective, the soul is eternal. This world is one of actions and the next life is where we experience the reality of what we have achieved in this life. Ultimate reward or justice is found in another dimension. Clearly then there is a strong belief that death is not the end, but beyond that there is room for conjecture. For example, it is possible for some Jews to believe that the souls of the righteous go to heaven and the souls of the wicked go to hell; some to believe in reincarnation; and others to believe in a day of final judgement and the coming of the Messiah.

In general, being more concerned with actions in this life than beliefs about the next, Judaism does not have much dogma about the afterlife. How you live, act and think in the here and now is what truly matters and will decide your destiny on the other side. Having said that, heaven is thought to be a place where the individual soul enjoys the greatest pleasure imaginable – being close to God. In addition, a person's experience of heaven is determined by the way he or she has lived their life. If you have become spiritually aware in your life – by studying the Jewish text, the Torah – you will experience the greatest pleasure in heaven; whereas if your life has been very materialistic, you will not achieve this level of fulfilment.

Furthermore, there is the belief that when a person dies the soul will be given the opportunity to review their life's every thought and deed. If their life has not been entirely good, they will also be shown how it might have been, which will cause regret and give the soul an opportunity to cleanse itself. Some souls, however, are too evil for this purification and will be punished eternally.

Native American beliefs

Native American beliefs are deeply rooted in the culture of indigenous North American peoples. There are many significant variations between different tribes and peoples, and it is only possible here to skim the surface and generalise, but one common theme is that everyone and everything is sacred and has a soul, from the smallest insect to the highest mountain. All experiences and all things can teach us a lesson and everything, however insignificant it may seem, has a meaning and a purpose.

Above all, Native American spirituality is about love and respect. The Creator or Great Spirit is loved and respected. The Great Spirit is everywhere in everyone and everything, and hears whatever is in our minds and our hearts.

We believe that the spirit pervades all creation and that every crea-
ture possesses a soul in some degree, though not necessarily a soul
conscious to itself. The tree, the waterfall, the grizzly bear, each is
an embodied force, and as such an object of reverence.

Ohiyesa, Sioux 1902, aka Charles Eastman

Native spirituality is also about getting in touch with the world around and within us, and understanding that we are a part of everything and everything is a part of us.

Native spirituality has great respect for ancestors or elders, believing their example and their spirits can teach many crucial life truths. Reincarnation also plays a part, perhaps because it expresses a sense of family continuity so central to tribal societies. In certain traditions, it is believed that a new baby is a recently deceased relative reborn. As far as belief in the afterlife is concerned, again there is great variation from tribe to tribe. In certain tribes there is really no afterlife at all, just an endless cycle of reincarnation. In some, the souls of the dead pass into a spirit realm and can communicate now and again with the living through dreams or the work of medicine people, known as shamans. In others, there is a land of the dead ruled over by a god of death, and then there are tribes where the dead become stars or part of the earth.

Although there are differences, most tribes do believe that death is not the end but the beginning of a journey into the next world or underworld, because the spirit never dies. There is also the belief that spirits or ghosts of the dead can visit us. Death is revered and embraced rather than feared because it is a part of nature, and various rituals may be performed to make sure a soul has safe passage on its journey into that realm or is protected from harm in the afterlife. The spirits of deceased relatives may be asked to join the rituals by the medicine man or shaman leading the ceremony.

It could be said that Native spirituality believes in a hidden spirit world or deep, underlying connection that interacts with this earthly plane. Many people remain oblivious of this unseen world and the highest spiritual goal is to become aware of it and connect with it deeply. In the words of Black Elk, a Lakota Sioux medicine man:

The first peace, which is the most important, is that which comes within the souls of people when they realise their relationship, their oneness with the universe and all its powers, and when they realise at the centre of the universe dwells the Great Spirit, and that its centre is really everywhere, it is within each of us.

Paganism

This term refers to a diverse number of religions that have in common a great reverence for nature. Wiccans, shamans, druids and heathens, to name but a few, all consider themselves pagans. Pagans have had a lot of bad press over the years, so let's set the record straight from the outset. They do not worship the devil or practise black magic; they are not sexually perverse and their rituals do not involve harming anyone or anything.

Modern paganism is based on the indigenous religions of ancient Europe as well as belief in pagan gods, goddesses and spirits. Most believe that nature is divine and that a number of spirit beings can reveal eternal truth to humans. It is unclear whether all these spirit beings are connected and can be referred to as a divine unity or God.

It might be more accurate to say that if there is an idea of god within paganism, it is the concept of the sacred, divine female. Pagans are most likely to worship the goddess, manifesting herself in Mother Earth or revealing herself through religious figures such as Mary or Brighid. Goddesses are thought to offer blessings, strength and courage as well as purification and guidance.

When it comes to the afterlife, pagans believe in the existence of Summerland – a place of divine beauty and harmony where our souls go to after death. What makes Summerland unique is that it will appear different to everyone, but for each person who enters, it is a place of reflection, rest and renewal. Lessons are learned from our life on earth and decisions are made about where the soul will travel next. This might be a new life on earth, as many pagans believe in reincarnation.

Every person goes to Summerland, regardless of how evil they have been on earth. This is because in pagan thought, constant learning outweighs moral judgements about what is good and what is bad. In fact, because of this emphasis on learning rather than judgement pagans avoid using any terms with connotations of punishment. There is a strong belief that everything in nature and in humanity has both a dark and a light side. We are all part of the cycle of birth, life, death, decay and rebirth, and will naturally have both dark and light characteristics. The path to eternal summer is, therefore, to accept the dualistic qualities within ourselves and to learn to connect with and mature in wisdom within this natural cycle of light followed by darkness, followed by light.

Raëlism

Founded in 1974, so a relatively new religious movement, Raëlians deny the existence of supernatural gods but believe in the otherworldly powers of an alien race called the Elohim. They also believe that various prophets and spiritual leaders, such as Jesus and Buddha, were chosen and sent by the Elohim to reveal their message to humanity.

The founder of the Raëlians is a man called Claude Vorilhon. He claimed he'd been abducted by the Elohim, who gave him the new name Raël and instructed him to be their prophet. Raëlians believe that the Elohim planted all life on earth around 25,000 years ago. Using the argument that the Elohim are generous creatures who want humans to enjoy themselves fully, there is a strong belief in sexual freedom, or free love – and this controversial belief is what they are probably most known for.

The creation of an embassy for the Elohim to reveal themselves is high on their list of priorities, but the Elohim will only do so when humanity is ready – they will never force themselves on us. The goal of the Raëlian movement, however, is to get the human race to a point in our evolution when we are ready to welcome the Elohim. Initiation to the Raëlian movement involves a baptism known as the transmission, where the new member's DNA is communicated to an Elohim extra-terrestrial computer.

Raëlians do not believe in an afterlife, but they are fascinated by the scientific idea of cloning as a key to immortality. They also think that certain exceptional people have already been cloned by the Elohim and live on another planet.

If all this sounds like science fiction, you could argue that every religion has elements of the fantastic and downright weird – rising from the dead, hearing voices or reincarnation spring to mind. Raëlians may have taken things just that one stage further in the fantasy stakes, but many believe their lives are more fulfilled and pleasurable as a result.

Rastafari

This philosophy developed in 1930s Jamaica following the coronation of Haile Selassi I as king of Ethiopia. Rastafari believe that King Haile is the Living God and he will return to Africa all members of the black community who are living in exile because of the slave trade.

In much the same way that Jews believe they are the chosen people of God, the Rastafari devotee believes that black people are the reincarnation of ancient Israel and chosen people of God. Religious ceremonies consist of chanting, dancing, drumming and meditating, as well as the inhalation of marijuana to heighten spiritual awareness. Eating processed food is frowned upon, as is doing anything unnatural to your body, which is regarded as a temple. Forbidden to cut their hair, members grow it and twist it into dreadlocks. The colours red (sacrifice of past Rastafari), yellow (wealth of Africa), green and black (returning to their roots) have symbolic significance, and devotees also have their own dialect. The lion is the symbol of the faith: it stands for King Haile and dreadlocks represent a lion's mane.

Many modern-day practitioners have distanced themselves from earlier racist beliefs that black people are superior to white people. In the 1970s, a more modern approach to Rastafari belief began to emerge, which emphasised the divinity of God revealing Himself through humanity. God can be found in every man but most supremely in Haile Selassi. Although he is still regarded as a latter-day Messiah to some devotees – with his death in 1975 described as a disappearance because they refuse to believe he can die – belief in the divinity of Haile is no longer central today. Salvation is earthly and not heavenly, and followers continue to believe they are the chosen people on earth to promote God's peacefulness and supremacy. After death many believe a person reincarnates endlessly, making this life eternal.

You may have noticed in this short outline that I have not used the terms Rastafarian or Rastafarianism. This is because followers do not like to be referenced in this way, believing that any '-ism' or '-ian' represents corrupt systems of the West that oppress people. Nor do they like the term religion, preferring to think of themselves as a philosophy.

To understand this movement properly, it's important to remember that it began in Jamaica, in the Caribbean, where most of the black population had come from Africa and been forced to work there as slaves. As a people oppressed by Western society and colonisation, it was a form of empowerment for black people and a way to claim back their own culture. The Rastafari do rely on the Bible for many of their beliefs, but when it comes to heaven or paradise they have their own unique ideas about salvation on earth rather than in some otherworldly realm. Members feel that being removed from Africa – their homeland – against their will is a living hell and that Africa is paradise on earth. Therefore the goal of many is to move back to Africa – making this movement more about cultural leanings or yearnings, and celebrating and reconnecting with a way of life that colonial powers tried to destroy.

Scientology

Scientology was founded in the 1950s by the American science-fiction writer L. Ron Hubbard. He wrote a book on Dianetics and within a few years Scientology churches were formed.

Scientologists believe in a Supreme Being and that people are immortal spiritual beings with unlimited – but not yet realised – potential.

They believe that God helps those who help themselves. According to their writing:

> Scientology is a religion that offers a precise path leading to a complete and certain understanding of one's true spiritual nature and one's relationship to self, family, groups, Mankind, all life forms, the material universe, the spiritual universe and the Supreme Being.

In many respects Scientology is close to Eastern religions in that salvation (heaven?) is achieved through knowledge of self and the universe. The goal of life for a Scientologist is to learn about and understand oneself better as a spiritual being. Scientology means 'learning how to know'. They believe a person can be reborn over many lifetimes to continue the learning process, and only once past mistakes or crimes have been dealt with can he or she progress. The idea of heaven or hell is, therefore, all about future life, as the experiences there will have been earned by past behaviour. The thetan (spirit or soul) will travel through numerous lifetimes in an attempt to purge itself of traumatic images that create fear and irrational behaviour. Once the Scientologist has removed these negative and harmful images, he or she becomes an 'operating thetan' and can control thoughts, feelings, life, energy, matter, space and even time itself.

Over the years Scientology has had its fair share of controversy. Members swear a billion years of allegiance. Stories of followers being held against their will and the group's fierce rejection of psychiatry and psychology (because it is thought that these practices deny human spirituality and promote false cures), as well as the belief that a mother should be silent in childbirth (so her cries of pain do not alarm the spirit of her baby), have all been widely criticised in the media. High-profile celebrity followers such as Tom Cruise, Juliette Lewis, Kirstie Alley and John Travolta have also contributed to Scientology's mystique, but members don't see themselves as a cult or as controversial. Like everyone devoted to a religion or philosophical system, Scientologists truly believe they are on the right path to heaven and it is those who criticise who are confused, deluded and lost, unable to grasp the truth.

Shamanism

Shamanism is not a religion but a family of ancient, traditional beliefs and rituals that concern themselves with communication with the world of spirit. Although there are variations in shamanism all over the world, it is possible to identify a number of shared beliefs.

Principal among them is the conviction that an alternative reality or world of spirit (referred to as Dreamtime) exists and can interact with and play an important part in human life. Our visible world is permeated with invisible spirits or energies that impact the living. Some of these spirits are helpers and teachers. The belief that everyone and everything is part of an intricate pattern and interconnected is another core tenet, as is the belief that everything and everyone has a soul – not just humans but also animals, plants, rocks, mountains and so on. It is also thought that everyone and everything has an energy body that can be perceived by psychics as an aura. Animism is the term often used for the view that there is no separation between the world of spirit and this world, and animism is a fundamental aspect of shamanism.

The shaman is a healer or medicine man who can treat physical illness, but he or she is primarily a psychic who can achieve transcendental states of consciousness. A trance-like state is induced by dancing, meditating, chanting, singing or drumming, and in this condition shamans can commune with or control spirits and ask for their assistance or healing for an individual or community. The shaman's spirit can also leave his or her body and walk freely in the world of spirit. Supernatural powers, such as controlling the weather, have been credited to shamans, who may also be skilled at dream interpretations, divination and spirit travel, or astral projection. Animals often act as omens as well as spirit guides, and spirits – and sometimes the shamans who communicate with them – can be both good and bad.

In shamanism, life is a continuum that does not end with death, and one of the most important tasks of the shaman is to assist the dying as they make the transition from the material world to the world of spirit. In many shamanistic traditions, the realm of the afterlife is believed to be almost indistinguishable from our own. The next life is simply a continuation of this world where we will meet departed loved ones and family members. There may be less suffering and more light but in many respects the dead carry on with their lives in much the same way as they did on earth. Spiritual development continues to be of great importance, and once the soul or essence of the person has crossed over to truly experience heaven it must continue to evolve spiritually until it reaches the very highest level. So it could be said that a soul that does not continue to grow spiritually after death will not fully experience the blissful unity of the afterlife.

Shinto

Founded around 660BC, Shinto – meaning 'way of the *kami*' – is the indigenous religion of the people of Japan. The power of the *kami*, or gods, in nature and the world is central to Shinto thinking. Aside from belief in the *kami* and that every aspect of the world is imbued with deep sacred meaning, it is not easy to list other Shinto principles as this religion is more of a philosophy, best summed up perhaps by the phrase '*mono no aware*' – literally, 'the pathos of things'. This refers to an ability to see with the heart into the natural beauty and goodness of things, or a sensitivity towards beauty and emotion, sad as well as blissful, as a foundation stone for approaching life and the world. This approach to life can be seen in the focus on beauty, harmony, balance and nature in both the practical and the artistic world – for example, in landscape gardening and the interior design for the famous tea ceremony.

The concept of *makoto*, meaning sincerity, underpins Japanese ethics. It is thought that those who are sincere of heart will behave in moral ways. Sincere people will not lie or steal or try to kill, or do anything that could bring harm to others. The phrase *kannagara-no-michi* references the concept that goodness is a life that is lived in harmony with nature. In this way beauty, sincerity, goodness, morality and truth are all intertwined. And purity of heart goes hand in hand with sincerity of heart, and cleansing rituals using water, such as bathing, standing under waterfalls and so on, symbolise the purity from within that is essential for a fulfilling human and spiritual life.

Interestingly, although there is such a strong emphasis on purity and cleansing in Shinto, there isn't a strong concept of sin. The utmost indiscretion is not doing wrong – as it is accepted that there is both a good and bad side to *kami* – but rather leading a life of extremes and showing disrespect and a lack of humility. Shinto is all about balance between humans and nature and the importance of maintaining that equilibrium in our lives.

Every human being contains *kami* or eternal spirit or soul, and this is what lives on after death. After death a person becomes a spirit deity eventually joining with ancestors, which is the manifestation of the Great Divine. The Shinto afterlife was originally a dark underworld, but over time and with the influence of Buddhism, salvation now depends on avoiding impurity or pollution of the soul. When impure deeds or thoughts are committed, rituals must be performed to cleanse the doer or thinker. Once this has been done, the soul can join with its ancestors in the Great Divine.

Sikhism

Sikhism is rooted in Hinduism although Sikhs believe there is only one God. They also believe everyone is equal before God and can have direct access to Him. This is a religion that places the focus on both action and belief. To be a good person, a Sikh must become aware of God and also do good works.

Like Buddhism and Hinduism, reincarnation is a key theme in Sikhism. The quality of a person's present life is determined by how well or how badly they have lived a previous life, and this is called the law of karma. There is also great emphasis placed on the redeeming or condemning qualities of the last thought a person has before death. Evil is human selfishness, but if a person leads a good, honest life, performs good deeds, and meditates on God, they will be released from the cycle of reincarnation and become one with God.

Becoming one with God is a state of union and liberation (*mukti*) that can only be granted by God's grace. However, God will reveal through sacred texts and the examples of saints, gurus and prophets the best ways to achieve liberation. Sikhs believe that it is impossible to fully understand God, but they can experience the divine through love, meditation and worship. Sikhs search for God within their hearts and souls and in the divine order of the world all around them. They believe that most humans struggle to find God within themselves and around themselves because they are blinded by the evils of selfishness and materiality.

Everyone, no matter how evil, has God inside them and therefore is capable of changing for the better. The following rather lovely quote sums this up far better than I can: 'Just as fragrance is in the flower, and reflection is in the mirror, in just the same way, God is within you.'

Sikhism teaches that worshippers must find and understand God within themselves and also learn to see God in the world around them. In addition, they are required to lead a good and honest life, to care for and serve others as much as possible, to give to charity and to avoid the sins of anger, lust, pride and greed.

There is no direct belief in an afterlife but there is belief in a state of eternal liberation. The soul reincarnates when a person dies, and good or bad actions in life determine the quality of the next life. Souls that are ego-centred may be destined to suffer agonies in a dark under-world. A soul that conquers its ego by meditating on God will be liberated from the cycle of reincarnation and experience salvation in an eternal realm of radiant light and truth.

Spiritualism

I am on home ground here as I was born into a family of spiritualists and, from as early as I can remember, was taught to believe in and live my life according to spiritualist principles. It is therefore hard for me to give a completely accurate picture of spiritualism because I may be slightly biased, but it is also difficult because spiritualism is so diverse it does not have a universal code of beliefs.

Having said that, absolutely fundamental to spiritualist belief is the continuous existence of the human soul or spirit. We are spirit before we are born, spirit on earth and spirit after death. The world beyond this is referred to as the world of spirit and can also be called heaven.

On death of the physical body, the spirit joins the world of spirit – a realm in a different dimension that is intertwined with the material world. In the world of spirit, we have a spiritual body that is a replica of our physical one, and we also take across all our memories and our character. Spiritualist churches are places for communication with the dead, through mediumship, to take place. Church attendance, however, is not compulsory and some people call themselves spiritualists without belonging to a specific organisation or attending services.

There is no debate in spiritualism. It is taken as fact scientifically proven by the phenomena of spiritualism that the human consciousness survives death and communication with the dead is possible in a number of different ways. These ways include mediumship, telepathy, clairvoyance, electrical voice phenomena or EVP, Ouija board, table rapping, death-bed visions and apparitions. There is the belief too that, as well as people, animals that have been loved will also continue after death.

An infinite intelligent force (God) that created everything and everyone and can reveal itself in the world of nature is fundamental to spiritualism. Morality is defined by the ideal of doing unto others what you would have done to you and the universal principle of reaping what you sow. Personal responsibility is therefore another key theme, and an individual is believed to be responsible for his or her own spiritual development in both this life and the next.

The main aim of our lives is to get closer to God, and the way to do that is to learn the lessons we need to develop our soul. Countless spirits work close to the earth realm to help and guide us during times of stress and grief – and sometimes these spirits are referred to as angels. Spiritualists also believe we have a guardian angel, who stays with us from birth to death. We can ask our spiritual helpers for guidance and aid whenever we need it and they will reply through our intuition or sixth sense. They cannot lead our lives for us, but they can help us cope with the cards life has dealt us. In this way, spiritualism is more than a religion – it is also a way of life. It is finding spirit within and finding your God, whatever your culture or background, and this will bring peace and love into your heart.

On passing over, the spiritual realm we go to will be in line with the vibrations created by actions and thoughts we had when we lived our life on earth. The majority of people are said to go to the Third Realm, which is a place of light, peace, beauty. In that realm there will be opportunity to continue to develop spiritually and progress to even higher and more beautiful vibrations. Those who have lower vibrations because they have been bad, cruel or selfish go to the darker, more painful astral realms. They will not stay there forever, though, as spiritualists believe in progress and the ability to rise from the depths, even if it takes centuries to do so.

The origins of the modern spiritualist movement could be said to date back to 1848 New York and to the Fox sisters, who demonstrated that spirits could communicate with them by rapping on tables. The rappings directed the sisters to search the basement where they lived and records show that a body was actually discovered there. However, communication with departed loved ones is a phenomenon that has been recorded since the beginning of time. Today, there are millions of believers worldwide, and it is incredibly exciting that modern science is no longer automatically dismissing the claims of spiritualists and mediums but taking them very seriously indeed as a legitimate subject for credible scientific research and investigation. Indeed, a growing number of scientists are coming to the conclusion that there is mounting evidence for the survival of human consciousness after death (of which, more in chapter 3).

Spiritism has similarities to spiritualism but differs in that it is a collection of principles allegedly revealed by superior spirits. This codification is contained in a number of works by Allan Kardec, of which perhaps the most notable are *The Spirits' Book* and *The Book on Mediums*. There is also a belief in reincarnation.

Christian spiritualism is spiritualism that includes Jesus. Christian spiritualists believe that Jesus taught us the perfect way to lead our lives. We should be gentle and peaceful, love one another, forgive those who do us wrong, be humble and compassionate, not judge and love others as our neighbours regardless of colour or creed.

Sufism

Known as 'The Way of the Heart' or 'The Way of the Pure', Sufism dates back to the eighth century, when a more mystically inclined sect of Islam incorporated the transcendental teachings of Buddhists and

Hindus into their Islamic faith. Often mistaken as a sect of Islam, it is more accurately a dimension of Islam – a mystical dimension focused on achieving spiritual purity in the eyes of the divine.

The cornerstone belief is to ascend towards the Divine Light (God) that permeates the universe. There are a number of ways to ascend to the light, but the essence is to look within yourself for a connection to the divine, because if you know yourself and can purify your heart of everything bad, you can know God.

Perhaps the best way to describe Sufis is to say that they are devout Muslims. They pray five times a day, fast, chant, recite and glorify God, and faithfully observe other outward rituals associated with Islam. But what sets them apart is their desire to look within and nurture the spiritual, mystical dimension of their religion. Their hunger to seek the pleasure of God and find peace and love within themselves as well as harmony with all creation – humankind, animals, nature – is their path to spirituality.

While Sufis hold that the path to God is to look within, orthodox Muslims believe that only after death can humans achieve that level of closeness with the divine. Finally, even though Sufis go to the mosque to worship like any other Muslim, mainstream Muslims tend to disagree with the suitability of many Sufi rituals, especially those that contain music and dance, which they do not regard as a legitimate form of veneration. (See also Islam.)

Taoism

Also known as Daoism, Taoism takes its name from the ancient Chinese word 'Tao' meaning 'the way' – the principle of order and cosmic harmony in the universe which unifies and connects all things.

The *Tao* is present in the world – especially in nature – and is the natural way of life humans must follow.

Strongly influenced by ancient Chinese philosophy dating back two thousand years, the *Tao* is not God and is not worshipped as such. There are many gods in Taoism and they are venerated, but as part of the *Tao*. It is unclear what the *Tao* actually is – and words fail to describe it because it is 'everythingness', and not so much an object as a system of guidance.

> *The Way is to man as rivers and lakes are to fish, the natural condition of life.*
>
> Chuang Tzu

The focus is more on how the *Tao* works in the universe and how humans should relate to it. To experience deepest harmony a person must live in the here and now and learn to surrender to what is – to be in tune with the flow of reality. A significant concept is the principle of non-action, or the avoidance of actions and decisions, to allow the natural flow of life to take control. In Taoist belief the universe is working perfectly and there is no requirement for us to change things, so suffering starts when we fight to control our lives. This does not mean a person should not be proactive in their life, but their actions need to go with the natural flow of the universe; they need to be detached and not ego-driven. The Taoist does not struggle, oppose or strive.

This religion is all about unity, naturalness, non-action; achieving harmony with nature and spiritual immortality through self-development; and searching within yourself for answers. It is also a religion based on complementary principles, as expressed in Yin and Yang, which describe how seemingly opposing forces balance each other; for example, night and day, cold and hot, masculine and feminine, and so on. Feng shui, meditation, acupuncture as well as fortune-telling and reading the philosophical text, *Tao Te Ching*, are all Taoist practices.

Death is considered to be a natural Yang to Yin transition from a living to non-living state and is therefore not regarded by Taoists as something to be feared. Death is simply a natural balance to life and a part of the unchanging *Tao*.

Since life and death are each other's companions, why worry about them? All beings are one.

Chuang Tzu

After death there are thought to be blissful and painful otherworldly realms, the former for those who have followed the Way in life and the later for those who have not lived in harmony with the Way. However, as heaven is believed to be living in complete harmony with the universe, it can be experienced in both this life and the next because spiritual immortality is achieved by living in accordance with the *Tao*, in both this world and the next.

Unitarian Universalism

This is an extremely liberal religion which encourages its followers to believe anything they want about heaven and how to get there. Unitarian Universalists do not share a creed but they are united by their search for enlightenment and spiritual growth in this life. Followers seek inspiration from all major religions as well as atheism and humanism, but it could be said that the deepest roots of the movement are liberal Christian beliefs.

Unitarian Universalism actively encourages people to find their own spiritual path. This path may be to follow a particular religion or it may be entirely personal. The important thing when seeking spiritual truth is for a person to use their reason, and to draw on their experience and to follow the dictates of their conscience. Then when a path has been selected it is important to take that choice very seriously and live accordingly. In this way, belief becomes personal and autobiographical. A person believes what they feel is true and not what they have been told to believe is true.

Unitarianism – freedom of choice when it comes to belief – and universal salvation – every human soul can be saved – are belief systems that go back centuries but it wasn't until the early 1960s that the movements merged to form the Unitarian Universalist Association. It was around this time too that a very loosely held set of beliefs began to emerge.

First and foremost is the concept that a person should have the freedom to choose their belief according to the dictates of their conscience. The idea that a merciful God, or higher power, exists and is constantly revealing Himself in the world is also prominent, as is the idea that the kingdom of heaven can be created here on earth. In the end, God's mercy will reconcile everyone and everything. Humanity is essentially good and sin is a path that is chosen because of pain or ignorance. Jesus is believed to be a prophet of this merciful God, along with many other prophets from other religions. Lastly, but importantly, love is believed to be more important than doctrine.

Given that diversity of belief and independence of thought are encouraged it is not surprising that concepts of the afterlife are equally diverse. Some believe in heaven and hell, but most hold that these are symbolic and not actual places. Others believe in reaction or that heaven and hell are states of consciousness in both this life and the next. Then there are those who deny an afterlife exists and believe it is what we do in this life that really matters.

Voodoo

You may be surprised to find voodoo in this A to Z but it's been included for good reason as around fifty million people follow the voodoo faith worldwide. Also known as vodou or vodun, this religion developed from ancient African tribal customs that travelled to the New World. Today, it can be found in New Orleans, Ghana, Haiti and Nigeria, and blends African traditions with Catholic Christianity.

There are a number of variations in form, mainly because voodoo doesn't have standard rules and practices and is largely based on emotional and psychological states. It is also decentralised, with no organisational structure to connect followers together. Power and authority tend to lie with local priests or priestesses, who have healing powers as well as psychic/mediumistic abilities to communicate with dead ancestors and spirits. In fact, the word voodoo refers to spirit energy or mysterious forces that govern this world and the next.

Followers believe in a supreme and unknowable power who is served by loa, the spirits of good people, who share certain similarities with Catholic saints or angels in that they are believed to protect and guide people. As well as the loa, there are also evil spirits or demons. Ecstatic trance, drums, chanting and dancing are key features of voodoo worship, which takes place in a temple called a humfort. Followers typically gather around a pole placed in the centre, and believe that the loa can communicate with them through it. The aim is to create enough ecstatic energy to trigger a trance-like state where communication with the world of spirit is possible.

There is a strong belief in the existence of an afterlife. Death is not the end. Followers believe each person has a soul that has both universal and individual essence. After death the soul hovers close to the body and various rituals are performed to protect it from being captured by evil sorcerers. The soul, however, is not completely safe until a year and a day after death when, if the correct procedures are followed, it can be released to the cosmic community of ancestral spirits, where it may be worshipped by family members as a loa. Then, when the final rituals are completed, the spirit can continue to live on earth in the natural world. Sixteen incarnations later, it will finally merge and become one with cosmic energy.

The belief that has attracted most attention over the years is the idea within voodoo that a person's dead body can be revived by magic; that the dead person is a zombie who has no will of its own and can be controlled by magicians. The zombie myth has done much to stigmatise voodoo with black magic – and the ritual sacrifice of animals has done little to lessen this stereotype – but the majority of followers practise white magic and would never put a curse on anyone, alive or dead.

Voodoo can appear alarming to outsiders because of its emphasis on ecstatic trance and its endorsement of exotic spells, blood rituals and possessions. However, with its belief in the afterlife, a supreme being, saint-like helpers and invisible spirits to guide, comfort and protect humans, it really isn't that much different from other traditional religions.

Zoroastrianism

Founded in ancient Iran around 3,500 years ago, Zoroastrianism is one of the world's oldest religions. Although it was once the most influential religion in the world, today it has fewer than 200,000 adherents.

Followers believe there is only one compassionate and just God, called the Wise Lord or Ahura Mazda. The Wise Lord made the universe and is the creator of life. He is unchanging and unknowable and the source of all bliss. Everything the Wise Lord created is sacred and pure and should be treated with love and respect. This includes the world of nature and Zoroastrians are passionate about the environment. Fire is a symbol of the Wise Lord's light and wisdom. The truth about the Wise Lord was revealed through the prophet Zoroaster. Worship and prayer take place in a fire temple.

Zoroastrian dualism is manifested universally in the enemy of the Wise Lord: Angra Mainyu, or destructive spirit, who is the source of evil and death in the world. Dualism is also reflected in the opposing forces of good and evil within the mind. It allows for a profound understanding of day and night, good and evil, light and dark: life is a mixture of opposites; one cannot be understood without the other. The Wise Lord's gift to humanity was free will: we can choose to follow the path of evil or the path of righteousness. When all of humanity chooses the path of righteousness, evil will be destroyed and there will be heaven or paradise on earth.

While the Wise Lord resides in heaven, the destructive spirit reigns in hell. When a person dies, how good or bad they have been in this life determines whether they go to heaven or hell. It is thought that Christian concepts of heaven and hell owe much to Zoroastrian belief.

Zoroastrianism may have been the very first religion to suggest that a person's fate in the afterlife very much depended upon the way they'd lived their life on earth. The emphasis is very much on choice. There is no belief in reincarnation; instead, a few days after death a judgement takes place. However, if a soul does get sent to hell the doors to heaven are not firmly closed. There is still a chance for redemption, which makes this ancient religion a compassionate one.

As well as being compassionate, Zoroastrianism is also optimistic: there is a basic premise that humanity is essentially good and that one day this goodness will overpower the bad. In this way, humanity is not so much subordinate to God but a helper of God, making the religion one of empowerment too. In addition, everyone – male, female, young, old – is regarded as equal in the eyes of God. It is a religion that can be summed up as follows: good thoughts, good words and good deeds. Those who live their lives by this creed will be on the right path to heaven.

Ending this A to Z list with a religion that is compassionate, optimistic, empowering and has a firm belief in the equality of all humankind is very affirming and inspiring. There is irony here, too: perhaps the world's oldest known religion is showing us that we may have got a lot of things right from the start and, over the centuries, haven't progressed quite as much as we'd like to think we have.

Your choice

I'm sure that certain religions or movements spoke to you more clearly than others as you read the entries. I'm also sure that some didn't appeal to you at all. Perhaps you could make a list in your mind of your top two or three choices?

If you are a devoted follower of a specific religion you may find this exercise extremely hard as, of course, your allegiance is to your chosen faith, but perhaps you could try this as a hypothetical exercise? Be as objective as you can about religions other than your own. Try to understand them, and see if there are one or two others, apart from your own, that you are more favourably disposed to. Open your mind and go with your gut instinct!

You'll find that the religions that intrigue you reveal quite a lot about you and your spiritual needs. For example, if you are drawn to religions that place strong emphasis on group worship, it suggests that human interaction inspires you. On the other hand, if you are attracted to movements that stress an individual relationship, it suggests you are a more independent spirit. If you thrive on rules and instructions certain religions will appeal to you, but if you are more of a free spirit you will be drawn to other movements. Don't fall into the trap of thinking that one route to heaven is better than another. Every route has its merits as well as its downsides. The reason I'm asking you to try to narrow things down to your top two or three is that you will learn a lot about yourself in the process. You may also find that one religion or movement probably can't satisfy all your spiritual needs and what is missing from one movement you can find in another.

After you have settled on your top two or three choices, I would then like you to consider if there is one movement in particular that you are most drawn to. Don't try to force things; just go with what your heart tells you and make a choice. Your choice may not be realistic or suitable, and may not fit with your current lifestyle, but that doesn't matter. This is a completely hypothetical exercise and the choice you make does not commit you to it at all. I just want you to begin your journey of spiritual self-discovery, and perhaps the best place to start is with what is already on offer.

Be prepared – the choice you make now may shock you. I was completely taken aback. Obviously spiritualism was among my choices – and if you've read any of my previous books over the years you will already know that – but my other choice and the one I was most drawn to was (and please don't throw down this book now!) . . . Jediism.

I know it sounds crazy but I am being totally honest and open here. Jediism just struck a chord with me. I liked everything about it and didn't even mind the *Star Wars* connection – after all, most religions draw inspiration from stories that stretch the limits of your imagination or stories that can't possibly be true but which have profound meaning. It was also humbling to discover I could be a Jediist at heart because I have spent my life devoted to the serious, academic study of religion and spirituality and yet my final choice was for a movement that can't really be taken seriously. But this doesn't mean I don't take my spiritual journey seriously – I do. Indeed, as you saw in the previous chapter everything about my life has been wrapped around that search.

My choice also taught me that all the reading I'd done and knowledge I'd gathered over the years meant very little. I have worked closely with professors in my time, and attended count-less lectures, but none of that comforted me or convinced me that I knew anything.

When I was a university student with the typical arrogance of youth I thought my book learning made me a cut above the rest.

I'm ashamed to admit it but I felt a little superior. Working with undergraduates when I was doing my masters really boosted my ego. I thought I knew my stuff – after all, I'd read a lot of books – and liked that my students admired my cleverness. In reality I can see now that I knew very little at all. What I knew were books and the words in them, but words are not the same as life or experience. For example, I did studies of supernatural phenomena and read everything I could about the subject. I was a walking encyclopaedia. I knew so much but I had not had a supernatural experience myself. I hadn't lived it. It is the same with the word that every religion draws inspiration from – the word love. You can know everything there is to know about love from reading books, or in these days Googling, but unless you've fallen in love completely or had your heart broken or devoted yourself selflessly to the wellbeing of another, you will not know what love is.

The message I am trying to get across here is not that knowledge is wrong. It isn't – learning is to be highly recommended as ignorance is not bliss, but just make sure that what you think you know is not stopping you from *experiencing*. Life is your teacher. The reality of your experience is your guide. Don't ever lose your connection to your reality.

Discovering that my first choice was Jediism was a very welcome reality check. It taught me that positive thinking and light-heartedness were absolutely crucial for my spiritual growth. Being in control of the creative forces within me and the invisible forces around me, and understanding that there is more to this world than meets the eye, were also essential requirements for me.

However, I realised too that I didn't actually need to become a Jediist to live by all those principles. There were also aspects of other religions or movements that appealed to me and which I wanted to incorporate into my beliefs. For example, I totally respect the idea of reincarnation and karma. It makes a lot of sense to me. I also believe strongly in the idea of service to others – doing unto others as you would have them do unto you – as a route to heaven, and am passionately devoted to the concept of being able to communicate with departed loved ones in an invisible spirit world. I also think that there is divine energy hidden in the world of nature and a spark of divine essence in each one of us. I could go on and on picking bits and pieces from every belief group. I can even find myself agreeing with certain aspects of the atheist and humanist positions; namely, their honest admission that we simply do not know what happens after death, as well as their complete respect for the discoveries of science relating to the survival of human consciousness after death.

Basically, every movement has some magic for me, and I love the community spirit that many religions encourage because we all need to feel we belong. But, on top of all that, I could also add some of my own unique beliefs. For example, I have always believed that we become stars when we die and can look down on the earth. I don't know why I think that. I just believe it. I also think heaven can reach out to us through animals or through messages in dreams at night or subtle signs like a white feather crossing our path at just the right moment. I am convinced there is incredible power in coincidences, and that our thoughts and words have a power and an energy about them that can quite literally change lives. I think when we are asleep our spirits leave our bodies to help others cross over to the other side.

No religion or movement really contains all my personal beliefs, so perhaps the only way forward for me is to create my own religion. If I was fortunate enough to get others to agree with me on most of my beliefs perhaps Cheungism would be born!

And if someone ordinary like me could start a new religion, surely anybody could? Which proves my point entirely. All the ways to heaven listed in this chapter are ways that have worked for one person originally, or one group of people, and over time others have agreed (or been forced to agree) and a movement was born. The movement then went on to survive the test of time because of the profound and uplifting truths it contained, and because there is comfort to be gained from sharing a common bond of belief. If I were to be cynical and take the 'opium of the masses' line of argument, it may also have survived in some cases because it's easier for leaders or rulers to control large numbers of people if they have a shared belief.

But as each movement comes across as valid and profound in its own right, how on earth is it possible to claim that one is superior or better than any other, especially when thousands, or in many cases millions, even billions, of other people may be convinced their way is right?

You can't!

Just because one person or group of people believe they are right does not mean to say they are. All of us are in the dark really. We can't know for sure, so the sanest approach is to find your own route to heaven. If one of the A to Z speaks to your heart and spirit then by all means follow that spiritual path, as long as you do no harm to others and feel that it gives your life deeper meaning. However, you may also want to open your mind to the following thought:

> *Why copy what works for someone else? You are not that person. You are unique. Why not consider finding your own path?*

Of course, it is easier to follow the path set by others because it is already prepared, the work of discovery has been done for you, but sometimes following the well-travelled path isn't always the best path. Just because something works for other people, doesn't mean it has to or will work for you.

I am aware that what I'm saying here may be controversial but I didn't want this book to be a safe and comforting read. I wanted it to challenge you in every way, so that by the end you can be fairly sure that the spiritual path you have chosen is exactly the right one for you. If the right path for you is to adhere to the guidelines of a religion or movement then nothing I say in this book will change your mind or make you doubt your choice, because you know deep in your heart that you have found your truth. If, however, what I say gives you pause for thought then perhaps it suggests your search for spiritual meaning and fulfilment is still ongoing. Perhaps there is more for your spirit to experience and discover. Perhaps . . .

Pause for thought

Finding your own path to heaven isn't easy. However, if you join a movement or religion and follow the principles and examples set by others, this will make things easier, as your job is to adhere to the guidelines, not set them. Even if the rules set extremely high moral and spiritual standards and require a high degree of discipline and dedication, most of the creativity and hard work has been done for you already by other people. You are not an innovator but an imitator.

I'm not criticising, as imitation is not wrong in itself. But imitation is a stage not a destination. Imitation is the natural way to learn but it is not the way to foster a creative or innovative spirit. It is also not the way to mature and grow. Many of us have achieved great success by imitating successful work done by others, and children learn correct behaviour by imitating the examples of older children and adults. However, there comes a point in all our lives when we have to stop copying others and think about who we are and what is right for us. If we don't stop copying, we have no sense of who we are. We will not grow up. It is exactly the same with spiritual development. Imitation or doing what has been done by others makes us complacent.

If you follow a religion, movement, group or ideology you become just that – a follower. You impose on to your own uniqueness the ideals and practices you have watched or been taught. You become a part of that movement or group. You follow the example of people who are venerated by that group. For example, Christians follow the example of Christ, Buddhists the example of Buddha and so on. You try to become like these people and there is nothing inherently wrong with that, as they were awe-inspiring role models. The problem is, the universe knows and relates only to uniqueness. Each one of us is a complete original; even identical twins or triplets have differences. So, however hard we try to become like Christ or Buddha or Muhammad, we are setting ourselves up for failure. There was only one Christ, one Buddha and one Muhammad, and the universe will never see anyone exactly like them again.

It is the same for you. There is only ever going to be one you.

The universe will not see another person like you again, so why dilute what makes you remarkably original by trying to become someone you are not, however inspiring, pure, spiritual that person may be? Be inspired by that person, by all means, but if you want to truly discover your spiritual path and who you really are, perhaps the most important thing to do is to stop copying other people.

Again, I'm not saying copying is wrong. Far from it. When you are young, vulnerable, in need of guidance or support, copying may be exactly the right path to follow, but sooner or later the individual spirit inside you will demand to be recognised. There will come a time when you need to find out who you are. You will need to discover and become yourself – just yourself. This can feel disorientating and confusing at first. You have become so used to following, obeying and copying that feelings of uniqueness will feel strange, but you will also notice how alive, fresh and new you feel. It is intoxicating to become yourself, to truly be you.

The process of self-discovery is lifelong. You may find you get moments of illumination. Moments when you feel totally free, unique and alive. These are the moments when the true you is shining through. Learn from them and treasure them. They are pointing you in the direction of your heaven.

Billions of people all over the world right now are living their lives according to the beautiful and good examples set by religious leaders, but I want to ask you to think about what all of these spiritual leaders have in common.

They all share a wonderful secret.

And that secret is simple . . . These spiritual leaders did not follow or copy anyone.

Christ did not imitate and neither did Buddha or Muhammad. These great men found the path to heaven that worked for them. They followed their own beliefs or their divine calling. If they had followed in the footsteps of those before them they would not have become Christ, Buddha or Muhammad. They would not have reached their full potential.

It is the same for you. Become an original. Don't lack confidence in yourself or just follow the herd. History is littered with examples of people who blindly followed spiritual or political leaders, with often disastrous consequences for humanity. You don't have to be like that. You can discover your own spiritual path, and the best place to start is to stop becoming like other people and become who you are.

Depend on yourself

Depending on yourself and trusting your own heart is incredibly empowering, but there is no denying it can also be terrifying. Suddenly, all the familiar words, ideas and routines have gone and it is you standing alone and vulnerable beneath the stars. You may find you have an irresistible urge to pray for guidance, because prayer is something we associate with spirituality and religion. But instead of pouring your heart out to some invisible being that you can't be fully sure exists, why not pour your heart out to what you can see, hear, touch and feel? Instead of praying or trying to believe in something invisible, try loving something or someone you can see, hear, feel. Try being a loving person.

Every one of us can love. If there is one thing that followers of all the A to Z belief systems in this chapter possess it's a heart, and these hearts can all love. Love is not exclusive to a spiritualist or a Christian or a Buddhist – love is something we are all born with. We don't have to learn it – it is something we just instinctively know. We aren't born with religious teachings ingrained in our heads or hearts, but love is part of who we authentically are. It is there from the start. It is there until the end and probably after that.

So, to discover who you really are perhaps the best place to start is with your own heart. Love does not need a religion or a belief system to authenticate it. Love just needs you to believe in it and be guided by it. Love is life and love is the path to heaven.

When you reconnect to the love that is your birthright you will immediately feel more alive and full of joy because you are being true to yourself. You will feel unique and authentic. You will understand that every single human life is a miracle, not a sin, and no human being is superior or more special or inferior or less special than you are. Stories or texts which tell you otherwise are ridiculous and insulting. You are a miracle.

Not convinced?

Think about your amazing mind and body, for example. Even the greatest scientists in the world have failed to unlock fully the secrets of the human brain. It is a breathtaking and intricate piece of work that defies logic and yet supplies us with logic and magic connections. Your body is another masterpiece of engineering that looks after you your entire life. It does so many wonderful things to keep you alive every single second you are breathing. And it not only links you to the miracle of nature and your existence in this universe, it also makes you the unique person that you are. If you asked a scientist to create a human mind and body they would not be able to because such a creation is impossible. But you are possible. The universe has made you possible. You are a living, breathing, walking, talking and feeling miracle.

You are a fragment of heaven.

Recognising the presence of heaven within is an unending process, but it is possible to recognise certain stages of spiritual development and this may help you to understand where you currently are on the belief continuum. Some of us may move through each stage with ease and speed, whereas others may take far longer, but the potential for higher or lower levels exists within us all. You could compare spiritual growth to climbing a ladder – sometimes you climb as high as you can but then you might feel uncertain again and want to settle on a lower level for a while. The goal always, though, is to climb to the very top – to find heaven.

When your spirit is calling out to you to fulfil your potential and take a leap of faith you may go through periods of great uncertainty and confusion. But as I tried to explain with reference to my own spiritual journey in chapter 1, such periods of hesitancy and doubt, rather than signalling disillusionment and despair, are in fact signs of true spiritual awakening; signs that you are ready to evolve. In chapter 4 of this book I identify some other signs which I believe are sure-fire indicators of the need for spiritual awakening, but for now you may want to think about which stage of spiritual development you are in.

From being to bliss

The first stage is one of **being** and self-interest. You can be loving but your relationships are often self-serving and chaotic because there are no clearly defined principles for your heart to trust in and live by. If you form relationships with people who are principled and living in a higher stage, your life can find structure, meaning and purpose; but if you mix with people who are also in stage one of their faith development, confusion may be the result.

The next stage is one of **belonging** and dependence on a formal group for direction and guidance. This is the stage where followers of many of the religions and belief systems discussed in this chapter belong. However, guidance and structure may not necessarily come from a religion but from an institution, such as a business or the military. If you are in this stage, you may find it hard to open your mind to points of view other than the ones you have been taught to live by. There is nothing wrong with that if it makes you compassionate and understanding towards others. In fact, some of the most amazing acts of generosity and kindness are undertaken by people because of a cause or belief they follow.

This stage is only negative if you start to think it is your way or no way, or you discriminate against or belittle others who do not share your beliefs. However, if you respect the opinions of others whatever their beliefs and find joy, companionship, fulfilment and a sense of community in your chosen belief, then right now you are on the correct path for you. There may come a time when you want to rethink your options or that time may never come. Either way, heaven is revealing itself to you through belonging to a community of like-minded people who are your spiritual family. You take care of one another and, in a world where loneliness is a growing problem and compassion in short supply, this is a truly miraculous and wonderful thing.

Belonging is a stage that typically attracts young people looking outside themselves for a sense of identity, and it also appeals strongly to those who feel alone or vulnerable and in need of support and community.

The third stage is one of **becoming.** I suspect a lot of you reading this book right now would be either entering or living this stage. You are someone who questions what you have been taught and who wants to discover your own answers. Perhaps you have abandoned religion or are seeking answers within your faith. Either way you are a truth-seeker. You may also be a scientist, student or sceptic. You could have moments of great clarity and illumination but feel frustrated that these glimpses of the truth behind all things are so fleeting.

The final stage is one of **beauty** or **bliss**. It is the highest stage you can reach on earth and for some people it can only be achieved in dreams, in meditation or in flashes of inspiration. Others may not experience it in this life at all. Near-death experiences typically describe this stage of belief. If you are lucky enough to glimpse this stage on earth, you begin to see beauty, wonder and magic within and all around you. You sense a connection and unity between all people and all things, in both this life and the next. Love is your teacher and your guide. You love mysteries and paradoxes and have no problems understanding and accepting that spiritual growth is an unending process. You could be described as a mystic, a true individual, a free spirit, a true spirit who brings glimpses of heaven's beauty to earth.

As mentioned above, there are a number of signs which suggest that you are ready to move from one stage of your spiritual development to another, and you can read all about those signs, and decide where you really are, in chapter 4. For now, bear in mind that during our lives we will often fluctuate between stages, going backwards and forwards on the ladder of faith depending on our needs and life circumstances at the time. For example, if you feel vulnerable and alone and in need of guidance and the support of others, you may drift forwards or backwards to the belonging stage. You may catch a glimpse of bliss but this stage is extremely hard to sustain in this life, so you may step back towards becoming. Moving between stages in this way is perfectly natural and healthy. You need to experience and fully understand all four stages to grow closer to heaven.

Life before death

You don't need to wait until you die to find heaven because you are a part of heaven already. Many religions and beliefs focus on the idea that this life determines how we will spend the next life. A lot of time is devoted to thinking about what happens when we die and how best to prepare ourselves for the other side. But we don't fully understand the miracle of this life yet, so how can we even begin to understand what death is?

Wouldn't it be better when you are alive to focus on that? Wouldn't it be better to try to understand ourselves and our amazing planet, and to leave thoughts of death to when it actually happens to us? Wouldn't it be better to channel all our energy into what is alive within us right now? Perhaps thinking about the other side is taking your energy away from what is heavenly about this life and what is heavenly about you.

There is nothing more miraculous or heavenly than this life. The life you are living right now as you read this book. The life you lived yesterday has vanished and the life you hope to lead tomorrow does not exist yet. The only thing that truly exists and is truly real and deserves your utmost veneration, worship and respect is the magic of the present moment.

And don't assume that you need to do great or significant things. Life is often made up of the tiniest things. It is about the small things that make up your existence. It is about all the precious moments that fill your heart with joy. It is about watching a sunset or glimpsing a rainbow. It is about the laughter of your children or the warmth of a hug. It is about going for a walk with no particular destination in mind. It is about spending time with family or friends or beloved pets or flooding your heart with happy images of departed loved ones. It is about so many wonderful, small things – but when you put all these small things together they make up the wonder and the miracle of your existence. Respect that existence. And from that respect you will instinctively discover a respect for the existence of others.

You will understand that although you are utterly and completely unique, you are seeking the truth of your existence just like everyone else on this planet. After all, isn't the search for heaven – or feelings of fulfilment, love, certainty and bliss, if your preference is to avoid using any word that has associations with religion – what drives each one of us? Isn't the search for contentment and inner peace what unites young and old, rich and poor, atheist and priest?

The search for bliss is a desire that lingers in everyone's heart. Two people from different cultures, backgrounds and belief systems may be convinced that there can never be a meeting ground between them because they speak different languages, have different social norms and read different sacred texts, but in essence they are not so very different after all. Both long to find heaven or whatever word they use to describe a feeling of belonging, truth and connection.

Problems of communication only arise if both have fixed ideas about the right or wrong way to find heaven, but if they could only respect that a person who appears different is seeking truth and meaning and life – just taking a different route to the same destination – what an enlightened and harmonious world we would live in.

Indeed, a wonderful world where each one of us respects the right of another to be themselves and find their own life-affirming spiritual path would come as close as I can imagine to experiencing heaven on earth.

It would truly feel like home.

Sadly, such a world isn't likely to be created overnight. There is a lot of darkness, confusion, stupidity and ignorance to be overcome first, and this may take centuries. There is no point focusing on some distant utopia which may never come to pass. All we have is the present, and in the here and now each person who takes the road less travelled by discovering who they truly are and what heaven means to them becomes a light and a beacon of hope and progress.

Prepare yourself

In the next chapter you will not only find answers to some frequently asked questions about the afterlife to help prepare you for your spiritual journey, but you will also read a collection of intriguing stories sent to me by people who have become total originals in their search for heaven. They will share with you how they found their own path to heaven or caught a glimpse of heaven on earth. Prepare to be moved, amazed, shocked and inspired. Prepare to smile and prepare to shed a tear. Prepare yourself for the road less travelled:

> *Two roads diverged in a wood, and I –*
> *I took the one less travelled by,*
> *And that has made all the difference.*
>
> Robert Frost

CHAPTER THREE

Taking the road less travelled

Do not go where the path may lead, go instead where there is no path and leave a trail.

Ralph Waldo Emerson

In the previous chapter the different paths to heaven, or bliss, that religions or belief systems endorse were laid out for you, but this chapter is not about religion or following any kind of movement – it is about *you*. It is about becoming a total original in your search for heaven. It is about finding your own path, not taking the one that others have trod before you. It is about becoming rather than following. It is about finding rather than searching.

Think about all the people in life that you admire, respect or worship. In the great majority of cases these will be people who have not copied others but who have come forward with their own unique voice, style, approach, message or insight. Remember,

Socrates, Copernicus, Lao-Tzu, Da Vinci, Mozart, Mother Teresa, Steve Jobs, to name but a few, did not imitate anyone. They challenged convention and found enlightenment. They all took the road less travelled.

As we've seen, espousing a religion or spiritual movement does have its benefits. Your shared beliefs are validated by the group you have joined, and that can be very comforting, especially during times of loss or grief because we are social beings. You can give yourself a label and others can instantly understand where you are coming from because of that label.

So, from a social angle, joining a group with shared beliefs can be extremely beneficial and should be encouraged. However, when that group starts to tell you what to think and believe, and that their way is the only way, this could stunt your spiritual growth because all the thinking about what heaven is and how to get there has been done for you. But that is the problem. Spiritual growth is unavoidably an individual thing and undoubtedly challenging and difficult. It shouldn't be easy.

It's a bit like growing up, really. As much as you would want your children to always be looked after and not have difficulties, the wise part of you knows that this would rob them of invaluable life lessons and experience and make them pretty immature and dependent adults. Making your own decisions, taking the rough with the smooth or treating Disaster and Triumph just the same, as the famous Rudyard Kipling poem 'If' recommends, helps mature a boy into a man or a girl into a woman. This insightful quote says it far better than I can:

Sometimes you have to sink, in order to understand what it means to rise. You must fall apart, to understand what it means when you are whole. Experience loss in order to truly appreciate what you have. Be in the grasp of true despair, to remember what it means to be happy. Go through Hell in order to find your way to Heaven.

Nathaniel Butler

In much the same way, habitually avoiding self-examination, creativity, originality and responsibility in your spiritual development is tempting because it offers immediate gratification and an easy, comforting life. There is also comfort in the knowledge that others are travelling along that road so you won't ever be alone. The trouble is, the path of least resistance if travelled too frequently will eventually cripple you emotionally and spiritually. You will be doing all the conventionally right things in life and following all the rules – but still feel empty inside.

So, when choosing a spiritual path you are faced with a clear choice: take the road travelled by others and avoid independent thought, or take the road less travelled and examine who you really are and what truly matters to you. The road less travelled is harder, longer and more painful and challenging because you are going against the grain of what is considered acceptable or usual, but the life of self-examination or self-discovery has the potential to be extraordinary. It all depends on what you want.

Do you want to believe what others tell you about heaven and how to get there or do you want to discover the path to heaven yourself? Do you want to believe in the extraordinary because you have read about it or because you have searched deep in your heart and know it to be real?

I'm hoping your answer will be the latter in each case, but if it isn't that's okay too because you are making a choice about your spiritual development and discovering who you are and what you want in the process.

However, as a number of well-travelled routes have already been discussed the rest of this chapter, and indeed this book, will be devoted to the road that is less travelled – a road where spirituality is distinguished from religion and where self-examination and a heart full of love are the only requirements. I'll begin the journey by sharing with you some stories sent to me recently by people with ordinary but extraordinary lives.

Leading lights

Stories from people who believe they have glimpsed something magical on earth will show you that the route to heaven can vary significantly from person to person. There are as many different ways for heaven to speak as there are people on this planet, so this selection can only focus on some of the most commonly mentioned or recognised ones – and even then there will be variations in how one revelation appears or is interpreted by different people. Please don't think that the doors to heaven are closed to you if you've not had any similar spiritual experiences. Believe me, your path is out there, you just need to know how and where to look – and, hopefully, chapters 4 and 5 will help you search in the right direction.

For now, though, sit back and let the stories that follow open your mind to the invigorating idea that the road to heaven is one that only your heart can find and only you can walk down.

This first story is one of those that offer perhaps the closest anyone might get to direct proof of heaven.

Subliminal cuts

Dear Theresa, my name is Lawrence and I had a near-death experience in 1973. This all happened after my dentist had given me a drug. I had a heart attack, but I believe it was healed in heaven. I recently had an angiogram and doctors were amazed at how good my arteries are for a 62-year-old man.

In my near-death experience I came out of my body, saw myself dead on the floor and was taken through a tunnel by a ghostly white car into another portal tunnel towards a stunning bright light. At the end of the tunnel I was greeted by a young lady and a boy. The light was so bright I couldn't see their faces clearly so I had to squint. They welcomed me, speaking in my mind as in telepathy. They asked me if I wanted to enter the garden ahead which was a beautiful scene of flowers, trees, greens and built-in streams. I saw glass marble structured mansion-type buildings ahead and was in awe at the sight.

All the time I felt elated and happy. I wanted to stay there but then suddenly I was lifted up several inches from the floor and I saw people and animals running about. They all had solid bodies. I knew I had died but I didn't care as there was so much love and peace. At that point a cinema screen appeared in my mind and I saw my life. It started when I was around five and ran to my current age. Everything was at great speed with subliminal cuts. I was asked several times if I wanted to go back and I said I might. The screen didn't just showcase my life, it also showed me clips of wars in the Middle East and earthquakes and tsunamis in Japan and the Philippines. After that I saw good and beautiful things like medical cures and laughter.

Suddenly, without warning I began to descend to the ground and floated to the gate. The two beings of light asked me if I wanted to go through the gate because if I did I would go back to the realm of earth. I half-opened the gate and entered slowly, and as I did I felt myself turn into solid body form again. I felt eighteen again! A blue, violet light came towards me and I was mesmerised. I felt the light feeding knowledge into my mind. I could feel it teaching me about the universe around me. I feel I have so much understanding of this life and the next, the garden of bliss and how beings of light assist us when we cross over. It has changed my life and filled it with a sense of wonder and awe.

Near-death experiences like Lawrence's are gripping to read. Equally sensational are actual sightings of spirit. Becky, a young nurse at the time, sent me this story.

Night shift

I was on night shift and doing my rounds. I went to check up on one of my patients and it was about 4.30am. When I went into her room, she became wonderfully alert, as some people do very near the end. I sat by her and held her hand and she looked to one side, staring into vacant space. As time went by, it was clear she could see someone there I couldn't. Then her face lit up like a beacon. She was staring and smiling at what was clearly a long-lost friend, her eyes so full of love and serenity that it was hard for me not to be overcome by tears.

Then she closed her eyes and I knew that she had died. I sat for a while in silence, giving the moment the dignity and respect it deserved. When I looked up I saw something rise from her body. It was absolutely beautiful. A whirl of pastel colour, vibrant in not only appearance but also movement, was leaving her chest area. It was so comforting. Like I said, I was a very young nurse – we are talking 1970 and I'm close to fifty-five now – and at the time I thought that this was probably the body letting off steam or something, but I don't think that now. I believe I saw that old lady's spirit leave her body.

I've also been sent vast numbers of magical stories like this next one. Linda didn't actually see her father but she knew he was there.

Calming

I was never one of those people who know where they are going in life. I dropped out of school and just drifted from one dead-end job to another; one dead-end relationship to another. My mum had passed when I was a little girl and my dad raised me by himself. We were very close but fell out when my dad didn't want me to leave school.

My dad always wanted me to go to university and get a good job but I was more interested in hanging around with my mates. I wouldn't listen. One morning after breakfast we had a huge argument. I stormed upstairs, packed my bags and went to stay with my best friend for a few nights. I got a job at a clothing warehouse to pay my way. If only I'd known that Dad had just a few more months to live – that was typical of him, he never wanted to burden me with his worries.

After my dad passed, I was totally overcome with depression, grief, anxiety – you name it, I had it. I cried all night, begging my dad to come back and help me. I hated that the last time we had really spoken we had argued. I felt guilty and lost. I could not imagine getting on with my life without him; getting married; having a child or living any kind of life. This went on week after week. I went to my dad's grave during my lunch breaks, where I sat and cried.

Normally it took me ages to get to sleep but one night, as soon as my head hit the pillow, I fell into a trance. I couldn't move or open my eyes. I was aware of where I was, but I felt frozen. At that moment I knew my dad was in the room. I did not see him; I just felt his presence and then I felt the side of the bed go down as if he was sitting on it. I felt him lean against my cheek and I heard him whisper in my ear. I couldn't understand what he was saying but I felt an unfamiliar calm come over me. I drifted off to sleep and woke up the next morning determined to turn my life around.

For the first time I didn't cry on the way to work. I knew what I had to do. I handed my notice in and put my applications in for college. Then I visited Dad's grave and sat there, still savouring a feeling of calmness. It was the most astonishing thing. I couldn't explain it exactly but I felt as if a weight had been taken off my shoulders.

Although I haven't felt his presence since, I know Dad was there that night. He knew what I was going through and came to comfort me and give me some good advice. To this day my encounter with my dad gives me hope and strength. I'm a qualified secondary school English teacher now. I'm determined to make a difference and help other kids find a sense of meaning and purpose in life. I know I'm making my dad proud.

Leanne really saw a spirit. Here is her remarkable story:

Stay with me forever

The most recent experience I've had was by far the most incredible and will stay with me forever.

In early 2011, my husband was diagnosed with stage 4 non-Hodgkin lymphoma and my world collapsed. We had four-year-old twin boys and had just got our lives back on track financially – this could not be happening to us!

About three weeks after his diagnosis, my husband was undergoing massive doses of chemotherapy and was feeling so dreadfully ill, he began sleeping downstairs on the sofa, instead of coming to bed, as he was unable to sleep most of the time. Night-times were the worst for me, as I lay there imagining the possibilities for the future, crying myself to sleep and asking heaven for help and guidance.

One night, after sobbing myself to sleep, I woke to find a figure sitting on my husband's side of the bed, leaning towards me on an outstretched hand, as if watching me sleep. I sat bolt upright in shock and shifted quickly away from the figure and as I did so he (as it felt so like a male presence) stood very slowly, moving gently away from me, as if to reassure me that he meant me no harm. I noticed, as he stood, that he was very tall, at least seven or eight feet, and he wore a brown habit, tied at the waist with a yellow cord. His hood was up so that his face couldn't be seen, but he placed his hands slowly together, as if in prayer and I immediately felt that everything would be okay. Despite my initial fear, I lay back down and fell into the most deep and peaceful sleep I'd ever had.

My husband has now been in remission for almost three years and I thank heaven every single day for listening to my prayers and helping us through the darkest time in our lives. It is great to read that others have had these experiences too, as although I knew in my heart that I was not imagining it, there have been times when I've doubted – but not any more!

By an amazing coincidence, as I was working on this section of the book a news item flashed on my screen with the heading 'Guardian angel "ghost" photographed at dying grandfather's bedside'. I scrolled down and read the story of 76-year-old Bob Large, who had been diagnosed with terminal bladder cancer and kidney failure. The hospital had given him just days to live and a vicar was summoned to read him the last rites. His grandson, Chris Leadbetter, used his mobile phone to take what he thought would be a last picture of his grandfather, and the photo clearly showed the image of a veiled woman watching over Bob – his 'guardian angel'. Incredibly, Bob's health started to improve soon after, and he's now out of hospital. If you Google those names you can see the picture for yourself and it is awesome.

For some reason the media got hold of the story, but my mail-bag contains many similar pictures of hazy faces or balls of light that just can't be explained. I also get lots of stories about unexplained sightings of spirits or ghosts that shock, surprise, confuse and delight those who witness them. All of these accounts would make great news items but the people involved didn't make them public. I am so honoured that they choose to share them with me. The photographs I've seen suggest that cameras are picking up something the human eye cannot detect. Sure, in some cases there could be a logical explanation, such as reflections of light or a fault in the camera, but the people who send me their photos often tell me they have checked that there is nothing to reflect the image off and their cameras and film cannot be faulty because no other picture was affected in the same way. And what strikes me in many cases of spirit sightings is how surprised people are by what they saw. Many describe themselves as feet-on-the-ground kind of people, who actually didn't believe in the supernatural before their experience.

As well as possible spirit sightings, miracle rescue stories where the only possible explanation seems to be divine intervention can also grab the imagination and tug at the heart strings like nothing else. A number of these stories are so amazing that they make it to the newspapers. This was the case for a woman called Charlene Deherrera, who was rescued dramatically when driving her car in a flood. If you Google her name you'll find a number of uplifting video links so you can see the rescue for yourself. It seems that she didn't see or couldn't stop in time and her SUV was submerged in water. It started going under. Her windows were rolled up, and she couldn't swim, so she panicked and froze. A man who dove in to try and help her started beating her window with a stick to break it, and it never gave. Eventually another man felt her grabbing at his arm through the front window, so he pulled her out. When they dragged the car out, the windows were all rolled up, unbroken. How do you explain that – if not miracle intervention?

Leanne's story wasn't reported on the internet but that doesn't make it any the less spectacular. She is convinced a miracle saved her life:

Around the corner

This is nothing short of a miracle and I have no doubt that it saved my life.

Aged about twenty, I was driving to my boyfriend's house along the same route as I had used hundreds of times before. I was driving too fast, singing along to my music, when suddenly I heard a clear voice in my head say, 'You should slow down – you never know what's around the corner.' I immediately slowed right down, much slower than I usually would have, as I was approaching a blind bend in the road. As I bore left with the bend, I hit the brakes hard – there was a

Transit van parked on double yellow lines, right in my line of travel. Had I not slowed, I would certainly have ploughed right into the back of it and probably, due to the speed I was travelling, wouldn't have been here today. Needless to say, I now drive carefully!

Reports of near-death experiences, along with sightings or images of ghosts and miracle rescues, strongly indicate that heaven is for real but, in my opinion, such dramatic stories, however convincingly they appear to offer proof of the reality of heaven, are not the catalysts for the current wave of belief in life after death. Far more compelling is the increasingly large number of people who haven't been saved from certain death or survived against the odds or seen spirits but who, for a variety of different and powerful reasons, have come to the firm conclusion that this life is not all there is. People like this lady, who prefers to remain anonymous, but whose story is below. She is convinced heaven saved her life in a different way. For her, divine intervention was not obvious or dramatic, but invisible to everything except her heart.

Heart without a beat

Twelve years ago I didn't like living at all. I didn't want to live. The details would bore you but to cut a long story short my husband had left me and my son, who has severe learning difficulties. I blame myself because I was an alcoholic when I conceived him and drank throughout the pregnancy, very heavily. It was the only way I could get through the day at the time. My husband – if I can call him that as he never lived by his vows – made me feel deeply unloved and unhappy. Stupidly, I stuck by him until he left me.

Well, there I was, standing on top of a multistorey car park. I had my son with me. If I jumped I would take him with me. I started to walk towards the edge, ready to climb over. My aim was to pretend it was a game as I knew my son would follow everything I said. I grabbed my son's hand and as I did everything just stopped. Hard to explain but it was like I was in a freeze-frame and time stood still. Before, my heart had been beating heavily and noisily in my chest but suddenly it just seemed to stop. I stopped breathing, too, and my son stood still like a statue. It must have only been a few moments that life stood still in this way and there was only silence, but when I snapped out of it and could hear my heart beat again I knew that I was going to live. I grabbed my son and hugged him.

Today, I look back at that terrible moment and can't believe how far I have come. My son is a pure joy to me. He has made so much progress and has lots of friends at school. I've also just finished my midwife training. Nothing gives me more joy than to tell expectant mothers there is a new heartbeat inside them. A beating heart that is the purest joy and I know from my experience that when the heart physically stops beating it keeps on beating in a spiritual sense.

Huge numbers of people have written to me to tell me how they know they have sensed, seen, heard or felt reassuring signs of the afterlife. Sometimes reassurance comes through an other-worldy feeling, as it did in the story above, but other times it can come from a sign or message from a departed loved one received at a significant moment. The sign can be anything; the important thing is the meaning it holds for the person observing or receiving it. Here's Alexandra's story, which, in her own words, illustrates this phenomenon perfectly.

Signs from above

I have just lost one of my favourite aunts on Tuesday. We are still reeling from the shock of losing her so suddenly.

What you said about a deeper connection with departed loved ones came true for me. I have received two signs from her so far.

The first was after I remembered and was missing the dumplings she used to make, was just thinking I didn't get to try hers this year and, a few hours later, I saw a fallen bamboo leaf near my car, which is the same type used to wrap the dumpling which she used to make. There were no such bamboo trees in the area I was.

I thought it was just a coincidence and thought to myself that if there was another sign, then I'd know it is my aunt. This morning at 1 am, I was in my study and one of the lights flickered for a while. I thought maybe it was going to burn off, then it stopped flickering and suddenly I felt goose bumps and then I was embarrassed if my aunt saw me because I was a little underdressed.

I quickly went into my room after that. I hope that if it was her, she wouldn't be offended by my reaction. My cousins have had some signs as well. We all believe she has moved on to a better place and those signs are her way of telling us she is alright.

Here's Catharine's touching story:

Valentine

I lost my beloved husband Gerard in August 2012 on his eightieth birthday. It was a sudden death and a dreadful shock for me and our son and daughter, particularly since he had recovered well from an operation a few weeks before. He had suffered over the years with major heart problems, but was a strong, determined man and with great fortitude always fought his way back to health after setbacks. I, being thirteen years younger than him, was able to care for him and, although at times difficult for both of us, we coped. We both have a strong faith which helped and his love of music and gardening kept him focused and determined to carry on. I felt his dying on his birthday was very sad, but somehow poignant, as if he had lived the full circle of his life.

Shortly after his death we were to celebrate our forty-sixth wedding anniversary and one day when I was really upset I found a card standing against the back of my cupboard. I thought it was maybe a Valentine card as it had a single red rose on it, but when I opened it I realised it was an anniversary card which said, 'To my beautiful wife with my love forever, Gerard.' I realised later it was a card he sent me many years ago but I had forgotten all about it. To find it in this unexpected way, when I was feeling so upset, was amazing. I was in tears all day.

So far I've mentioned signs that are personal and unique to the observer but there are some that are so often reported that I like to call them divine calling cards. Of these, the most common has to be the perfect white feather. Here's a lovely story sent to me by Wendy:

Blown away

I lost my dad four months ago. My daughter-in-law was diagnosed with terminal cancer. I have been helping my mum more due to her failing health, looking after numerous grandchildren, and I managed to upset someone I love dearly. Life hasn't been too good lately and I was beginning to lose the plot a little. I woke up during the night and with my head in my arms asked heaven to send me a sign that I wasn't alone. I desperately needed to know angels were with me.

My husband bought me an iPad for my birthday tomorrow. Last night I found an angel picture and used it as the wallpaper. Today when I came home I checked my emails and discovered my fourteen-year-old son had changed it for a picture of three beautiful white feathers. I just cried when I saw it.

I asked my son why he changed it and he replied that he knew I loved feathers.

They couldn't have come at a better time.

That was just what I needed.

Do you think heaven gave my Joe a helping hand?

He's never done anything like this on my old iPad.

I've had feathers before, falling at my feet. On the floor in my dad's bedroom at the care home when I collected his belongings after he passed and in coat pockets. Those feathers today on my iPad just blew me away.

A white feather appearing at just the right moment offers so many people great hope and comfort. Jean sent me this short but perfect story.

Floating down

Just recently I was dusting a framed photo of my dad, who died in 1995, and I kissed the photo and told him I missed him, only to turn round and see a white feather float down and land at my feet. Reading your books helps me realise that these things are real, and not my imagination. My dad often comes to me in dreams, too. Once again, many thanks, you have helped me so much.

Even though a white feather is a commonly reported sign, the way each person responds to it is totally unique – for some it can offer reassurance, for others inspiration or a sense of being watched over.

Elaine believes heaven spoke to her through a rainbow.

Rainbows every day

Today is my dad's anniversary and I had been thinking a lot about him during the day. Just after my dad died I was feeling very upset and asked for a sign. Almost immediately a beautiful rainbow appeared in the sky. On the day of my dad's funeral there was a rainbow across the cemetery. For at least a month after my dad died my mum and I saw rainbows every day. Rainbows have become very significant to my mum and me.

Butterflies are the theme of this next account, from Chloe.

Flying around

I had been offered a last-minute au pair job in Cannes (South of France) in mid-July of this year. I flew home from a family holiday and a day later flew out to my new home. In that short day at home I quickly picked up three books to take with me on my travels – yours being one of them. I am a bookworm and tend to read the blurb and first page of every book I purchase … But for some reason I just picked yours up and felt I had to have it, without reading anything first. That evening I went to say goodbye to my family and my grandpa, who was very unwell with cancer. He told me that he was very proud of me for going and doing something new and challenging. He also said, 'If for any reason anything happens to me while you are away, I want you to know I am immensely proud to call you my granddaughter and I love you very much.' I told him I would see him soon.

I started reading your book as I flew out and was immediately drawn into each chapter, each experience. Unfortunately my amazing grandpa passed away on my fifth day in Cannes. Straight away I felt like the chat we had before I left was perhaps because he felt he knew. The day after my mum had called and given me the news, I was having lunch on my terrace when a beautiful red admiral butterfly flew around my table for ten to fifteen seconds. I felt straight away that it was a sign from above saying my grandpa was safe and free from pain. I decided I would fly home to Cornwall, England, the following week on my nineteenth birthday (29 July) and attend the funeral on the 30th. On the night of my birthday, my boyfriend took me to a beautiful secluded spot for a picnic. As he asked me how I felt about the funeral and if I was feeling okay, a red admiral flew around the two of us and stayed with me for about thirty seconds. We both felt that again it was a sign about Grandpa.

Finally, the day of the funeral arrived and I can honestly say it was the hardest and most emotional day I've had. We decided to have a small, intimate family dinner afterwards at my gran and grandpa's local golf club. I felt emotionally exhausted so decided to leave the meal early. My mum later relayed to me that when I had left (leaving an empty chair at the table; all the windows were shut in the restaurant) a beautiful red admiral flew around the table, settled behind my gran, flew back around the table and disappeared out of the room. The whole table was silent and they had finally felt what I had experienced in Cannes.

I flew back to the South of France and am now nearly at the end of my summer here in Cannes. These sightings/

feelings I had/have, alongside reading your book, have brought me great comfort in feeling that my grandpa is no longer in pain and in a safer, more beautiful place. Although I have my own anxieties and uncertainties about the afterlife … I feel I am connected to something beyond life on earth. I thank you massively for helping me feel that way …

I've mentioned three commonly reported signs from heaven: feathers, rainbows and butterflies. However, there are many others I could have included, such as coins appearing in unexpected places, lights flickering, unexplained balls of light or orbs in photographs, and sightings of birds at significant moments, but the sign could be absolutely anything that has personal meaning for the individual involved, perhaps even this book you are currently reading. I am deeply humbled whenever I get emails like this one sent to me by Suzanne:

Light in the room

Some years back I literally found myself in a dark, dark hole, one that I didn't even realise I was in till I was given one of your books by my lovely younger brother. Anyway, the first night I began to read your book, hand on my heart it's like the light in the room illuminated beyond any light I had ever experienced and slowly I was being lifted up out of that dark hole. There are many reasons for falling into that dark place, a lot of it was feeling disconnected from the truth, and thankfully your books set me on the path to rediscovering the real truth of life. Thankfully today I have a lovely husband

and two beautiful babies that just fill my heart and soul with such love and goodness. I now trust that life is happening exactly as it should be and that heaven is leading the way for my family and me.

Thank you again for sharing your books with the rest of us, you have helped my family so much. My brother and mother also read your books and through a lot of bereavement in our lives we needed hope and you gave us that hope, so thank you kindly from the bottom of my heart.

Of course, you could argue that all these so-called signs are just coincidences, but have you ever considered the possibility that coincidence might be the language that heaven speaks?

Dreams can bring heaven closer for many people. I think this next story is pretty extraordinary. It was sent to me by Elizabeth.

Another place

I do have a story that I am pleased to share with you. It concerns a strange dream!!? I had many years ago ... forty to be precise. Dreams tend to fade over the years but this one is as vivid as if it happened only yesterday. Anyway to cut a long story short:

I had an uncle that I was very fond of when I was a child. He and my aunt had no children of their own and always made a great fuss of me. When I was in my early twenties he was diagnosed with terminal cancer. During this time he and my aunt needed extra support so every evening after work I went to their house and slept there. After several weeks my uncle passed away. I and other members of the family were with him at the time.

About a week after the funeral (I was still sleeping at my aunt's house) I had a very vivid dream. I should tell you that my aunt and uncle each had a rocking chair. Both the chairs were identical. My uncle sat in his to the right of the fireplace and my aunt always sat opposite on the left ... it was something of a joke, neither ever sat in each other's chair. One morning just before waking I had this vivid dream. I dreamt that I walked into the living room and my uncle was sitting in my aunt's chair with his foot on the coal scuttle the way he always did. Laughing, I said to him, 'You're in big trouble, you're sitting in auntie's chair.' He looked up at me and said, 'Oh no I'm not, my love' – he always called me that – 'this is my own chair.'

I woke up then, got myself ready for work, said goodbye to my aunt and left. That evening when I returned from work my aunt seemed less grief-stricken and started to talk about my uncle, and about the good life they'd had together. Because she seemed more like her old self I decided to mention the dream that I'd had that morning. When I did her face lit up and she told me a strange thing. She said, 'That's made me feel so much better.' When I asked why, she told me that the day after his funeral, unbeknown to anyone but herself and when she was alone, she swapped the chairs around and so for the previous week she had been sitting in his chair. How could I have known that? The chairs were identical. Did my uncle return to let us know that he had just moved on to another dimension known as heaven?

Intuition can also be a bridge to the other side. Intuition is that small voice inside you which, if listened to, can change your life in big ways. It is knowing something without the use of reason or information from your senses. Intuition figures strongly in the next story, sent to me by Sally.

Wake up

One morning, I was playing with my little daughter Lily on the living-room floor after a sleepless night. She was still waking four or five times. The doorbell rang and I went to get it – a large bunch of flowers from some of the girls at work. I remember feeling touched but rather ungratefully also a bit put out as I really didn't need something else to look after. I opened the baby gate that guarded the stairs and quickly nipped upstairs to place the flowers in the bathroom sink ready to put in my bedroom later.

Then I went back to my daughter and after changing her lay down with her on the floor and fell asleep. It was a deep and heavy sleep because I was so, so tired. I didn't dream but I heard a voice within me waking me up. It sounded as loud as a fire alarm and it was shouting for me to wake up. My initial thought when I woke up was that there was a burglar in the house. Then I looked for Lily. She was not in the room.

I ran to the front hall and saw immediately that I had forgotten to shut the stair gate. Then my heart stood still when I saw Lily balancing and looking precarious at the top of the stairs. I grabbed her just before she fell. It wasn't a dream, it wasn't a 'sense' that I should wake up: it was some-body who deliberately jolted me awake because my baby was seconds away from falling ten steps down on to a hard floor. I can't prove it but I absolutely know it and I am forever grateful to whoever and whatever it was.

Scent that has no explained source is something that features a lot in the letters I receive. The smell of flowers is often mentioned, as is the aroma of vanilla. Kaisha told me:

Lemons

When I was twenty, my departed Nannan appeared in my dream. There was an olive-coloured swirling background, and she appeared in front of it, clear as day. Her message was short and clear: 'I want you to name your first daughter after me.' A part of me knew I was dreaming, and I also knew that this wasn't a normal dream. I woke slowly and I could smell lemons for about thirty seconds after I woke, before I opened my eyes. There were no lemons in our house or anything that could be mistaken for a lemon. I used to bake cakes with Nannan as a young girl and we always made lemon icing, so I am sure she put the scent there to ensure I took notice of the dream.

Music – especially songs played at significant times that remind you of a departed loved one – is another recurring theme. Numbers, especially the repeating number 11.11, also keep cropping up in my mailbag. Here is Jackie's experience:

Death is not the end

I lost a very close friend a year ago and miss him so much. Sometimes the loss is overwhelming – we had been child-hood friends and had known each other for over forty years. He was diagnosed with cancer in February 2013 and died five months later on 16 July. Knowing that his soul lives on brings me some comfort, although I long to see him again.

The experience which reassures me death is not the end is that I continually see 11.11. It happens quite a few times a week – I feel compelled to glance at a clock and that's the time shown. When I used to work until recently in a shop, I would often get 11.11 on someone's till receipt or the amount they'd spent would come to £11.11p sometimes.

Sometimes heaven manifests itself in human form. Even though the situation has a logical explanation, for the person involved it can feel like divine intervention. It certainly did for Maggie – here is her story:

Wrong exit

In the summer of 1991 when I was twenty-six I was on holi-day in America, staying with a friend in Philadelphia. We had planned an evening boat trip with dinner and we had arranged to meet at the hospital she worked at when she finished and go on from there. I was excited about the evening and, being single, thought I might be lucky enough to meet a nice guy, so took care with my make-up and hair, which was highlighted blonde and curly. I decided to show off my newly acquired tan with denim shorts and a black bodice top and after finishing with a nice pair of heels and a bag I was set to go. My friend had given me directions to her hospital from her home using the underground train, explaining which exit to take when I arrived.

Some areas of Philadelphia are heavily populated black communities and she and her brother had told me of how fearful they felt driving through these run-down areas, having to stop at traffic lights and so forth. She and I had no racist tendencies but we seemed to have an element of paranoia about ending up stranded in this black community, so she told me to be careful which exit I took as one led into one of these areas. Guess who took the wrong exit! As I walked along the street wondering where the heck I was going, I noticed how deserted the place looked. I think I saw one or two people but that was it until I turned a corner down a side street, when my blood froze – I saw a number of guys (I think there were about five) lounging against a car across the street to my left and when they saw me they shuffled about and sat up with interest.

I thought about retreating but felt I would be followed and besides I couldn't run far in my heels, so I ventured on down the street with my heart thumping in my chest. I was cursing myself silently for taking the wrong turn and thought I must look like a prostitute to them dressed as I was! One of the guys sauntered over to me so I slowed down, and when he approached he asked me in a lazy tone if I was lost. I bumbled in my Northern Irish accent the name of the hospital I was looking for, but he either didn't understand or didn't seem that concerned in helping me, saying something like 'Whaa?', and I really didn't like the look on his face.

I noticed the other guys were all standing up at this point, looking over expectantly. In my mind I was thinking, 'This is it, this is how I'm going to go, another statistic found up some alleyway, you stupid idiot!' I felt so frightened as there was no one else around. Just as I was about to repeat the hospital name to the guy thinking how futile this would be, an ambulance pulled up alongside me to my left with a black male paramedic driving it. I never felt so much relief in my life! Assessing the situation quickly, he had pulled over and shouted to me, 'Need a lift?' I looked up gratefully and said yes, and gave him the hospital name I needed to get to. He told me to jump on, he was going that way, so I did this quickly, leaving the intimidating guy standing there. I got a mild reprimand from the driver (who I viewed as my saviour) about not walking around these parts dressed like that etc. I thanked him when he dropped me off and met my friend, who yelled at me for being so stupid!

It is only since my recent insights into spiritual matters that I have connected this event with possible heavenly rescue. What do you think? The more I think about this, the more it seems to be the case. For example, if any guy (black or white) had pulled up in a car to offer me a lift, I would have been caught between a rock and a hard place, I feel. Also, if a white guy in an ambulance had offered help, he may have got set upon by the group on the street. It seemed so suitable given the location for my rescuer to be a black guy in an ambulance, which immediately made him respectable to me and perhaps less of a threat to the group on the street. I don't think it was a coincidence and now feel strongly that divine intervention took place that day for me.

Sometimes I'm sent stories about human angels which are less easy to explain away as coincidence or 'right time, right place'. I call these 'vanishing stranger stories' because the helper appears from out of nowhere, typically with exactly the right skills or knowledge to help in a crisis, and then is impossible to trace afterwards, inviting speculation that he or she was an angel in disguise. Here is Nathan's story:

Water babies

Five years ago I took my ten-year-old twins – Josh and Jonah – to our favourite beach in Cornwall. It was a beautiful sunny day and the sea was calm, and my boys were strong swimmers so I had no worries about letting them take a swim. I've got skin allergies and have never been great at swimming so I stayed on the beach watching them laughing and splashing in the waves. I remember feeling very content with my life and grateful for the gift of my sons. My wife, Suzanne, and I had tried for seven years before we conceived with the help of IVF. That feeling of happiness turned to panic and terror when I saw the boys were getting carried away and going too far from shore. I ran to the water's edge and yelled and waved at them to come back, but I think they thought I was larking around so they waved back.

And then both their heads disappeared under the waves. I couldn't see them. I ran into the water but because I didn't take my shoes off I couldn't swim fast enough. At that moment I heard someone shout at me from behind. I glanced around and saw a young boy. He looked about the same age as Josh and Jonah. He swam next to me and told me he could go and get them. I was in such a panic I didn't even reply. I just helplessly watched him swim towards where I had last seen my boys.

A few moments later I saw Josh swimming towards me. He grabbed me and I grabbed him. But there was no sign of Jonah. I told Josh to get back to shore but he just clung to me so again I couldn't move. For what seemed like eternity I trod water, desperately calling out to Jonah. And then suddenly from out of nowhere he appeared and grabbed me as well. It was a struggle to keep my head above water as both boys were clinging on to me, but eventually I made it back to shore.

I was so deliriously happy that the boys were okay that I forgot about the boy. Eventually, when we had all got our breath back I asked them what had happened and they said they had both been playing and then felt themselves being dragged under water. They had been very scared but then they'd felt me pull them up. They told me I was a hero. Much as I would like to take the credit, everyone knows I am a terrible swimmer so I told them I thought it was another boy who had rescued the, but they had not seen another boy.

To this day I wonder who that boy was. Sometimes I worry that he didn't make it back to shore but if that had been the case the local coastguard would have put out an alert and I would have known about it. The beach had also been deserted that day, apart from myself and the boys. I often asked myself if I imagined the boy but I know I didn't. He was real and he saved my boys. I hoped there was a heaven before this happened but now I know there is a heaven.

And then I get a whole load of stories sent to me by people who found heaven not in a particular event but through their hearts – or a feeling of unexpected warmth and comfort that changes everything. Here is what Mike told me:

Heartache

I can't explain this rationally but then I think most great things don't make sense. A few months ago I was going through a difficult but not terrible time in my life. I had split up from my girlfriend of seven years and was not coping very well. The relationship had run its course so I knew there was no going back but my heart ached a lot. I missed being with someone. It can be a lonely world sometimes and is especially hard for us guys as we have to appear tough and independent a lot of the time.

It was a Friday evening and I was biking home from the gym after an intense workout and a heavy, tired, bored, lonely feeling I was getting used to. I came to some traffic lights and as I got there I noticed that a blind guy was trying to cross the road with his guide dog. They weren't having much luck. I felt too despondent to offer to help so just sat there watching them. Then an elderly, frail lady who surely must have had vision problems herself offered to help the guy across the road. The dog started to look nervous as she pulled the guy's arm, indicating it was time to cross. It really was a case of the blind leading the blind. The guy was trusting the woman not his dog and I knew that this was a mistake, but still my apathy stopped me intervening. I couldn't be bothered.

And then just as the lights changed to orange the lady pulled the guy and the reluctant dog into the road. At that moment I jumped off my bike and ran towards them just in time to save what could have been a terrible accident.

After I had guided them both across the road and been thanked, something rather incredible happened. The guide dog sat on my feet, making it impossible for me to leave. As I bent down to stroke the dog it started licking my hand – as if saying thank you as well. It was incredibly touching and as I watched the man and his dog and the elderly lady walk away I got this massive surge of energy. I can't quite describe it, but it started from inside my chest and spread all over my body. For a few moments I felt like I could fly. I was that elated.

The feeling of warmth and energy stayed with me for a good few hours afterwards and I shall never forget it. Again I can't explain it but ever since it happened I haven't felt lonely any more when I'm alone. It's incredible and I have never felt so happy. Do you think it was because my heart muscle got a much-needed workout that day? I'd been to the gym and lifted weights but I'd forgotten to pay attention to the muscle that most needed my attention – my heart.

I love Mike's story because I truly believe that the journey to heaven always starts, and goes on forever, in the heart.

I could carry on listing amazing story after amazing story but that is not the aim of this book. There are many collections of true-life stories like these from ordinary people whose lives have been transformed by a glimpse of heaven or a message from above – and I have written a few such books myself! – but I hope what I've included here will give you the general idea.

A running theme in all these accounts is that nobody discovered absolute proof of heaven's existence. The evidence is personal, anecdotal. But despite this the people who send me their stories are absolutely committed to the idea that they were touched by the divine, and this trust gave them the happiness, strength and courage they didn't think they would have been able to find on their own. It is like something within them becomes independent of their being.

Indeed, from my own life and from reading the insights and stories of thousands of people, it is clear that the path to heaven is not so much about miraculous healings or dramatic rescues, hearing voices, visions of the other side or other such proofs of heaven, but far more about coincidences, subtle signs and gentle dreams – and, above all, a powerful sense of not being alone when all hope seems to have gone.

Even though I don't have indisputable proof of heaven myself I know that heaven has intervened in my life many times. This lack of proof used to distress me and make me think I wasn't special or gifted enough, or that heaven had no interest in me, but as I move into the second part of my life dreams, coincidences, insights and other signs from heaven have changed my perspective entirely. They have shown me that even though I may stumble and lose direction at times, I am on my path to heaven and death is most certainly not the end.

And clearly I am not alone with this transformed perspective. There are a lot of people out there, like me, who feel the same way.

But why now?

Why are more and more people today believing in the possibility of heaven?

Throughout history there have been stories of encounters with the world of spirit and visions of the afterlife. Near-death experiences (NDEs) have also been consistently reported. Recently, however, a number of bestselling books about people who claim to have actually seen heaven have coincided with developments in scientific understanding about the survival of human consciousness after death, as well as exciting progress in the field of quantum physics. Combine all this with the phenomenon of the internet connecting people all over the world and allowing them to talk about their belief in heaven and a moment in time has been created today where speculation about the afterlife and its existence has exploded in popularity.

Recent global polls and surveys show that on average between 50 and 80 per cent of adults believe that heaven or an afterlife exists. Such surveys clearly show how important a spiritual life is to the world's citizens, with a staggering half of us (at least) believing that heaven is real. And of the remaining half about a quarter of those typically say they aren't sure what they believe, with the remaining quarter saying they don't think heaven exists. I used the word staggering because aren't we supposed to be living in an increasingly secular, materialistic world where logic, reason and science are triumphing over faith and belief in the supernatural?

The surveys and polls inspire rather than surprise me. When my first book about the world of spirit came out several years ago the reaction from readers was instant. The book flew into the *Sunday Times* top ten despite very little marketing. I realised instantly that I had touched a nerve. Countless people wanted to share their experiences with me and to date the number of astonishing letters, emails and messages I receive from people, not just in the UK but all over the world, continues to take my breath away. I believe it is a unique combination of factors that has brought about this sudden resurgence of belief.

Separating talk of heaven from mainstream religion certainly plays a part, and this is reflected in a wave of books about the afterlife which have regularly been topping the bestseller lists in recent years. It all started with *90 Minutes in Heaven* back in 2004 and other notable bestsellers – which are all well worth a read – include: *To Heaven and Back, I Believe in Heaven, The Boy Who Came Back from Heaven, Heaven Is for Real, Proof of Heaven* and *Journey of Souls*. Some of these titles, *Journey of Souls* for example, reflect multiculturalism and belief in reincarnations, whereas others have a recognisably Christian slant. *Heaven Is for Real* is a notable example. This multimillion-selling account tells the true story of a four-year-old boy who suffered a ruptured appendix and 'died' for three minutes. Before being brought back to life by doctors this little boy sat on Jesus' lap and met a miscarried sister he had not been told about. Written by a middle-aged neurosurgeon, *Proof of Heaven*, another multimillion-selling book, could not be more different.

Eben Alexander, author of *Proof of Heaven*, is a Harvard-trained neurosurgeon and not the kind of person you would expect to say he had seen the other side. In 2008 Alexander fell into a coma for seven days when bacteria attacked his brain and shut down his cortex – the part of the brain that controls thoughts and emotions. During that time, he was guided by a girl riding a butterfly and experienced the invisible spiritual world. He also met God, whom he refers to as 'Om', as it is the sound that evokes the essence of an omnipotent and unconditionally loving divinity.

When he woke up from his coma Alexander was never the same again. He no longer held the standard scientific view that the cortex creates consciousness and we live in a universe without emotion. He had seen the unconditional love of the invisible world of spirit and he knew it to be real. And the girl on the butterfly? She turned out to be his deceased natural sister. Alexander was adopted and only saw a photograph of his sister after his NDE. He instantly recognised her as the girl riding the butterfly.

The reaction to Alexander's book was intense. Christians objected to the term Om for God, and were disapproving of the fact that there was no mention of Jesus and angels. Scientists attacked his story with science, saying he was dreaming and his cortex could not have fully shut down because if it had then he would not have had such dreams. Others argued that if he'd had these visions they were the result of unexplained chemical changes in his brain, lack of oxygen or firing of neurons, which created the illusion of a tunnel of light, and they were not of supernatural origin. A few brave scientists came to his defence, pointing out that chemical changes and lack of oxygen in the brain tended to create wild confusion and not the lucid visions that Alexander reported.

Heaven Is for Real and *Proof of Heaven*, along with other titles, have brought to public attention as never before the phenomenon of NDEs, which have in fact been reported for centuries. One of the reasons they are enjoying the limelight now is improvements in resuscitation techniques, which means increasing numbers of people declared clinically dead are being brought back from the brink. Typically a person is 'dead' for just a few minutes, but there are now reported cases of people being 'dead' for up to ten hours. A decade or so ago these people would have remained dead and not returned to tell their stories. Indeed, there are currently so many reports of NDEs that scientists can no longer dismiss the phenomenon as an anomaly. The continuation of human consciousness after death is now the subject of hot debate in scientific circles, with the study of NDEs at the forefront of this research. Out-of-body experiences during operations, or when a patient is clinically dead, are also being reported in ever-increasing numbers.

Sceptics naturally have an army of counter-arguments to challenge the belief that NDEs are real. In addition to chemical changes occurring in a dying brain, other explanations offered are that NDEs are triggered by sleep disorders, cardiac arrest, medicines and drugs. False memory syndrome, hallucination, wish fulfilment and temporary madness have also been put forward, but as I showed in my previous book, *The Afterlife Is Real*, where I argue the case for the existence of an afterlife, none of these explanations is convincing.

For example, during a hallucination a person is out of touch with reality, but accounts of NDEs suggest they are accurately able to report what is going on in their immediate surroundings. Also many NDEs occur when a person has a flat EEG, meaning they are brain dead. But if they'd had enough brain activity to produce a hallucination, it would have been registered by the EEG. Also, a dying brain or delirium are not convincing explanations as they would not be recalled as a positive experience or a spiritual turning point. Similarly, whereas mental illness typically leads to depression and an inability to cope with everyday life, NDEs have the opposite effect and are likely to lead to a renewed zest and passion for life. And finally, the wish fulfilment theory is just too flimsy as it does not explain the similarity of NDE accounts. Surely people would have different memories from a tunnel or a life review? A beach in Hawaii for example? Moreover, none of these arguments can fully explain cases where a person has 'died' or been in a medically induced coma and they have been able to report seeing or hearing things they can't possibly have seen or heard. For example, recounting the conversations of loved ones or relatives outside the room; or describing exactly what doctors are doing for several hours during an operation.

A common theme in NDE accounts is that the world of spirit is about one thing and one thing only: love – and that love is eternal and unconditional. There is also a noticeable lack of judgement and harshness. The popularity of these books suggests that NDEs are giving hope that there is life after death not just to people from a religious background but to scientists, too. They reveal the extent to which we are moving away from collective ideas of punishment or reward in heaven or hell to more personal, non-judgemental beliefs about the afterlife.

The gradual and steady decline of organised religion has undoubtedly contributed to this trend of personal spiritual development. Since the 1960s increasing numbers of people have become disillusioned with religion or abandoned the idea of religion altogether. This is hardly surprising when you consider some of the scandals that have emerged over the years and how extremists within certain faiths have misinterpreted and butchered their message – making religion feel repellent, twisted, cruel and ugly rather than comforting, inspiring, peaceful and uplifting.

In his 2006 bestseller, *The God Delusion* – which again is well worth a read because an open-minded person should consider all viewpoints – Oxford scientist Richard Dawkins puts forward a convincing case against religion. He shows religion to be a man-made, controlling and divisive force in history and from my studies at university it is hard for me not to agree with him. However, what his argument lacks, in my opinion, is a convincing counter-argument that the world would be a more peaceful, happier and better place without religion. Yes, religion is responsible for some terrible crimes and misdirections, but at the same time it can also inspire compassion and selflessness in followers, not to mention the benefits of community spirit it encourages.

Perhaps this explains why interest in spiritual development and what happens when we die has not declined when interest in religion has. Disillusionment with religion has left a feeling of emptiness or hunger within people's hearts and, for many, personal spiritual development has filled that void.

Humanity has always needed reassurance that there is a spiritual element to this life, a divine presence, and that goodness and love are stronger than evil and death, even if at times that presence feels invisible and irrational. Belief in an afterlife is an expression of this deep spiritual hunger, but discussions about the reality of heaven aren't just for those who have moved away from religion. The search for heaven is a much-needed uniting force, which in today's war-torn world has never been more necessary. As I tirelessly try to explain in my books, heaven is a spiritual goal that is for everyone and it can fit into any religion or belief system – even atheists and scientists can now embrace it.

Remember, science is no longer the enemy it used to be when it comes to proving the existence of heaven. In fact, you could even say that modern science has increased the popularity of belief and strengthened rather than weakened the case for life after death. Take a look, for example, at quantum theory, the theoretical basis for modern physics which offers an explanation for the nature and behaviour of matter or energy on an atomic and subatomic level. By itself quantum physics does not suggest the existence of a world of spirit, but it could provide a framework by which spiritual beings could exert their influence on the physical world.

I am no scientist, so forgive me if my explanation appears crude. You would be far better off reading a remarkable book called *The Tao of Physics* by Fritjof Capra. This book, published in 1975, brought the mystical implications of subatomic physics to public consciousness for the very first time. Capra demonstrates that both modern Western science and traditional Eastern spirituality

reveal the same elemental truth: that the universe is one interconnected whole, an endless flux of living energy of which we are all
part. He opens up the possibility of the interconnectedness of all
mind and matter and, by drawing parallels between physics and
mystical views of the universe as a creation of the mind, suggests
the possibility that the afterlife could actually exist. From a logical
viewpoint, heaven can't exist but from a quantum perspective it
could. Science and spirituality are not incompatible and people
who believe in heaven could be right after all.

Another factor that has undoubtedly contributed to a recent
surge in belief in the existence of heaven has to be the miracle of
the internet – an astonishing tool of communication uniting
people from different races and religions and viewpoints all over
the world. It has opened up new avenues for writers, artists, scientists, religious leaders, thinkers and individuals to talk freely about
their spiritual development as never before and they are doing so
in unprecedented numbers. Just type in the words afterlife or
heaven and be astonished at the sheer volume of hits you get. The
ether is an invisible superhighway of communication and it most
certainly is playing its part in the spiritual revolution.

I'm giving my personal opinion here but I believe that heaven
may well have chosen this moment in time to reveal itself as
never before, to launch a new campaign. In a world that feels
confused, cruel and unjust so much of the time we urgently
need to believe in the power of goodness and love. We may have
made astonishing advances but time has not always brought
with it wisdom and compassion, because the world we live in
today is too crowded and distorted by suffering and injustice.
You just need to turn on the news every day to see images of hell

on earth – children starving, religious groups tearing each other to pieces, and pollution – and we urgently need reminding that there is still goodness within ourselves and others, and that love and hope are strong enough to defeat cruelty and injustice. We urgently need to be reminded that heaven is possible, and that it can exist not just in the next life but in this life, too.

Today, heaven is making itself known through the voices of ordinary people with extraordinary stories of spiritual experiences, because the human race is crying out for them. And the more we listen to their voices and trust in them, the closer we come to creating heaven on earth because their stories remind us of the goodness and love we have forgotten within and around us. It is easy to dismiss sentimental stories of belief in heaven transforming people's lives for the better, but instinctively we know that heaven is another word for what is good and loving and eternal.

Centuries ago people didn't doubt there was a heaven because they knew they had to choose between that and hell. Today, with so many of us battling our inner demons, due in large part to the wealth of choices modern life offers, we need to trust that when the time is right we will choose what's honest, right, compassionate, loving and true. Before we say or do anything, we all need to look within ourselves and ask if our intentions are heavenly.

The greatest fear

In my mind and my heart, the time has never been more right for us to know that whenever we feel afraid, conflicted, hurt or lonely it is always best to choose the path of love, compassion, grace and peace – which, if you think about it, is surely the path to heaven. But why then do so many still choose not to follow it? Why is it that some of us want to grow spiritually but others don't? I hate to sound clichéd but I think again it comes back to love. Love is the desire to grow. Truly loving people are people who are always opening their minds and hearts, forever learning and growing.

The capacity to love is something that every human being has. Sometimes our ability to love is damaged by traumatic childhood or adult experiences, and that is an unjust tragedy, but however tough life has been there is always something deep inside us urging us to reach higher. That is why it is possible for some people to rediscover their loving and compassionate hearts after experiencing the most terrible suffering and hardship.

You could say a resilient character gives a person the ability to rise above adversity, or you could say it is divine grace or an external spiritual force that acts through a person's heart and through the hearts of others supporting them and through other mysterious ways we cannot understand. Whatever you call it, some people can emerge from the deepest pits of despair with renewed spirit, whereas others remain stuck and unable to move forward. As I write this I am reminded of the courage of teenage cancer sufferer Stephen Sutton. Diagnosed at the age of fifteen, Stephen approached the final years of his young life with incredible courage and positivity and without a hint of bitterness. He wrote an inspiring blog, compiled a bucket list of all the things he wanted to do and raised millions for charity in the process. Before he died, aged nineteen, he told the world, 'Cancer sucks but life is great.' His bravery and tenacity in the face of such adversity took the world's breath away.

But why is it possible for one person, like Stephen, to rise above the bitter blows of fate and for another to be crushed by them?

Is it perhaps because evolving spiritually requires discipline, independent thought and courage, whereas standing still, giving up or giving in is much easier? I know this to be the truth from my own spiritual journey. There have been so many times in my life when I have chosen to curl tight into a resistant ball and let fear, self-doubt and anxiety stop me in my tracks. I blame everyone and everything except myself. I try to convince myself I am powerless, when I am anything but.

I'm reminded of the *Spider-Man* movie and that profound line: 'with great power comes great responsibility'. To evolve spiritually is to become aware of your responsibility to yourself and others to be loving and compassionate and a light in the darkness. This is an enormous responsibility and it is far more comfortable to shy away from that burden: to remain a spiritual child rather than a spiritual adult.

Marianne Williamson described this brilliantly.

> *Our deepest fear is not that we are inadequate. Our deepest fear is that we are powerful beyond measure. It is our light, not our darkness, that most frightens us. Your playing small does not serve the world. There is nothing enlightened about shrinking so that other people don't feel insecure around you. We are all meant to shine as children do. It's not just in some of us; it's in everyone. And as we let our own lights shine, we unconsciously give other people permission to do the same. As*

> *we are liberated from our own fear, our presence auto-matically liberates others.*

In other words, with spiritual growth comes great responsibility as well as great obligations to yourself and others. You will be required to think for yourself all the time and that means not blaming circumstances or other people for your condition. You are responsible for your thoughts, words, feelings, actions and choices in life. This realisation of your own freedom and power to choose – of the heaven or God inside you – can feel frightening and lonely.

Becoming an adult is not so much about what you say, do or experience, but about who you are – about coping with the demands life throws at you and not running away from responsibility. Finding the path to heaven that is right for you is much the same. It is a call to spiritual maturity and don't be surprised if at first you feel daunted rather than overjoyed.

Because spiritual growth is going to involve hard work and facing our deepest fears the impulse to run away or hide is only natural, and many of us choose to do exactly that. As you saw in chapter 1, I have done it so many times I have lost count. There are so many places to hide – in work, in self-pity, in drugs, in alcohol, in obsessive behaviour, in depression, in sex, in family, in other people, in friends, in material things, in celebrity, in religion, in self-absorption, to name but a few. Journeying to all these places can help us discover who we are and what matters to us, but ultimately the only path to spiritual fulfilment is to rediscover the power and light of love, peace and truth within ourselves and to take responsibility for the life choices we make.

I have no idea why some people are able to set a shining example and discover within themselves the discipline, courage and humility to grow spiritually and take the harder path in life. From the numbers of letters, emails and messages I receive every day from people who are on their spiritual journey, I know that they come from every walk of life. Some have respected jobs, others are still searching for their role in life. Some are wealthy, some are struggling to survive. Some have by their own admission led a charmed life, while others have experienced deep loss, grief and trauma. Some are very young, some are very old. Some are deeply religious, others are not. It is impossible to predict who will become a truly loving individual and answer their individual call to power. It is life's greatest mystery. It is also one of life's greatest paradoxes.

As I know only too well sometimes putting in the hard work and discipline isn't enough. Feelings of utter peace and contentment can't be earned. They are often bestowed on us like a gift – perhaps from some mysterious force or perhaps from heaven. I don't know how it happens but what I have learned is that we can increase our chances of receiving this gift by opening our minds and our hearts to the possibility.

In other words, we need both to choose the path of spiritual growth and put in the effort but at the same time to let spiritual growth just happen to us. We need to look for heaven and not look for it at the same time. This is a real paradox and very complicated, but for now just know that it goes back to the notion of trust I talked about earlier in the book. There just comes a point when we need to let go and trust completely that the mysterious, spiritual forces that underpin our lives and the universe will point us in the right direction.

Spiritual beings

Remember, the path to spiritual growth requires independence of thought and action as well as courage, discipline and a loving heart. It isn't going to be easy. While sacred texts, rituals or religions can offer profound advice and assistance along the way and maybe point you in the right direction, they cannot take you there. You must choose your path and then you must walk your path alone, working things out in the context of your own life and your individual relationship with heaven.

It is easy to feel discouraged, insignificant and invisible in a universe so vast it is beyond our comprehension, but once we truly understand that we are spiritual beings having a human experience and that there are mysterious forces inspiring and guiding us from within and all around us, it becomes obvious that our lives are not meaningless. It also becomes obvious that spiritual development is the most important thing in our lives.

Seen in this light every person's life (or lives if you believe in reincarnation) carries great meaning and significance, because each one of us has the power to bring the love, peace and compassion we associate with heaven, or a state of bliss, closer to earth with every thought, action and decision we choose to make. There are no words, rituals, actions or teachings that can deliver us from personal responsibility or the need to find our own way to connect with and reveal heaven. In the words of Gandhi: 'Be the change you wish to see in the world.'

Frequently asked questions about heaven

More and more people want their lives to have deeper meaning. They are looking heavenward for inspiration and guidance in their lives. I know this from the stacks of questions in response to my afterlife books. I will try to answer as many of the commonly asked questions as space will allow here, so that we can get them all out of the way before beginning your spiritual journey in earnest in chapter 4. Hopefully, answers may also be found elsewhere in the book. If anything isn't clear or you have a burning question you want answered, please do get in touch with me – details can be found at the end of the book.

Where is heaven?

The idea of heaven being a higher place or 'up there' came from earlier times. In ancient Greek and Hebrew the word heaven means sky. It seemed appropriate in centuries past to place God in the skies because the world was thought to be corrupted with sin and not a suitable place for God to reside, but fast-forward to the modern day with our expanded view of the universe and such a simplistic view can no longer be taken seriously.

Today, even religions that talk about God residing in heaven don't see heaven as a place somewhere up there in space. What they are really talking about is the transcendent nature of heaven, which means it transcends this world and exists outside our limited human experience. Most believers these days don't think of heaven as a place at all but a spiritual experience in which a person connects deeply to feelings of bliss and loving attachment to everyone and everything in the universe. Going to heaven is a never-ending journey that our hearts can begin on this earth and continue after our death.

Of course, many people still talk about 'going to heaven' as if it were a destination, and this is understandable because it is a different dimension of reality that can't be described or understood in human terms. In other words, it is a transcendent state of eternal bliss we can experience in this life but not be able to fully understand and become a part of until we cross over to the other side.

Does heaven really exist?

I believe it exists. Other people don't and that is their choice. Scientists are starting to gather evidence that it actually exists but, since there is no definitive proof yet, it can only really exist if you believe it to exist. If you accept the reality of heaven it becomes your reality. For all I know, just believing or trusting in heaven could make it a reality when you die.

No one really knows for sure if heaven exists but the closest we have got is the descriptions of people who believe they have seen heaven in near-death experiences. In a stunning coincidence, as I was attempting to write a coherent answer to this eternal question up popped on my computer screen a news item that took my breath away . . .

>*First hint of 'life after death' in biggest ever scientific study*

Southampton University scientists, led by Dr Sam Parnia, have found evidence that awareness can continue for at least several minutes after clinical death, which was previously thought impossible.

The feature went on to talk about the world's largest-ever study into near-death and out-of-body experiences, and how it had proof that some kind of awareness did continue after the brain had shut down completely.

The scientists from Southampton University examined 2,060 people over a period of four years who had suffered cardiac arrest in fifteen hospitals in the UK, US and Australia. Approximately 40 per cent of these people experienced some kind of awareness when they were clinically dead and before their hearts were restarted. Although many could not recall everything in detail, one-third said time had slowed or speeded up, and one-third said that they had felt an unusual sense of peace. Others recalled a bright light or golden flash, and some said they experienced the sensation of being dragged through water. Around 13 per cent said they felt their senses were heightened and the same number described having an out-of-body experience.

One 57-year-old man recalled leaving his body entirely and watching the resuscitation from the corner of the room. He was able to describe accurately what the nurse did and the sounds in the room.

The brain can't function when the heart stops beating but research leader, Dr Parnia, a former research fellow at Southampton University and currently at the State University of New York, is quoted in the *Telegraph* as saying:

But in this case, conscious awareness appears to have continued for up to three minutes into the period when the heart wasn't beating, even though the brain typically shuts down within 20–30 seconds after the heart has stopped. The man described everything that had happened in the room, but importantly, he heard two bleeps from a machine that makes a noise at three-minute intervals. So we could time how long the experienced lasted for. He seemed very credible and everything that he said had happened to him had actually happened.

This is not the first study into NDEs, but it is the first to use a really large sample size and this gives the work a lot of validity in scientific circles. It also paves the way for more extensive research into what happens when we die and shows that so far NDEs are the best proof we have that human consciousness can survive bodily death.

In my book *The Afterlife Is Real*, I present the case for the existence of heaven in great detail, but here's a brief summary of my defence:

- Since ancient times millions of people have reported NDEs and scientific data shows that around seven hundred people experience them every day in the United States alone.
- NDEs are not limited to any one religion or culture and can be found in Europe, the Middle East, India, Asia, Africa, the Pacific, United States and basically everywhere in the world.

- In the great majority of cases there are striking similarities and consistencies in NDE accounts regardless of a person's age, sex, religion, culture and so on.
- People who didn't know anything about NDEs also report consistent experiences.
- NDEs are also consistent with deathbed visions – visions people report before they die but in this case they don't revive.
- Children under the age of five who could not possibly have any expectations of the afterlife report consistent experiences. (Interestingly, in this age group there have also been compelling studies of reincarnation that have been verified.)
- People who have been blind since birth describe similar visual experiences.

Over the last few decades a number of highly respected scientists have studied and verified the reality of NDEs. To take just one of countless examples: Pam Reynolds had a brain aneurysm that lowered her body temperature dramatically, stopped her heartbeat and breathing, flattened her brain waves and drained the blood from her brain. Clinically dead, she had an NDE as well as an out-of-body experience (OBE) and later was able to accurately report in great detail what had happened in the operating room when the medical team was trying to revive her.

Dr Parnia's research is the latest in a long line of similar studies, all of which suggest that consciousness can exist separately from and independently of the brain. In addition, resuscitation research also proves that consciousness exists independently of the brain by showing that a person can be technically dead – no heart rate or brain activity – but their personality and memories (their spirit) can be revived hours later. All these studies suggest that consciousness is a non-physical quantum reality.

Those who have had an NDE describe it as a mystical experience: there is typically a transcendence of time and space, a sense of cosmic unity, overwhelming love and positivity as well as a feeling of sacredness and intuitive illumination. Afterwards, those who have had an NDE – in contrast to those who were close to death but did not have an NDE – report an increased sense of sacredness and spirituality without the need for religion in their daily lives.

On top of this there are all the polls and surveys which suggest that up to two-thirds of people believe in an afterlife, or reincarnation or ghosts, or have had an afterlife encounter. These polls certainly can't be used as proof, but surely that many of us can't be deluded? They also suggest that the afterlife is a topic definitely deserving of serious consideration.

Sceptics waste no time discounting the work of respected scientists, and the mounting evidence they are gathering for the existence of an afterlife as not valid, because it is impossible to prove the reality of these experiences. What they seem to forget is that a lot of scientific theory is based on uncertainties and theories that are impossible to prove or validate. For example, string theory is pretty mind-blowing. This theory of the universe suggests that separate dimensions exist but this can't be proved. Quantum theory is equally unprovable, as is the parallel world theory. And what about dark matter and energy? Scientists think our world and the sun, moon, stars and planets and galaxies we know about make up around 4 per cent of our universe, and the remaining 96 per cent is made up of dark matter and energy, but they don't know exactly what dark matter or dark energy are. They also can't prove it exists.

It is crucial for scientists to always try to find proof, but there also comes a point when a leap of faith has to be made in the name of progress. Remember in chapter 1 I talked about medieval times when everyone thought the earth was flat. Copernicus put forward the theory that the earth revolved around the sun and was ridiculed for his views, as were other great innovators in history who believed in something considered impossible at the time; for example, electricity, air travel, space travel, telephones, and so on. Sometimes you have to take a risk and believe in the impossible.

Perhaps one day we will have absolute proof that heaven exists but until then we have to make do with what we've got: compelling and scientifically validated testimonies from millions of people who believe they have glimpsed heaven, and our own gut feelings, beliefs and intuition.

And right now, the only person who can tell you if heaven is real or not is you. I'm not going to try to convince you any more. All I hope that reading this book will do is give you the information you need to make your own decision. Of course, I hope you trust in the existence of an afterlife but ultimately whatever choice you make I hope it brings you happiness, fulfilment and inner peace. If you have those three things then I don't think you need any proof – you may not see it as such, but you have your proof of heaven.

And last, but by no means least, for all of you who have problems believing in a world of spirit, I want you to think about love, goodness and kindness. You can't see or touch these things but you know them to be real. You can't measure love scientifically but you can see it transform lives. It's the same for heaven.

Heaven is a spiritual dimension so it is unlikely its existence can ever be proved in a rational way to those who have closed their minds and hearts, but even the most sceptical of people have to admit that there are things in the world that exist but cannot be explained. It is the same with the spiritual dimension or heaven. It might help to think of it as radio waves or the ether: you can't see or feel it, but when you tune into it miracles can happen.

What is it like in heaven?

Having not had a near-death experience myself I can't speak from personal experience, but from my extensive research of other people's stories I've been able to identify a number of similar characteristics for you – although do bear in mind that heaven reveals itself uniquely to each person.

Time and time again I have read or been told that human words just can't convey what is being felt or experienced. The brightness, beauty, bliss, peace and illumination have no words to describe them because they are beyond human experience. Sometimes people talk about glistening fields and meadows and flowers and trees that display colours not seen on earth. One little girl said the flowers were singing and that is such a beautiful thought. There are also sparkling rivers and streams, enchanting birdsong and sweet music – but music not heard on earth. Such a setting has the aura of a fairy tale, but the overriding theme of all these idyllic descriptions is that everything feels more alive and vibrant than it did on earth. Many people have said that when they return to earth it feels as if their earthly life is the dream and heaven the reality.

There is mention of cities, gardens and palaces and magnificent libraries or places of study and healing. Knowledge is highly prized and there are opportunities to learn and grow spiritually. Another intriguing notion that recurs is the idea that spiritual reality in heaven seems to match the spiritual awareness a person had on earth. So, if you've lived a life of love and good intentions on earth, you will experience beauty and light in the afterlife; but if you've lived a life of selfishness then your afterlife will be more shadowy, grainy and darker, making it hard to see anything with clarity.

Material accomplishments on earth vanish in heaven, as it is clear that what goes on in a person's heart and how they treated others are all that matter. The only true measure of success is love and compassion. If someone has been unkind or cruel they are not punished as such, but will experience the suffering they caused others because in heaven everyone and everything is interconnected.

So it seems that on earth our thoughts, feelings and actions create the kind of heaven we will inhabit. What an incredible and potentially life-changing thought!

Will I reunite with departed loved ones in heaven?

Yes, according to NDE accounts you will, and not just loved ones, close family and friends but people of all ages because, although we carry our individuality with us into heaven, in spirit everyone is interconnected.

Contrary to popular thinking, I truly believe that the existence of an afterlife where we are reunited with departed loved ones is perfectly logical. Just think about it. Modern science tells us that everything – you, me, this book, your mobile, your keys – consists of energy. Everything in the universe consists of pulsating units of energy and the manner in which it pulsates determines how it will manifest on earth. Is it so irrational then to believe that when our body dies, the energy that sparks us into life, the energy that creates our thoughts and makes our hearts beat, continues to exist? And is it such a stretch of the imagination to think that this energy could live in another realm of existence and continue to interact with the living?

Do our loved ones look down on us from heaven?

Yes, but only if we open our hearts to them.

Remember, heaven is really a state of mind and not a place and even on earth we can live in heaven and feel the presence of departed loved ones. The choice is yours. The place your loved ones went to after death is not up there in the sky. It is around and within you, interpenetrating your life all the time. And those you've loved and lost are not far away, looking down on you; they are close by your side on earth, striving to help and guide you, and loving you as they did before they crossed over.

This is a question I'm asked so many times and in chapter 4 there is plenty of information about the subtle – and sometimes not so subtle – signs the spirits of departed loved ones are constantly sending us.

What about angels?

This isn't a book about angels but a book about heaven. However, whenever there is talk of heaven there is usually talk of angels too. I've written books on angels – as I believe them to be invisible messengers from heaven who serve only what is good, loving and pure within and around you. Sometimes they appear in traditional form, complete with wings and halo, but most of us meet them in our dreams, thoughts and feelings, or sense their presence in subtle signs or calling cards, like the appearance of a white feather. Angels may also manifest through the spirits of departed loved ones or through other people consciously or unconsciously guided by heaven.

Although angel experiences can vary significantly, a telltale sign of their presence is a deep inner certainty, light and joy, or feelings of peace and comfort that were not there before. Remember, the term angel is interchangeable with the term heaven, and if your path to heaven involves encounters with angels they will inspire and transform your life in magical ways. You will not feel doubt, anxiety or anger. The glow of love is their calling card and you will feel comforted and warm in their presence.

Some people believe that each one of has a guardian angel who is with us before we are born, accompanies us through life and in everything we experience on earth and is with us as we leave this life and return to heaven. This is a beautiful concept, but what it really means is that heaven or what is loving, pure and good always lives within us in this life and the next. Whether we choose to connect with what is really important in life is another matter. Heaven is always watching and whenever our personal decisions or actions don't come from a place of love and goodness, this is what gives us that feeling of unease which is very hard to ignore.

Just one more point about angels: many people think that when departed loved ones die they become angels with wings and halos and watch over them. Strictly speaking, this isn't correct as the term angel refers to a spiritual being that has never lived on earth as a human being but, that said, spirits of departed loved ones may well be guided by angels. At the end of the day definitions are pointless because angels and spirits are pieces of heaven, or ways for heaven to reveal itself to us.

What about prayer?

Millions of people all over the world pray on a regular basis to their God and there is absolutely nothing wrong with that. The last thing I want to do is stop anyone connecting with their concept of goodness and love, or heaven. As I've stressed throughout, heaven is for everyone regardless of belief system and if talking to your God comforts and heals you then keep doing it.

Indeed, there may be great power in prayer if it helps connect you to the invincible and immortal love and goodness that define heaven.

Prayer is a word I was initially reluctant to use because for many people it is so closely associated with religion – and, at the risk of repeating myself, heaven is non-denominational. There is no doubt, and certainly nothing wrong with the fact, that many people do find great comfort and strength from traditional forms of prayer, but prayer is really just a way of connecting with the force of goodness and love within and around you. Your thoughts are a form of prayer and because heaven knows what goes on in your mind and your heart your thoughts can have great power.

If you aren't convinced of the power of positive thinking, take a look at the recent studies conducted around the world that have shown the healing effects of prayer. If, as modern science believes, all matter and life consists of units of energy – including our thoughts – then it is feasible that through an intense concentration of thought in prayer, this energy can be directed to influence the health and wellbeing of others.

Sure, you could call this the power of positive expectation, rather than the power of prayer, but whatever name you give it, it really does seem to work. And it doesn't just work on other people. The power of reflection can work on you, too. Just taking a few moments to pause and gather your thoughts can lead to moments of profound intuition, inspiration and illumination. Moments when we just sense, feel or intuit something we did not know and our thoughts trigger a connection with heaven.

I believe in heaven so why am I still afraid of dying?

This question goes quite literally to the heart of the matter. When the heart stops beating, what happens? Even though the overwhelming feedback from people who've been close to death but come back to life is that the experience is peaceful and illuminating, the uncertainty of it all, the not knowing for sure, is frightening.

I'll be completely honest with you here. Despite all my writing about the afterlife I'm still anxious about dying, but my research has taught me two very important things. First of all, the kind of afterlife I will experience will be very much determined by the life I'm currently leading, so I try to put most of my focus and energy on what I am creating for myself in the here and now. Secondly, reading all those inspiring accounts of people who have crossed over to the other side or glimpsed heaven on earth makes me think that perhaps it's not anxiety I'm feeling but anticipation or even excitement.

It is only natural to fear death because it is the great unknown, but I sincerely hope that what you read in this book will help take the sting out of death. The fear you have is simply a fear of change or entering a new phase of existence. Compare it to an expectant mother nervous about giving birth but excited about the experience, too. If you can think of death not as an ending but as a new beginning, your whole perspective will change.

It is disappointing that our society celebrates birth but shrouds death in a cloak of secrecy. As a result, few of us are prepared for it. We don't talk about death or even like to think about it, but we are spiritual beings and death is not the end. It is just another phase in our existence and there is so much waiting for us on the other side.

Of course, if you think about it, you actually start dying the moment you are born. But this is an energising not a depressing thought because it means that every second of our lives heaven is calling us back to our true home. Even when you sleep at night your consciousness leaves your body and travels to the world of spirit. In the morning, you may recall some of the dreams you had but, even if you don't, it shows that every day of your life you are dying and living again whether you realise it or not.

Life is not killed by the death of your physical body. Death is a natural process so should not instil dread. It is fear, anger, hate and guilt that can end life, not death. Despair of the heart and emptiness of the soul are what really kill and, if you allow negative feelings and thoughts to take control, you become one of the walking dead. In much the same way, the spirit of a person whose heart is full of love and compassion will never die.

As such there is no death, only darkness without light; and in the light there is no death, only goodness and love.

How do I keep on going now the love of my life has died?

How to ease the heartache following the loss of a loved one is a question I've been asked many times and it is never easy to answer. Whether the loved one is a soulmate or a family member, child or friend, the suffering and sense of loss can feel intolerably painful. You wish to be with the person you've lost but at the same time know that you need to continue your life for your own sake, as well as that of your children or others who rely on you.

But how to get through each day without the person who gave your life meaning? Decades ago, when I was less experienced in life, I would try to comfort other people who had lost loved ones by sharing my belief in an afterlife. I would tell them that death was not the end. I remember when I was sixteen one of my best friends lost her father to a sudden heart attack. A few days later I went round to see her. She looked pale, thin and so haunted. I sat with her and talked about my beliefs but they didn't seem to comfort her at all. I just made her cry so I stopped talking and listened to her instead. I left feeling that I had been no help whatsoever and for months afterwards I avoided her.

Years later, she got in touch with me to ask me why I'd dropped out of her life. I told her that I felt I'd let her down because I made her cry. I had so wanted to make her feel better. She told me that I had, that it was incredible to have someone just listen to her. Nobody else at the time had listened. They all gave her advice and told her what to do and think and to be brave, but all she wanted to do was cry.

Even then I didn't fully understand – not until I experienced the first great loss in my life, the death of my mother when I was in my mid-twenties. I understood my friend completely then. I just wanted to cry, too. I didn't want cheering up. I didn't want comfort. I just needed to cry. Being told about my mother living on and watching over me in some invisible realm was no comfort at all when what I wanted was to hug my mother, hear her and see her again. I missed her physical presence and what I needed to do was mourn that loss. I needed my time to grieve and it was only when I'd given myself that time that I was ready to enter into a new relationship with my mother in spirit. Grief not only needs time – and there is no escaping that whatever people tell you – but it is a journey you will travel alone.

It is so tempting to try and offer words of comfort during times of loss but when a person is blinded by grief no words can really give any comfort. Nothing can make them feel better. They must go through the grieving process because, if they don't, entering into a new relationship with departed loved ones in spirit becomes so much harder. It is crucial that you first mourn the loss of the physical, the way things were.

During the painful grieving process all other people can do is be there for the bereaved – be a shoulder to cry on. Then, when the time is right, a miracle will happen and the bereaved person will gradually begin to understand that they still have their life to live. They carry on living their life for the sake of those they've loved and lost. Every time they wake up in the morning and see the world with fresh eyes, or enjoy a chat with a friend or take a walk with a beloved pet or take pride in their children's achievements, they are experiencing the world for the sake of departed loved ones. They carry those they have loved and lost with them everywhere.

I'm reminded here of these lines by poet Emily Dickinson:

> *Parting is all we know of heaven,*
> *And all we know of hell.*

Of course, hell refers to the numbness and pain of grief but what about heaven? Does it mean that when we die we go to heaven or does it perhaps mean that when a person dies we discover the real meaning of heaven? Let me explain.

Grief is something that never completely disappears. You never fully recover from the loss of a loved one and the sorrow becomes a part of your spirit – who you are. In other words, you carry that person with you always in your heart. Grief changes you forever. You will never be the same person again. Your heart will be bigger and fuller because it will be filled with longing for someone you loved and you will be one step closer to heaven.

The intensity of your grief is a response to the depth of love you experienced. Grief has shown you that you understand what real love is and therefore, whether you realise it consciously or not, you also understand the meaning of heaven because heaven is defined by love. Deep down you know that love is a miracle that transforms all our lives and after a person dies it continues. It doesn't die.

Can we see heaven in our dreams?

Yes, you can catch glimpses of heaven in your dreams and in the next chapter we'll cover this topic in more detail.

Can rich people find heaven?

From all that I have learned about heaven, one theme keeps recurring: in the world of spirit money or material things have absolutely no meaning. Heaven is not interested in money. It is spiritual wealth that matters there, not your bank balance.

Even in this world money does not buy happiness. One famous study of lottery winners showed that those who had won significant sums of money were not happier than those who had won nothing, and you only need to look at the examples in the media of rich, famous people who are desperately unhappy to realise that wealth is not a panacea. Having said that, there is no denying that material things and money can make this life more comfortable. Indeed, many people who trust in heaven have sent me wonderful stories about money, surprise gifts or unexpected financial relief seeming to appear out of nowhere when they were most needed. Sometimes the people have earnestly prayed or asked for help, but on other occasions it just seems to happen and when it does they feel on top of the world!

When you find yourself on the receiving end of pennies from heaven there is no denying it feels wonderful. It happened to me once when I was struggling to pay my rent and I found a bundle of cash in the street. I did the right thing and handed it into the police station, but nobody claimed it and eventually it became mine. However, although heaven can work in mysterious ways and there is nothing wrong with asking heaven for financial help in your hour of need, money and material things are not the language that heaven speaks and can never bring you true happiness.

So to answer the question, can a rich person find heaven? Of course they can. Heaven is for everyone, regardless of their income. The only rich person who cannot find heaven is the one who allows material wealth to block their spiritual development. What makes a person rich is not money but a loving and compassionate heart.

However, this doesn't mean that money is evil – far from it. Money can transform and enrich lives, and you can be deeply spiritual and still have an income for yourself. Indeed, someone who is spiritually healthy is loving and believes in abundance and generosity towards themselves and others. It's wrong to equate spirituality with extreme selflessness and renouncing everything. Indeed, money could be seen as a physical manifestation of the energy we give and receive from others. When you accept money you are acknowledging your contribution and when you give money you are acknowledging the contribution of others.

So don't hate money – love it instead.

Mother Teresa loved money because she knew it could help ease suffering and create a better world. Without accepting financial aid Mother Teresa would never have been able to set up her charities. Of course, there is a downside to money, as there is with everything in life. If you love money because you think the more you have the better person you are; or if you love money for the sake of it or use it in unproductive or morally wrong ways; or forget that the best things in our lives are always free – then it is not a positive or spiritually healthy energy in your life. However, when you realise that you can bring happiness to yourself and others through the choices you make with your money, you will understand that money is not the root of all evil at all.

Is there such a thing as a soulmate?

From a perspective of spiritual growth, I believe we meet many people in the course of our life, or lives if you believe in reincarnation, who could be described as soulmates. This doesn't mean that each one is a lover. The encounter is all about spiritual growth and connection, and friends or people from all walks of life can be part of that journey.

Indeed, every relationship in your life, even conflicted ones, could be seen as a possible soul connection where we can learn about ourselves, and make loving choices. Sometimes we may meet someone we feel emotionally, physically and spiritually connected to and we want to believe we have found 'the one', but searching for 'the one' can be counterproductive to fulfilling relationships if we use it as an excuse to move from partner to partner. So in many ways our task in life is to move every relationship we have along the soulmate continuum. If you can see each person in your life as a chance to learn about yourself and make positive and loving choices, then sooner or later you are going to meet someone who teaches you the meaning of love.

When two people are together and in a rewarding relationship it can often seem as if the hand of heaven has intervened to make sure the relationship happens. Ask any couple in a happy, long-term relationship how they met and they will often share with you stories of chance encounters or coincidences that brought them together at the right time and in the right place. There are billions of people on this planet and somehow their paths and hearts met at just the right moment for them both. Isn't that miraculous?

Miraculous yes, but are they soulmates? I'm aware that I haven't really answered the soulmate question directly and I'll be honest here, I simply don't know the answer. I do know, however, that believing you have found your soulmate can be a sign of spiritual awakening or, as I like to see it, your spirit calling out to you to find your own path, your own way to heaven – and we will explore this further, along with other signs of spiritual awakening, at the beginning of the next chapter.

Are there animals in heaven?

Over the years I have received countless stories from people who believe they have been visited by animals in spirit form and many people ask me if they will be reunited with beloved pets in heaven. According to some schools of thought animals cannot survive death because they do not have souls or spirits in the way humans do – and they are entitled to their opinion. But I completely disagree. Everything in the universe consists of energy and animals are made up of that energy just as humans are, so there is no reason why they should not survive death in the same way.

If you are an animal lover you will be acutely aware of the bond of unconditional love that can exist between human and animal. Love is boundless and connects every part of creation, including animals. Love is also the language that heaven speaks and I believe that animals can teach us many important spiritual lessons about empathy, healing, happiness and the power of unconditional love.

Are children closer to heaven?

Children have that wonder and open-mindedness which means they don't automatically shut out things that don't conform to logic and reason as adults tend to do. Sadly, as we get older doubts and fears stop us seeing magic in everyone and everything. It is the ability to suspend disbelief that makes heaven appear more real to young children, but age has nothing to do with how close to heaven a person is.

If you have ever been in the presence of a deeply spiritual person or mystic you may have noticed that they have a youthful twinkle in their eyes. And that is because finding heaven often means reconnecting with the child inside of you, and by this I mean the part of you that can see wonder and magic in the ordinary. The part of you that is passionate, spontaneous and living in the now. Children can appear closer to heaven because they instinctively know how to see the wonder in everything and their approach to life can teach us a great deal about finding heaven. Sadly, there is so much pressure on children these days to grow up fast and leave childhood pleasures behind. Of course, we all need to learn about responsibility and treating others with respect, but if we feel like singing, dancing, crying, laughing, running or dreaming we should not always restrain ourselves. You are only as old as you feel. As long as you are able to live in the moment and see magic in the ordinary, you are a child at heart and it is being a child at heart that draws heaven closer to you.

One of the greatest gifts my spiritual journey has brought me is the return of my childhood to me. As you may have gathered in chapter 1, I had a rather serious, disciplined childhood and I was rather anxious, old before I was young. I tried to control every aspect of my life, especially my spiritual development, but over the decades I have gradually learned to let go and recon-nect with the child within me. I have begun to realise that feeling truly alive is about living in the present and seeing magic in the everyday. With this approach to life my heart and mind have opened to the possibility of heaven existing, and love, laughter and magic have flooded back into my life.

I sincerely hope that after reading this book you will achieve something similar in your life. You will know you are on the right path to heaven because you will be reminded of everything that is wonderful about living. You will laugh more. You will love more and you will feel young again – and if you feel young, you will look young too.

What about hell?

Just as there is day and night, light and dark, it is impossible to talk about heaven without the concept of hell. If heaven exists, hell must exist too, right?

In many traditions, hell is where the spirits of bad people and the unconverted go after death. It is a place of fire, brimstone and suffering, and many religions have used the fear of hell to brainwash people into converting or donating large sums of money to escape eternal damnation.

I'm sure you won't be surprised when I tell you that I don't actually believe in hell or eternal punishment, as it doesn't equate with all that I have learned and experienced about the afterlife. I'm not alone in this. Interestingly, recent surveys suggest that while belief in heaven is on the increase, belief in hell is steadily on the decrease. It seems that our generation prefers to focus on the non-judgemental aspect of the afterlife rather than the evil in humankind and punishment for sinners in the afterlife. This is laudable but when you think of atrocities like the Holocaust or Hiroshima, or the murder of a young child, is it possible not to believe that hell on earth exists? And do we really want to dismiss so readily the concept of hell as punishment for dictators, terrorists and other monsters who seem to have got away with their crimes?

This is pure conjecture, of course, as I can't know for sure, but again from what I've learned I am inclined to think that the afterlife will be experienced differently by people who have been evil, selfish and cruel. There are spheres in the next life which are dark, confusing and unpleasant but these spheres are not eternal. They exist to reflect the life a person led and are there to encourage spiritual growth.

On earth nothing can interfere with our free will – our ability to choose between good and evil – but in the afterlife there is no place for evil and cruelty, and wrongdoers will have no say in the matter. Those who have chosen evil will go to a sphere that reflects their lives on earth and will not be able to find peace until they experience, feel and comprehend the acute suffering and pain they have caused others in their lives. They will also encounter great loneliness as they will not be welcomed by departed loved ones, only by those who exist on the same lower vibrations as themselves.

There is no place for evil in the afterlife. There is only an absence of light, so it could be said that hell is not really separate from heaven – they are layers of the same reality. The degree of hell-like experience is determined by the way a person lived their life and if they have inflicted pain on others they will experience that suffering until they are ready to evolve.

No person alive is completely good or completely bad and in the next life we will all be forced to confront our true nature, but this is not about punishment and reward. It is about learning, growing and evolving spiritually. In the next life, just as in this one, we develop spiritually by experiencing and learning from our mistakes.

And just as heaven is a state of mind, so too is hell. I'm reminded here of that famous Milton quote spoken by the devil: 'Which way I fly is Hell; myself am Hell.' Remember, we all have the gift of free will and if you espouse bitterness, anger, hatred, jealousy, guilt and fear you are choosing darkness rather than the light. You are creating your own personal hell on earth and blocking your own spiritual progress. Remember, too, that the more you focus on the idea of hell, the more power you give it if the findings of a 2014 survey are anything to go by. This University of Oregon study links believing in hell with lower levels of happiness and satisfaction in life. So if you have a choice, why opt for believing in something that is going to make you unhappy?

Choose the path to happiness instead. Trust in heaven.

My heart is broken, how can I believe in heaven?

If you have been through a bitter break-up or divorce, or had your heart broken by disappointment, heaven can seem very far away. As I know from bitter experience, when your heart is ripped in pieces talk of heaven really doesn't help. In fact, it just makes things worse because a part of you – the part that has been rejected, abandoned, left or hurt – doesn't believe or trust in it any more.

The journey to heaven after heartbreak is perhaps the hardest journey of all, but the greater the struggle to overcome, the greater the pain and suffering, the greater the spiritual growth. Heaven is calling out to you through your suffering to discover the real meaning of your life. Heaven wants you to grow taller spiritually. Of course, when all you want to do is cry and shut yourself away from the world because everything feels too painful, this is small comfort, so let's start at the beginning with a very simple piece of advice. Don't try to bottle everything up. Cry it out.

Tears, like many everyday miracles, are often taken for granted but crying it out can help heal us emotionally, physically and ultimately spiritually. Crying helps remove toxins, eases stress and boosts mood because it encourages the release of pent-up emotions. Research has been done into tears produced when peeling onions and emotional tears, and the latter contain toxins. Sad crying is healing. In the words of Shakespeare, 'To weep is to make less the depth of grief.'

Tears also help you let go of any notions you might have that things are going to return to what they were. Your tears are helping you accept the reality of your loss because until you are able to accept that your life has changed forever, you can't heal. You will be trapped loving someone who doesn't love you (why would you do that to yourself?) or denying just how much the death of a departed loved one has changed your life irrevocably.

Obviously, you can't walk around crying all the time – even though that is how you may feel – but when you deem it is safe to do so, you need to let the tears flow and not feel that you have to stop them. You may find, as I did after one heart-break, that it takes months to get past this stage. Eventually I did – I remember it clearly. After months and months of crying and not taking care of myself because I couldn't see the point of living, and endless days of not finding joy in anything or anyone and endless nights sobbing into my pillow, suddenly out of nowhere the heavy feeling began to subside. I still felt sad and bruised but my thoughts didn't automatically get stuck on my heartbreak any more, my heart didn't instantly hurt when I saw another sunset or sunrise and knew I couldn't share it with him. I cherished those moments of relief from the pain and the more I cherished them, the more frequent they became. In time, I started to feel extremely proud of myself. Finding happiness away from him empowered me. I realised then that my heart had grown stronger not weaker after breaking up because that is what the heart does. It is a muscle. The more you use it – even for feelings of sadness – the stronger it gets.

If you are in the throes of grief what I'm saying may seem unlikely, but I am just asking you to trust me. Please trust me. I hate to use the cliché but time does heal, and I'm going to go further and say time *and* tears heal. Recovery may take longer than you wish for, but I promise you the acute pain will pass. It will pass but before it does and a transformed you can emerge to take you further on your journey, you need to mourn the loss of your old self or way of life. You will know the moment of healing when it comes. It will come out of nowhere and feel sublime. The sadness, pain, panic and hurt you have grown accustomed to will be replaced by greater self-knowledge, wisdom, courage and compassion. Your heart will have enlarged rather than shrunk and you will know just how powerful and life-changing feelings of love can be. You may also discover within yourself a drive and a determination to live life to the full that you didn't realise you had. You will truly understand the meaning of that phrase, darkness comes before the dawn.

You will have grown spiritually and closer to heaven. And that is the purpose of your life, you see, to find heaven, however hard the path you are on may be.

I did something very bad, does that mean
I will never get to heaven?

Doing something bad does not shut the doors of heaven. Nobody is perfect. Heaven is for everyone; it will just be experienced in a different and darker way by those who have done wrong. And from what I have read and researched, if you have caused others suffering you will feel that suffering either in your next life or in the world of spirit. We all have our flaws and learning from our mistakes is the key to spiritual growth in this life and the next.

If there is a heaven, why do bad things
happen to good people?

If you believe in reincarnation – everything you do in your life will be rewarded or punished either in this life or in the next by the law of karma (what goes around comes around) – then you have the answer to this question. For example, someone who commits a crime and escapes justice in this life may find that in their next life they suffer as a victim of crime.

If you aren't sure you believe in reincarnation this might prove helpful. Perhaps in this life our human minds are not capable of comprehending why bad things happen to innocent, undeserving people. The answers will only become clear to us when we have evolved into spirit form. Perhaps then when a good person experiences struggles, injustice or poor health it is all part of their spiritual journey or destiny. Sometimes our greatest spiritual lessons are learned through difficulties.

On this earth we live in linear time but when we die we cross over to spiritual time where everything is different. So we can't understand why things happen as they do until we also live in spirit time. All we can do is live our lives in a loving and positive manner so that when we finally cross over to the other side we have left this world a better place and can settle into our new spiritual home without fear, regret or guilt from our previous existence weighing us down and stunting our spiritual growth.

If this explanation doesn't satisfy you, I completely understand. It does feel inadequate and unfair, but let me turn things on their head by asking you a question: What if you knew the answer? What if life's greatest mystery was solved and you understood the reason why innocent people suffer?

The reality is that knowing the answer might be even worse than not knowing it. If you knew the answer you might reach a place where you accepted suffering – made your peace with it. You would not shed a tear when you see others in distress or lend a hand to help them because you understand what is going on. A good comparison is a woman going into labour. She may scream in pain but her family won't be too upset for her; they may even feel joy because they know why she is in pain and her cries are a signal that the baby is ready to make its entrance into the world.

You see, the pain and suffering of others are easy to deal with if you know why they are happening. Imagine you've just had a pair of braces fitted to straighten your teeth. You will initially feel pain but you understand that the discomfort is caused by your teeth repositioning themselves, so you find a way to deal with it.

You take painkillers. You adjust your lifestyle. You put on a brave face and get on with things, trying not to let the pain distract you too much from the business of living.

Now imagine you understood why innocent children are murdered or undeserving people bombed in a brutal war or slaughtered by a natural disaster. If you could make sense of things, you would find a way to deal with it. You would accept the tears and broken lives of others because you could rationalise it. There would be no questions, no sense of outrage or injustice, or need for compassion because you would learn to live with it.

However, as long as the question about why bad things happen to good people remains unanswered, we refuse to accept that their pain is natural. We try to do all we can to help or ease the suffering of others. We believe that we can still make a difference in this world.

Instead of trying to understand or find an answer to this eternal question, maybe it would be better if we just keep asking it over and over again. Would any of us want to live in a world where people did not ask that question of themselves? I know I would not. So perhaps the best thing for us all to do is to take our sense of injustice and direct it into easing the suffering and burdens of others. Fight cruelty with love, and suffering with compassion. Do all we can to end suffering – because an end to suffering is what we all really want, isn't it? We can't just sit back and leave it to God to do that for us, or wait for heaven to intervene. Perhaps the world of spirit is looking down and wondering why on earth we don't take matters into our own hands and end the suffering we inflict on each other ourselves.

How can I tell when I am on the right path to heaven?

It's hard to explain but you will just quietly know that you are on the right track. Your thoughts will feel focused and convincing and you just know what you need to do and say. There may still be questions swirling around in your head but you welcome those because you understand that an open, questioning mind is a mind that holds the keys to heaven.

This paradoxical certain but open-minded feeling will bring a sense of peace and lightness into your life that is very different from the heaviness and noise that fear and rigid thinking create. If you feel tired and weighed down and judgemental, and anxious and worrisome thoughts clatter in your head, this is fear taking you in the wrong direction. When you are on the right path your thoughts and feelings will be gentler, kinder, fairer and non-judgemental.

If the voices in your head tell you there is only one option, if they tell you that you are a loser or can't cope or haven't got what it takes, or that nothing can be done, then fear is directing your life and not the search for heaven. When you are on the right path you will start to see yourself and the world around you in an uplifting, loving and inspirational way. If things aren't working out in your life, instead of feeling bad and beating yourself up, you will sense that it is time to make a change and find a new approach that works better for you. There won't be guilt and regret – just a gut feeling that it is time for a change.

If you aren't sure whether you are truly on the right path or headed in completely the wrong direction, be patient and wait a while. Don't force things. You will find that spiritual messages have a substance and reality to them and they will keep on gently but assertively repeating themselves, whereas the noise of fear burns itself out. There is a lot of advice in the next chapter about how to listen to heaven, as well as guidance on spiritual awakening and knowing when you are ready to discover your path to bliss.

Why can't I believe in heaven?

Paradoxically, perhaps, one of the main reasons is trying too hard to find heaven, as this gives your ego far too much control over things. I've made this mistake many times in my life and it is so easy to do. You think that if you just understand this, listen to that, practise hard, study diligently and be self-disciplined, the answers will come – but all too often they don't. As you will see in the next chapter, when it comes to finding heaven forcing the issue is not the way forward. What you need to do is relax and let go and trust that heaven will find you when the time is right for you.

Stop straining and trying too hard to make things happen. Simply keep your mind and your heart open to the wonder around and within you. As you will see in chapter 4, living in this receptive state can open the doors to heaven.

Another reason could be that heaven has constantly been revealing itself to you but you simply haven't noticed it, or have dismissed it because it seemed too simple or obvious and you didn't trust what your heart was telling you. Trust your heart – it always knows what is right. And sometimes you may not be able to believe in heaven because unhealthy lifestyle choices or toxic relationships or destructive habits, such as drinking or overeating, are creating a fog in your mind and obscuring the clarity of divine guidance.

It is also impossible to believe in heaven if you don't believe in yourself first. Trust me, I know how very hard it can be to do that. I have suffered all my life from lack of self-confidence and I know I am not alone. Countless numbers of people feel the same way for a variety of different reasons, ranging from toxic parenting to abusive relationships to problems with self-image. They find it hard to believe in themselves and it is this lack of self-belief that destroys their chances of happiness.

So how do you start believing in yourself?

Self-confidence isn't going to happen overnight. It is going to take time, sometimes a lifetime, but if you want to find bliss you need to find a piece of heaven within yourself first. There is no other way.

This may surprise you as you are probably used to associating religion/spirituality with selflessness and putting yourself last, but the most difficult step on the road to heaven is actually to put yourself and your spiritual needs first. Selflessness comes later on your spiritual journey, but before that you need to be self-centred because out of self-centredness true kindness can emerge.

You see, if you are selfish you are trying in every way you can to be happy. You are trying to find heaven for yourself. You are not on a voyage of spiritual discovery for the benefit of others or for those less fortunate than you – all your efforts are directed towards finding inner peace and happiness. Then, once you find your inner bliss, you are ready to share it, give it to others because happiness is your goal in life and sharing your happiness with others and being compassionate and of service to them feels joyful. You won't be helping others because you think you ought to or because it makes you feel less guilty or because it makes you feel good; you will be helping others because it is a happy thing to do. It has nothing to do with your ego and everything to do with spreading light and joy in the world.

It is much the same with love. If you don't love yourself first, you won't have any love in your heart to give to others. You may think you are in love but you are confusing love here with need. You need someone to love you and fill the emptiness within your heart. The only way to experience true love is to love yourself first, so then when you meet someone you can give your heart to them with no strings attached. You want their love but don't need it.

Of course, I'm not suggesting that you totally disregard the needs of others in your search for bliss or indulge in hedonistic pleasures. That would make the people you care about unhappy, and being the cause of unhappiness in others is not the recipe for true contentment. Also, simply seeking pleasure for pleasure's sake is an empty way to live. Your search for happiness needs to have real meaning.

I'm also not suggesting that from now on you try to avoid anything that might cause you distress or hardship. It is impossible and unhealthy to be constantly happy. You would not evolve emotionally and spiritually. Sometimes pain, struggle, loss and confusion are the greatest teachers and the key to spiritual growth and awakening. Someone who appears constantly happy is someone who is not fully engaging with life, denying themselves the opportunity to learn and grow spiritually. Life, both its highs and lows, has to be experienced fully because the insight, maturity and wisdom we gain from our struggles prepare our hearts and minds for the wonderful possibility of heaven.

So when I talk about the need for you to become self-centred, I don't mean self-serving, self-indulgent or 'happy' all the time. What I'm saying is that you need to be self-centred because until you can discover magic inside yourself, you simply won't be able to find it in any other way. Your journey to heaven must begin from the inside out.

Discovering heaven from the inside out is the road less travelled. It isn't an easy path to take but, if navigated properly, it is a sure-fire way to discover the real truth and meaning of your life, here and hereafter.

And travelling along this road is what chapter 4 of this book is all about . . .

Remember, though, that if you want things easy and don't really want to think about the consequences of your actions or the meaning of your life, the rest of this book probably isn't for you. The road to self-understanding, becoming yourself and evolving spiritually can lead you to your heaven, but it is going to be difficult and sometimes lonely and you are going to have to face up to your fears, doubts and other uncomfortable truths along the way. Just as things weren't easy for Gandhi, Martin

Luther King or any great human beings in history who challenged the status quo, they aren't going to be easy for you either, but if you want to find peace, a sense of meaning and true fulfilment then it is the only path for you.

> *There are always two choices. Two paths to take. One is easy. And its only reward is that it is easy.*
>
> Anon

CHAPTER FOUR

Fast track to heaven

People take different routes to find happiness and fulfilment. Just because they are not on your road does not mean they are lost.

Anon

The path to heaven isn't necessarily 'out there'. It can also be discovered within. Indeed, the journey within may well be the fastest and simplest route to finding heaven on earth so in this section of the book we will explore how to find meaning, purpose, comfort, hope, joy, love and peace (aka heaven) in your everyday life.

Before that, however, you need to know whether you are truly ready to search within your heart and begin your journey to heaven. If any of the following signs of spiritual awakening sound familiar to you then the chances are you are.

Signs of spiritual awakening

The first and by far most common sign of the need to turn inward and re-evaluate is one I am very familiar with – confusion. There may be doubt mixed in with your confusion, too – although you might not admit this to yourself – and you may find yourself questioning everything you thought was right. In addition, you may feel that your life isn't working for you or that you aren't making progress. For example, you may wonder if you've chosen the right career or relationship, or think there is no way round love, money or career problems. As I've tried to show throughout this book, the best way forward is to think of your confusion as a sign that you are ready to change and grow – letting go of rigid thinking and opening your mind and your heart to new ways of seeing and feeling will help.

Experiencing intense feelings that you are not familiar with is another sign. You thought you knew pretty much everything about yourself and then suddenly you find yourself feeling things you thought you weren't capable of. These feelings may be triggered by another person and you are convinced you have found your soulmate, or they may be sparked by a new-found passion for life. Either way, these feelings set you on fire and make you question everything you ever thought you knew about yourself.

Closely connected to strong and unfamiliar feelings, you may also experience unusual levels of anxiety and find yourself doing wild things, like wanting to have an affair or taking up a dangerous sport. Typically, this kind of thing happens as we head into our forties and fifties and is often referred to as a midlife crisis. As long as you don't hurt anyone who cares about you in the process, a midlife crisis can be an incredible thing because it is your spirit urging you to rethink who you are and what matters to you.

Another sure-fire sign of the need for spiritual growth is feeling stuck after a significant loss of a partner, job, friend, your health or anyone or anything that you really cared about. You may feel as if you can't rebuild your life and there is no way forward, so the temptation is to shut down and withdraw into despair, depression or cynicism. If you're able to view the loss as a sign that you are ready to grow spiritually, it can be easier to bear. I'm not going to lie to you: viewing loss in this light is incredibly hard and you will need to grieve for what you've lost before you are ready even to consider moving forward.

The theme of loss continues with the next – and probably most painful – sign of spiritual awakening, and that is the death of a loved one. Your life changes completely. You can decide to spend the rest of your life mourning the loss or you can celebrate that person's life and enter into a new life in spirit with that person. It is obvious which path offers the most healing and hope.

Confronting your own mortality – perhaps because you've had a brush with death, are suffering from poor health or because you suddenly realise life is too short – can also act as a trigger.

One of the clearest and most exciting signs of spiritual awakening is a fascination with matters spiritual and a passionate desire to discover your deeper self and live your life on a more meaningful level. You may notice that your gut feeling is more right than wrong and your psychic potential is developing.

Perhaps you sense or see things more clearly, or perhaps your dreams are becoming more vivid and insightful. Enjoy all these developments. Your spirit wants you to listen to them, to make contact with the invisible world.

Spiritual awakening doesn't always have to be dramatic and sudden. Sometimes the need for change can creep up on us unawares. In other words, you won't always know when you are ready or think you need to change. However, acknowledging that you are changing inside is crucial if you want to lead a deeper, more meaningful life.

Did any of the above speak to you? If you aren't sure, you may also want to glance at the stages of faith discussed on page 117 to give you another perspective. However, if any or all of the signs are definitely familiar to you then this is a powerful indicator that you are ready to live your life in a deeper, more meaningful way. The chances are you haven't quite found the answers or fulfilment you need through the traditional route of religion. And perhaps you also feel disheartened because you've read stories about people who have caught a glimpse of the afterlife through heavenly intervention or encounters with lost loved ones, but nothing like that, no personal proof, has ever happened to you.

Guidelines not rules

Please think of the advice that follows as guidelines not rules. I sincerely hope they will get you thinking and feeling along the right lines, and help you discover the magic of eternal life within you and around you. However, do feel free to disagree or go your own way if your heart tells you to. In fact, finding your own spiritual path and thinking through what works best for you is something I actively encourage, as it shows you have truly moved from belonging to becoming and believing in yourself in the faith continuum.

Heaven is such a mysterious, wonderful, incredible, miraculous, unending swirl of unlimited magic and potential that it simply cannot be contained and reduced to a set of rules, laws and beliefs. In much the same way, the amazing and unique person you are can't be completely in tune with principles and beliefs that were formulated by someone who is not you. Following those rules would do an injustice to your individuality. Remember, true enlightenment happens to individuals, not groups. All the great prophets of the world – Jesus, Buddha and Muhammad among many others – were individuals. They didn't take the easy, comfortable, heavily trodden path, and neither should you.

Of course, it is so much easier to follow rules laid down by others. If others are doing it then it must be right – how can so many people be wrong? And when you follow a group, you give that group the gift of validation and, in return for your devotion, the group welcomes you and you feel like you belong. At times in our lives we all need the security of belonging, but sooner or later this won't be enough and you will feel as if something is missing from your life.

And something is missing – your individuality. Let's see now what we can do to rediscover it . . .

What lies beneath

As we've seen, the most obvious place to look for heaven is within yourself. If you are unable to believe that heaven can exist within you then you have your first stumbling block to spiritual growth, because heaven tends to reveal itself first from the inside out.

You need to believe that within you lies the power to create happiness. You need to trust in yourself and feel good about yourself. I know that is far easier said than done. I often have problems thinking of myself in a loving, magical way. I'm sure I am not alone and many of you reading this may have also felt unworthy at various times in your life.

Trusting and believing in yourself is something everyone struggles with, and your level of self-esteem will likely ebb and flow throughout your life. It will always be a work in progress and that is perfectly natural. Even the most confident, contented person has bouts of low self-esteem, but there are things you can do or shifts in perspective that can help rebalance the scales.

All too often our self-esteem is based on external factors: how we look, having a partner, climbing the career ladder, getting qualifications, having money and so on. But all this is so fragile and rather pointless because, as we've seen, in the world of spirit material things are completely meaningless. Also, the problem with self-esteem that is built on impermanent external factors is that you only feel good when things are going well; but when things go wrong – which sooner or later they will because, let's face it, we all age, lose jobs, fail in relationships, make mistakes and know deep down that money can't buy happiness – you lose your self-esteem.

To prevent your self-esteem being controlled by external things it helps to be grounded in self-acceptance. The concept of self-acceptance is based on the knowledge that we are all fallible human beings. We all have flaws and weaknesses and need to learn to accept ourselves, warts and all. Sometimes we say or do things we regret. Sometimes we get things wrong. Sometimes we are weak and needy. Sometimes we disappoint those we love and, in a world with billions of people, there is always going to be someone cleverer, thinner, prettier, younger or more successful. That's life. So if you've convinced yourself that you just aren't good enough, you need to stop right there. Perfection in this life is not possible – indeed, it is not even desirable because if you were perfect there would be no room for growth and transformation.

Due to misinterpretation of religious doctrines many believe that only those who have lived a good, error-free life make it to heaven, but life isn't about getting it right all the time. Life is about getting it wrong some of the time and learning and grow-ing from your mistakes. It is about confronting your demons and accepting that there is always scope for improvement because nobody can or should be perfect. Just imagine how dull and limiting the world would be if everyone was perfect! How could you grow spiritually if you didn't have inner conflicts to resolve?

So, to improve your self-esteem focus on what truly matters in life rather than material things; practise self-acceptance and stop beating yourself up if you get things wrong – because, try as you might, you are going to get things wrong from time to time. Doing the best you can really is enough sometimes. It also helps to remember that whatever has happened to you, and whatever you think about yourself, the life you are currently living is your responsibility.

It is very easy to blame the past, your parents, your teachers, your boss, your partner, a stroke of bad luck, the economy, the climate, the world – but, at the end of the day, the harsh truth is that the way you feel about yourself is your responsibility. You choose how you feel about yourself. Even if you think you were born a self-doubter, you can change. You can't change other people but you can change yourself. I will repeat. You can change.

Thinking and feeling

And the best place to start changing is with your thoughts and feelings because the way you think and feel can sabotage your self-esteem. Believe it or not, you can learn to control your thoughts and manage your feelings so that instead of thinking and feeling negatively about yourself you can think and feel magic.

Sometimes it can feel as though you aren't in charge of your thoughts, but this isn't true. The big secret to boosting your self-worth is to understand that you are in charge of what you think about. This doesn't mean replacing negative thoughts with positive thoughts, as looking on the bright side when things are clearly falling apart around you isn't helpful at all; but it does mean replacing negative thoughts with more realistic ones that take into account both negative and positive outcomes. For example, 'I'm no good at anything' can be replaced by, 'There are things I'm not so good at but there are also things I am good at.'

So the next time a negative thought appears ask yourself if you are being realistic or if you are exaggerating, making unfair generalisations or predictions, blaming yourself unjustly, ignoring the positive or worrying unnecessarily. Start challenging your thoughts with realism and replace them with something more constructive. And, for goodness' sake, stop treating your thoughts as facts – just because you think something does not make it true. Challenge negative thinking and start recognising when you are losing perspective, worrying too much, being melodramatic and overly pessimistic.

Just as unrealistic negativity can damage your self-esteem, out-of-control emotional responses can also result in loss of identity. The first step is to understand that you are not your feelings. Feelings are temporary and you can learn to manage them. You may find it hard to understand or trust your feelings because they seem illogical and we have so often been taught to deny or suppress our emotions, but the very nature of our emotions is to be illogical. Sometimes, for instance, you may just feel sad, and, instead of questioning or denying it, simply allow the feeling to pass through you. You may find it painful to express certain feelings, but expressing your feelings – even the so-called negative ones, like anger, fear and sadness – can boost your self-esteem. When emotions are not felt they can cause even greater distress because you are not allowing your heart to express itself. This does not mean you have to act on your feelings all the time, but you do need to acknowledge that they are carrying messages from your inner wisdom, perhaps to alert you to an area of discomfort in your life. If such emotions are not worked through, this will cause tension.

Emotions are the only real way we have of perceiving what truly matters to us and what doesn't, and difficult emotions signal the need for some kind of change in our lives. They require us to change the situation or mind-set that is causing distress. Negative emotions are not bad emotions; they are necessary because learning to manage them helps us grow and develop.

Reconnecting with your emotions won't be easy if you've grown used to denying or suppressing them, but on your journey to heaven it is important that you start to become aware of what you are feeling and, most crucially, not to identify with that feeling. Understanding why you feel a certain way can help, but recognise that you may not always be able to comprehend why you feel the way you do. If that is the case, remember that sometimes you just need to feel a certain way without there being a reason why. Let yourself experience the emotion but don't let it control your life. You are always the one in charge of your emotions, not the other way round, and taking control of both your thoughts and emotions – seeing them as something that happens to you rather than defining you – will give you the confidence to be the person you want to be.

Take care of yourself

Last, but by no means least, it goes without saying that healthy living and watching your stress levels are crucial for healthy self-esteem. In other words, people with good self-esteem take good care of themselves physically, mentally and emotionally.

As I said earlier, building your self-esteem can take a lifetime (or more) to achieve, so don't feel despondent if you know you have a lot of work to do. I've received countless stories, and know from personal experience, that heaven certainly doesn't wait for self-esteem to be high. In fact, it often breaks through when feelings of uncertainty, desperation or despair shatter self-belief. But you don't need to go through that trauma, distress and shock to find your path. You can find it in quieter, calmer, happier ways and in moments of serenity and inner confidence, too.

So, feeling good about yourself is not essential for finding heaven on earth but it can certainly help. I haven't emphasised self-esteem because I think it is the most important requirement but because having self-esteem can free you from the mind-set that equates selflessness with spirituality. Not thinking of your own needs just makes you unhappy and unfulfilled – the very opposite of experiencing heaven on earth.

Far better to feel good about yourself first so that you have the energy to be there for others. Far better to be happy so that you are like a light in the darkness for others. Far better to love yourself first so that you have love to give. A heart that is constantly giving to others is running on empty. It needs to be refuelled with self-love. Moreover, if you accept and acknowledge how unique and amazing you are then you are more likely to be assertive and to make your own mind up about the things that really matter in your life. As I've repeatedly stressed throughout his book, being true to yourself is the key to your spiritual growth on earth.

Remember, as long as you don't break the golden rule of not harming others, what you think, feel and do has as much validity as any other human being who has walked this earth.

Watching yourself

The only way to be truly content is to trust and believe in yourself. This means letting go of all the confusing and noisy voices in your head that distance you from yourself and the experience of bliss. Meditation can be a wonderful tool for achieving clarity of vision and a receptive state of mind, but there is a warning attached: meditation is extremely hard to do and it may not work for everyone. It doesn't typically work for me as I often fall asleep whenever I make a concerted effort to try it, but perhaps one of the reasons I struggle with meditation is that I'm one of those people who always likes to be doing. I'm not very good at being, and meditation is all about being. It is all about being yourself, just you in the moment.

There are tools and techniques that can help you get into a meditative state. However, in a strict sense they don't help because in its purest form meditation is something that you cannot *do*. It just happens. And it can happen at any time, and not necessarily when you are kneeling on a yoga mat doing deep-breathing exercises. I've had moments of profound clarity at the most unexpected times, usually when I'm totally absorbed in an activity, daydreaming, feeling a sense of wonder or my heart is bursting with joy. And that is probably why I find meditation as a practice difficult. I'm straining to make something happen, thinking that if I learn certain techniques I'll get there, but, at the risk of repeating myself, meditation is about being not doing. So I'm not going to recommend any meditation techniques here. I'm just going to give you a new perspective – a perspective that works for me.

The meditative state is your natural state. It can't be created, learned or possessed; it just has to be noticed. It is already there for you and always has been. It is your being. It is you, and your task is to reconnect with it. A lot of people confuse meditation with contemplation or mind control, but meditation is not about thought at all. It is about the lack of thought. That's why meditation techniques, such as imagining thoughts turning into butterflies, aren't always effective because these methods just put more thoughts into your head. What you need to do is stop thinking and trying altogether. You must do, think and feel nothing. Just *be*.

Returning to just being is a challenge because so many of us lead busy and stressful lives and are used to doing, but if you are able to regularly set aside time to come back to yourself in this way you will experience remarkable inner clarity and vision. And this inner clarity could transform your life completely as you start to notice everything you say and do from the inside out. You become consciously aware of the energy within you and all your thoughts and feelings just vanish – all that is left is the silence of you.

Watching yourself from the inside out feels surreal at first but I urge you to give it a try. Spend a few minutes noticing every movement, action, word and feeling and thought you have from within. Pay conscious attention to everything you do. After a while something amazing will happen. You will notice that the real you is actually separate from all these things, and when you notice this separation you will gradually begin to distance yourself from your thoughts, feelings and actions. You will start to identify with your inner glow because you know it is truly you.

Then something even more remarkable will happen – someone else, typically someone sensitive, will begin to notice your inner glow. The light inside you will reach them. There may be no words or physical contact but they feel touched by you in some inexplicable way. There is a spiritual connection between you that you cannot explain and in time that bond will extend to another person and another and another and so on. Then it will extend to animals and the natural world and from there to everything in the world, and after that the universe and beyond. What you will experience then is a mystical connection between all people and things, past, present and future, living and in spirit. There are many ways to describe this mind-blowing experience but I call it heaven.

How to find heaven

The meditative, receptive, mystical state described above may only be fully realised in the afterlife, but it is possible to catch glimpses of it on earth and the remaining pages of this chapter will explain how. In many ways what follows is the true heart of the book because it shows that everyone, regardless of age and background, can find heaven through their heart, their intuition, their ears and eyes, in their dreams and in their daily lives.

As you read, I want to remind you one final time not to force things. Straining just creates stress and tension and shuts your mind to the possibility of heaven in the process. The attitude that can most nourish your connection to heaven is respect – for yourself, for others, for nature, for life itself, both here and on the other side. Whenever there is respect, feelings of tenderness, awe and wonder are never far behind, creating fertile ground for spiritual growth.

Working with your heart

It is fitting that we begin with your heart because it is the centre of everything. It is where heaven begins and never ends. When you are born your heart starts beating. When you fall in love your heart skips a beat. When you feel or sense joy your heart sings. When you die your heart stops, and in the next life it is your heart that people remember you by and in the hearts of others that you live on. What isn't real or true occurs in your mind. Everything that is true and real has a heartbeat.

Sensing paradise with your heart – your feelings – is perhaps the most typical way people connect to heaven. Earlier, I spoke about not identifying with your feelings and about managing them, but this doesn't mean you shouldn't notice them, listen to them or even trust them, because heaven can reveal itself to you through your emotions. For example, have you ever experienced a sudden and unexplained rush of euphoria or happiness, or sensed the presence of a departed loved one beside you, or noticed the atmosphere in a room change when someone walks in, or just had a feeling something wasn't right, even though you can't logically say why?

All of these are ways in which heaven can speak to you through your feelings, because your heart is captain of your feelings, but the chances are you ignored or dismissed them at the time because they are so subtle and irrational and not easy to explain. Another typical way for heaven to reveal itself through your heart is the feeling that someone has hugged you or embraced you, and this may be accompanied by a tingling sensation or the hairs on the back of your neck standing up. Sensing someone standing right behind you when there is nobody there is also fairly common, as is feeling light pressure on your head and heart and noticing certain scents, typically with a fragrant source but no identifiable cause. A cool breeze on your cheek, a light kiss on your forehead and a glowing sensation of warmth, as if you are wrapped in a warm blanket, are other regularly reported sensations but there are countless others.

Your heart reveals itself to you through your feelings and your senses, which are interconnected with your feelings. Although some of the most typical ways are outlined above, remember there is nothing more mysterious and magical than your heart, so expect the unexpected. However, even though your heart often speaks in irrational, indefinable ways, you will know when it is talking to you because the sensation will always feel warm, empowering and otherworldly, and there will be a swirl of joy for no reason. Your job now is to listen to your heart and trust it because your heart always knows what is real.

Opening your heart

So, if heaven lives in your heart what can you do to increase your chances of finding it there?

There are things you can do but first you need to determine whether receiving spiritual guidance through your feelings and senses is the ideal starting point for you or, as will be discussed later, whether your spiritual potential is more receptive to information received visually or aurally or through your unconscious in dreams. Remember, understanding yourself is the beginning of wisdom. If any of the following feels familiar to you then I'm guessing that emotions are going to play an important part in building your path to heaven:

- You are the kind of empathetic person who just understands how another person is feeling. Even if they haven't explained how they feel, you know what they are feeling.
- Sometimes you can walk into a room and feel the atmosphere without anyone explaining a word. The moods of people you care about deeply can impact on you to the extent that if they are anxious or tired you feel anxious and tired too. For no reason you can sometimes suddenly feel exhausted.

- The world can sometimes feel overwhelming to you, and when your senses feel bombarded you need to spend time alone or to take a step back to recharge. Your idea of a nightmare is being in a large crowd. As a child you may have been very scared of the dark and still feel nervous when everything is pitch black at night.
- As a child (and maybe even from time to time now) you were described as sensitive and may have burst into tears if you saw ugliness, injustice or cruelty, or sometimes for no good reason at all.
- You always cry when you go to the cinema. You cry when you are happy.
- Sometimes you are convinced someone is watching you or standing behind you, but when you turn around or investigate there is no one there. On occasion you can smell things with no discernible source. For example, roses when they are not in bloom or vanilla when there is no reason. If things are going wrong, you may get a tense, knotted feeling in your stomach or experience nausea you can't explain.
- You have a special rapport with animals of all kinds and feel most at home in the countryside, or park if you live in the city. For no good reason at all you often experience feelings of incredible joy – if you could fly you would.

Even if just a few of those statements resonated with you then it is clear that your feelings are your guide to heaven. When you start understanding your feelings better, you will find that you understand yourself and others better. Your life will feel richer and more colourful because your feelings will be sending intuitive messages about the path to heaven that is right for you.

I'm not keen on techniques and rules when it comes to spiritual development, but I hope the following guidelines will serve as a springboard and help you to develop the gift of 'clear feeling'.

Use your second brain

When it comes to your moods and feelings, your brain in your head is not the only one doing the thinking. Your stomach has such a complex nervous system that it has actually been called the second brain. It is believed to be the original nervous system, perhaps giving rise to the brain itself, and although you are not conscious of it, your gut thinking is particularly sensitive to emotion and plays an important role in your physical and mental wellbeing, helping you to sense and respond to your environment. You know that feeling you get when something doesn't feel right or when you feel excitement, fear or stress? We often call it a gut feeling and I'm going to ask that you pay more attention to your gut in the days and months ahead.

To stimulate your gut feelings and strengthen the clear seeing that is natural to you, try thinking about your stomach as your second brain. Listen to what it has to tell you. Do you feel tense, joyful or stressed? Remember, your gut feelings are often strong and almost seem physical. For example, a sinking feeling is a warning; an excited feeling might indicate you are heading in the right direction; nausea will suggest danger. Also pay attention to any physical sensations, as your gut communicates through these, too. Try keeping a record of your gut feelings and any unexplained physical sensations, such as an ache or a tingle. Then look back at them every now and again to see how many times you were right. Hindsight will typically show that your gut feelings were more often right than wrong.

Be someone else

After all the advice so far in this book about becoming yourself and discovering who you truly are, it feels weird to suggest that you put yourself in somebody else's shoes from time to time, but I'm going to do just that.

Empathy is a compassionate gift from heaven. It is the ability to sense or understand how someone else is feeling. It is the gateway to compassion and everything that is good in the world.

Empathy is a skill that can be developed and nurtured at any time or in any place. If you send a text or an email, imagine the person on the receiving end and how your words will affect them. When you are in conversation with someone really listen to what they are saying. Imagine you are them and what it might be like to live their life. If you are in a public place, do some discreet people watching and imagine seeing the world through their eyes. If you feel uncomfortable doing that, choose a picture of someone you don't know in a magazine or online and ask yourself what it might be like to be that person.

If you truly want to find heaven, empathy can open doors of divine communication. It comes with a warning, though: experiencing emotions that are not your own can be draining if you confuse other people's feelings with your own. When that happens you may start feeling overwhelmed, negative or tired for no reason and without realising why. If you struggle to disconnect with others, think of an invisible cord stretching between you and other people that you can cut anytime you need to detach. Wearing the colours black and gold will also help, as they have protective, confidence-boosting properties.

Think pink

While we are on the subject of colour, you may want to consider adding more shades of pink or emerald green into your life. I'm no colour therapist but I do know that studies have shown the therapeutic powers of certain colours, and pink and green can help you tune into your feelings more and open your heart. Why not buy yourself a bunch of pink roses or a vibrant green potted plant and take a moment every now and again to stop and smell the flowers? Wearing these colours may also help you tap into their energies. Emerald and pink (rose quartz) gemstones can also prove beneficial.

Light years

Eat well, sleep well, exercise regularly, avoid substances and activities that are damaging to your body, and watch your stress levels – in short, respect your body, mind and heart by leading a healthy lifestyle.

An unhealthy lifestyle will make it very hard for you to get in touch with your true feelings because fatigue, poor nutrition and stress will all be crying out noisily for your attention and you won't be able to hear the quiet voice of your heart.

Get to the heart of the matter

Finally, take a few moments every morning and night – that's all you need – to pay attention to your heart. Sit somewhere comfortably, close your eyes and listen to your heart beating. It may take a while but eventually, when the noise and bustle of everyday life and the thoughts racing in your head have calmed down, you will hear your steady heartbeat – the rhythm of your life. Focus all your attention on that heartbeat and then ask your heart what it needs and expects of you. Take your time and wait for an answer. It will come, I promise – and the chances are good that it will tell you it feels neglected because, although you consider the feelings of others, you aren't considering your own heart enough.

All the above will help you listen to your heart because it is in your heart that the love, hope and joy of heaven will appear. An open heart is an essential first leap towards heaven, and a double first leap – you guessed it – is an open mind.

Working with your intuition

From clear feeling we now move to clear thinking, or intuition. Also known as a hunch, vibe or sixth sense, it is a knowledge, understanding or insight that may not seem logical and you may have no idea how it came to you, but it gives you complete and peaceful certainty all the same. When a clear thought like that happens, heaven is speaking directly to you.

Perhaps you have already had experience of clear thinking but didn't recognise it at the time. Perhaps you had one of those amazing moments, I like to call them 'aha moments', when everything suddenly made sense or you could see a way forward when there was only confusion before. Or perhaps an inspiration came out of nowhere, or you wanted to remember something but couldn't and then suddenly you recalled what you had previously forgotten. Another example of clear thinking is when your mind is absolutely lucid and confident that something is a right or wrong idea, even if everybody and all the evidence suggests otherwise. You might also have a very definite sense of what is going to happen in the near future and your prediction turns out to be spot-on.

All these examples of clear thinking can easily be missed because they feel so natural, normal and understated. The chances are you will dismiss your insight as imagination or a stroke of good luck or something that jogged your memory, but these are all signs that heaven is talking to you. Here are some ways to help you listen:

Opening your mind

By far the most powerful thing you can do to boost clear thinking has been done already when you started reading this section of the book and were either introduced to or reminded of the compelling idea that divine communication can be transmitted to you through your thoughts. Simply paying attention to what you are thinking and not instantly dismissing your thoughts as irrelevant or random is a great place to start. In most cases, what you are thinking will be informative or insightful in some way and, most important of all, relevant to you and what is going on in your life.

It might be a good idea to keep some kind of written or verbal record, in a notebook or on your mobile phone, of the insights that come to you, even those that don't quite seem to make any sense at the time. Not only will this give you a chance to check whether your insights proved accurate, but it will also help you give expression to your thoughts rather than stifling them.

You may want to take a pen and paper or grab a keyboard and ask a question of yourself. Then for a few minutes write everything that comes into your head, even if it sounds totally ridiculous and off topic. Don't think about what you are writing – just write automatically and unconsciously. Think of writing as blinking, something you do without thinking. When you read it back, you may find that what you've written makes no sense at all, and maybe even sounds crazy, but it doesn't matter as you won't be sharing your thoughts with anyone. However, hidden in all those random thoughts you may just find a golden insight or see a pattern emerging. This exercise often takes several attempts, so give it time. It is well worth it.

Heavenly inspiration can strike at any time but it tends to happen more when your mind is relaxed and clear rather than crowded and stressed. Walking briskly in the fresh air is the best way for me to clear my head. The countryside or a park is ideal, but if none are at hand a walk down the street is fine. But you may prefer other methods, such as running or cycling. The aim is to clear your head so that you can hear what you are thinking and what heaven is trying to tell you. Meditation, of course, could also work for some but, as we saw on page 23, it makes me feel tired because when I close my eyes I want to go to sleep!

Here's a fun exercise. Find a place you can relax and think of a song – the first that comes to mind; it doesn't matter what the song is. Now play the song in your head and, as you listen, think about why that particular song came to mind, and perhaps your intuition will give you an answer and there will be a message in there for you somewhere.

Dreams are a wonderful way to tune in to your intuition. Just before you go to sleep think about the direction your life is heading in and what the world needs from you. Keep asking and asking until you fall asleep. Then in the morning grab a pen and paper (best to have them ready at your bedside) and don't write but draw what your intuition wants to tell you. You may remember some dreams you had, so draw them too; but if you've forgotten your dreams, it doesn't matter – just draw the first thing that comes into your mind and then think about what your unconscious is trying to tell you.

Finally, if you think a more direct answer will speak to you, try visiting your local library or bookshop in your imagination or in reality. Walk past the shelves of books until one title in particular draws you to it. Open the book randomly and see if a word or phrase on the page in front of you gives you an insight or answer of some kind, or at the very least pause for thought. This exercise may take a while to get used to, but I have done it many times and it really works. Trust it.

Trust yourself

Many of us discount guidance we receive through our feelings and thoughts because we don't really trust ourselves to get things right, but the most common ways for heaven to reach out to you are through your heart and your mind. Trust yourself.

Sure, there are some highly sensitive individuals who connect to the world of spirits through dramatic visions or voices, but I actually think heaven prefers to reveal itself quietly and subtly rather than in such an obvious manner. Heaven loves nothing more than for you to discover it quietly for yourself because trust without proof generates incredible spiritual energy. So if you think proof of heaven can only be revealed through visions of and voices from the other side, you are likely to miss out on the profound messages coming to you all the time. Of course, insight revealed through feelings and thoughts tends to be more subtle but this does not make it any the less potent.

I am aware all this sounds so much easier in theory than in practice. In the hustle and bustle of daily life, it can be incredibly hard to know if feelings and thoughts are from heaven or leading you in the opposite direction or, in some cases, in no direction at all!

Perhaps in the past you've been convinced you were right but actually weren't? Perhaps you thought someone had your best interests at heart but that didn't prove to be the case? Perhaps you thought you had a fantastic idea but in reality it turned out to be a terrible one? I think all of us can identify with these confusing scenarios. However, with hindsight I can look back on my life and the decisions I've made and see clearly how I have ignored divine guidance or misunderstood it. And the area in which there has been most frequent misunderstanding is in my relationships, not just with life partners but with friends and business colleagues, too.

As I mentioned earlier in the book, for a number of years I was involved in a very ugly relationship. At the time I convinced myself I had found my soulmate, but at every step of the way my heart and my mind were sending me clear warnings – I just ignored them. The warnings came in my inability to relax or feel good about myself, in the doubts I constantly felt I had to quash. All the time I was with him it was like I was having a conversation with myself, trying to convince myself that I didn't deserve to be treated better.

It's a similar story with my friendships. Early on there was always a moment – perhaps when a friend had arranged to meet me for lunch and then forgotten to turn up or, during conversations with me, been repeatedly distracted by texts or phone calls, or made endless demands on me that were unfair. I'd patiently wait or be unwilling to cause a fuss, or think I couldn't say no when someone asked for my help or my time, trying to convince myself that it didn't matter because it was only me. However, the tension and doubts I felt inside were trying to tell me that I did matter and I did deserve to be treated better.

Not surprisingly, I also misplaced my trust in colleagues at work. A part of me would know deep down that someone wasn't to be trusted but I would dismiss it as paranoia. Often these people would be glamorous high-achievers and I sacrificed any niggling doubts I had about them because they were so charismatic. I thought that if I proved my loyalty to them, worked hard and never complained they would see my worth. They didn't! They just saw someone they could manipulate because I didn't assert myself enough.

I opened my heart to people and trusted and gave all of myself far too quickly. If only I'd spent more time listening to my feelings and thoughts I would not have had my heart broken so many times. I still tend to give my heart freely because it is my nature to see the good in others rather than the bad, but I have learned to be slightly more cautious now and not rush in. I have learned that getting to know a person takes a lot of time and even then you can never know a person fully, and surprises can happen when least expected. I have also learned to either avoid a person or express how I feel to them politely if I have any doubts. If they truly want me in their life they will not be offended but embrace the opportunity to clear the air. If they do take offence, they either have something to hide or don't really want me in their life and it is better I find out sooner rather than later.

Levels of consciousness

Thoughts and feelings are by nature often confusing and illogical, and sometimes it can be hard to tell whether it is heaven talking to you through your unconscious mind, or self-doubt and worry talking to you through your conscious mind. Your conscious mind refers to processes in your mind that involve the here and now – the fact that you are reading this book – and your unconscious mind involves processes that you are not aware of.

Your conscious mind is logical, rational and a bit like a computer firewall that accepts or rejects information according to your beliefs, values and characteristics. Feelings of self-doubt, fear and worry will invade your life through your conscious mind. Your unconscious mind is emotional, creative and intuitive. It is in charge of memories, dreams and all mental processes that are outside your awareness. It can perform thousands of tasks per second and is the seat of learning. Convincing your unconscious mind that something can be done makes your conscious mind find ways to achieve it. Your unconscious mind holds the key to your potential and it is through your unconscious mind that heaven will speak to you.

Albert Einstein once said, 'No problem can be solved from the same level of consciousness that created it.' What he meant was that you need to delve deeper into your unconscious mind to find the answers you seek. I'm not going to lie to you – it can be incredibly hard to know if heaven is talking to you through your unconscious mind, or if your conscious thoughts and imagination are sending you on a wild-goose chase. However, in the many years I have been writing I have been able to identify some vital indicators and I hope the following will prove useful to you at some point.

The first is a feeling of rightness even if there is no evidence to suggest you are correct. There is just a quiet certainty, sometimes without any need for explanation, and this is the exact opposite of the long-winded, confusing conversations and constant need for detailed analysis and clarification that your conscious mind demands.

The second is clarity. Messages from heaven are absolutely clear. Minor details may alter but the central concept or idea will not shift, unlike the changes of direction conscious thoughts may generate.

The third is tenderness. Heaven will not judge you or tell you that you messed up or are stupid or a loser. Any self-doubt and anxiety are generated by your conscious mind. Heaven may urge you to move on or try something new, or tell you something isn't right for you, but it will never communicate this in a negative, belittling or judgemental way. Divine guidance is always tender, empowering and upliftingly positive about you and your life.

The fourth is a feeling of naturalness. The insight you have or the feelings that inspire you will feel like home – a place of safety, comfort and warmth. The communications of your conscious mind, however, will feel forced and make you feel anxious, cold and alone. Heavenly communication just makes you feel good from the inside out – like drinking a cup of hot chocolate on a winter's day.

The fifth is an element of surprise. When your conscious mind is doing all the talking, you may find yourself building up a case or argument that slowly and gradually convinces you over time. Divine communications through your unconscious, on the other hand, will often take you quite by surprise. You may be thinking or doing something entirely unrelated and suddenly an insight, solution or way forward comes to you and you understand it immediately without any need for interpretation.

The sixth is a leap of faith. When your conscious mind is in the driving seat a lot of your thoughts, feelings, actions and decisions will be designed to protect you from struggle, disappointment, embarrassment and failure, and to maintain the status quo in your life. Messages from your unconscious, however, don't always manifest that way. In the great majority of cases they will encourage you to jump outside your comfort zone, take a leap of faith, learn, grow, try something different, head in a new direction or challenge yourself in some way. They may also urge you to think about the needs of others as well as your own. You will be left feeling that the solution being offered is a refreshing change.

The seventh is discipline. Messages from heaven will almost always require hard work and discipline on your part. They are unlikely to provide quick-fix solutions because heaven knows that working through struggle and hardship is the key to finding heaven. You may get recognition or reward as a result, but only as an added bonus, since the main concern is always spiritual development. If the solution being offered seems to require little effort on your part you can be sure it is your conscious mind doing the thinking. Divine guidance only ever has one motivation and that is to enrich your life or the lives of others spiritually.

If any of the above helps you recognise when heaven is talking to you through your thoughts and feelings this is very exciting, because the more you recognise heaven talking in this way, the more you will hear it. You will just instantly recognise divine guidance and use your feelings of self-worth and good intentions towards others to guide you. Trusting in yourself isn't going to be easy and will take time, but the more you trust, the easier it will be for you to hear the voice of heaven coming from within your heart and mind. In time, you may also find that it gets easier to actually hear and see heaven on the outside as well as the inside . . .

The voice of heaven

Who hasn't given themselves a talking to from time to time? I know I have. I often catch myself talking out loud or in my thoughts to myself. Watch any competitive sportsperson and you will often see them motivating themselves by shouting or muttering. It's completely normal to talk to yourself from time to time. It's also completely normal to hear the voice of heaven.

My primary aim when writing books about the afterlife is to show that interaction with heaven is perfectly normal. However, I'm well aware that when this interaction involves hearing voices that are not your own, the automatic assumption is that this is slightly crazy. I worry endlessly about how to discuss this rare but valid mode of divine communication in my books so that it won't scare people away.

First of all, let me stress that, unless you are under medical supervision, hearing a voice in your head or calling out to you when there is no one about is not mad. It is heaven trying to reach out to you in a very direct way. If you've never experienced this, the voice will not be recognisable as your own and it will not feel like a thought. It will have a distinctness and a clarity and there will be no question in your mind that you must obey it. It is divine inspiration.

On one memorable occasion in my life I heard the voice of heaven talk to me directly and it saved my life. About fifteen years ago I was at a busy junction ready to turn left and clearly heard the voice of my departed mother telling me to take the 'right path'. Her voice was so clear and urgent and authoritative I instantly turned right, only to find out several hours later that if I'd turned left I would almost have certainly been involved in a fatal pile-up. The voice of my mother in spirit saved my life.

Yes, I've heard the voice of heaven and, yes, I know I can be eccentric and chaotic at times but, no, I am not insane. I have all my wits about me. I am also fully aware how crazy my heaven-saved-me story sounds and if someone told me the same I would probably question it myself. Indeed, for many years I didn't tell a soul for fear I would be labelled crazy. It took a lot of courage to finally tell my story in a book, but I'm so glad I did because in the years since I have received many stories from people who've had similar experiences. As far as I know these people are not insane, either. In much the same way as happened to me, they were having an ordinary day not thinking about or expecting anything remarkable to happen, but then something extraordinary did happen – they heard heaven speak – and they were guided, inspired, saved but, above all, surprised!

Opening your ears

Actually hearing the voice of heaven is extremely rare so please don't worry if it doesn't happen to you. In fact, that might even be a good thing because it can involve a lot of second-guessing and make you long for it to happen again and again. I still to this day wonder if I really heard a voice or if I was just remembering vividly one of my mother's favourite phrases, which was about choosing the right path – meaning do the right thing in life. However, I ask myself why that phrase should have popped into my head at that particular moment, because if it hadn't I would not be writing this book today, which incredibly is also about choosing paths in life. I also long a little too much to hear that voice again, but so far I've heard nothing similar and sometimes that can make me feel sad. And the reason it is not happening is probably because I want it too much, and that is something I need to continue to work on.

Although it is rare, sometimes heaven will talk to you directly. If it happens, you will hear a loud voice talk to you inside your head or, on even rarer occasions, outside your head. The voice may sound familiar or be that of a departed loved one, and very occasionally it will be your own, but if that is the case it will feel like something greater than yourself is using your voice to relay information to you. When heaven speaks directly don't be alarmed, take a few deep breaths and listen to what is being said. You will know the voice to be heavenly because, although loud and clear, it will sound friendly and not be threatening. What is said will typically be a statement in the third person. The word 'I' will not be used, although the words 'you' and 'we' might be. It will also be positive and loving and require an immediate reply or response. Voices that are generated by fear or substance abuse will be threatening, unclear and abusive and will require hesitation and procrastination. In other words, messages from heaven will not involve causing harm to yourself or others. Quite the opposite – they will always be about helping, inspiring, motivating or guiding you or others in some positive way.

Hearing a loud, clear voice ringing directly in your head is one way for heaven to reveal itself to you through the medium of sound, but it is not the only way. There are, in fact, a number of other more common ways but clear hearing can at times be even more subtle than clear thinking and feeling, so you may have been receiving messages already but not noticed them.

By far the most common and most neglected way is painless ringing in the ear that soon disappears. I'm not talking about the harsh, intrusive, constant, painful and grinding high-pitched sound you get from ear infections or tinnitus (if you are experiencing those symptoms, please visit your GP) but a gentle, almost inaudible high note that feels a bit surreal and only occurs for a few moments and then melts away. It happens to me a few times every month, and when it does I always think of it as heaven downloading information to my unconscious mind. I may not know what that information is, but I trust that it will inspire or uplift me when the time comes to reveal itself to me. If you ever hear this painless, gentle ringing you may want to stop what you are doing (if you can and it is safe to do so, of course, and not if you're operating machinery or driving) and take a moment to be still, to be receptive and let heaven filter into your thoughts.

Hearing music in your head is another way heaven likes to talk. In the majority of cases the music will be unfamiliar, but whether it is familiar or not it will be gentle and lovely. Sometimes it will not be music but a song or lyrics from a song that get stuck in your mind.

Many people write to me about hearing the voice of a departed loved one speaking to them in their mind or their dreams. Some hear their name being called but when they investigate nobody has called out to them, or they hear familiar sounds like a dog barking, a baby crying or a doorbell ringing, but there is no source. Others talk about a voice in their mind that gives them a solution to a problem or the location of a lost object. I get a lot of stories from people who have switched on the TV or radio and overheard a conversation or piece of information or music that speaks directly to them at just the right time.

In addition, the phone may ring and a person may hear the voice of a departed loved one at the other end. Phone calls from the dead are extremely rare but, trust me, they can and do happen and a number of people have been in touch with me about this over the years. More commonly, the phone may ring but there's nobody there when you answer, and no trace of the call on your phone.

If you are a musician or love listening to music or tend to pick up information about people from the sound of their voice, you are likely to be extremely sensitive to sound. If you hate loud noises and busy, bustling places and find the sounds of nature, in particular birdsong, magical then hearing divine voices will also likely come naturally to you.

Whether or not the above applies to you, the recommendations below can help you fine-tune your spiritual ear.

Listen consciously

In our everyday lives we tend to tune out noises and sounds that are potentially distracting to the task in hand, but one way to develop your spiritual ear is to pick a time when you do the opposite. Before you go to sleep would be a good moment. Typically, when you want to go to sleep you shut noise out, but try instead for a few minutes to listen really carefully to everything – every sound from cars or planes outside, to the cat or dog snoring, to the floorboards creaking or radiators hissing. Try to differentiate between each sound. Notice the differences between sounds made by things that are alive, such as your partner breathing, and sounds that are lifeless, such as a door slamming.

It is extraordinary once you begin consciously listening to sounds that you normally don't pay attention to just how much you've overlooked. There is a whole world of sound out there that you haven't been tuning in to.

This exercise will really help you develop your inner ear if you do it for a week or so. You may find that you have one ear in particular that is more sensitive to picking up subtle sounds and vibrations. If that is the case, put all your concentration into that side of your head when doing this exercise.

Orchestra of sound

Choose one of your favourite pieces of classical music – orchestral is best. Mine is Rachmaninov Piano Concerto No. 2. Now play that music, close your eyes and focus your hearing on just one instrument in the orchestra. You could take this a step further and play the music in your head whenever you feel inspired.

Feel the noise

We tend to think of sound as something external – something we hear outside of us – but try instead to feel sound from the inside. Fill yourself with the feelings of each sound. Notice what these feelings are and what they might be trying to tell you.

If you aren't sure how to get started with all this, one of the simplest and most uplifting ways to fine-tune your hearing is to listen to birdsong in a park, garden or the countryside at dawn or dusk. This time you do need to tune out of competing sounds, especially if your park or garden is near a road. Just focus on the birdsong and feel your spirit and your energy soar.

Heavenly voices

Sometimes you can hear the voice of heaven in your everyday life. You may switch on the radio or TV or go online and hear a song or a conversation that speaks right to your heart. Or you may overhear part of a conversation and gain an unexpected insight. I'm not suggesting you eavesdrop, though; I'm just encouraging you to listen to what is going on around you to give your spirit an opportunity to direct your attention to what you need to hear.

Conscious listening takes time and practice, but it is well worth the effort because it will open up a whole new world of heavenly communication. The only downside – although I think of it as an upside – is that noises that didn't bother you before, such as noisy chatter or loud car stereos, may now really grate. You may also feel the need to talk and move more quietly and gracefully. By becoming more sensitive to sound, your spirit longs to be lighter and quieter so that you can soar higher and higher spiritually.

Visions of heaven

Moving now from clear hearing to clear seeing: is it possible to actually see heaven on earth? To glimpse a vision of the divine?

Yes, it is possible. It is extremely rare because heaven tends to reveal itself in gentler, subtler ways, but it is most definitely possible. I'm basing my certainty on the vast number of stories I have been sent over the years from ordinary people who are perfectly sane and clear-headed. A lot of these people don't claim to be psychic or visionary, and a vision was the last thing they expected, but it happened all the same and changed their lives forever. They know their vision wasn't hallucinatory as they were not on medication or drugs and did not lose awareness of their natural surroundings, which is what tends to happen with hallucination. And nor was it wishful thinking. These people genuinely saw something they could not explain and, for fear of being ridiculed, a number told me this was the first time they had shared their story with anyone.

I'm sure there are countless exercises that claim to help you develop your spiritual eyes but I don't think this is something you can practise for. I believe external visions of heaven are a mystery and a gift. There is little we can do to increase the likelihood of them happening. We should just celebrate the fact that sometimes they do.

Don't despair if you think you will never be able to catch a glimpse of heaven in this way. I have never had a vision of the other side that I have seen with my physical eyes. This used to really trouble me. I longed to see spirits or angels and felt I had earned it, given the platform I had created in my writing career to promote the existence of the afterlife, but it never happened. I don't long for it to happen any more because I know now that you don't need your physical eyes to see heaven. Yes, there are some rare people who can see spirit outside themselves, but the great majority see it with eyes that are inside their head or in symbols. Let me explain inner sight first and then later we'll take a look at heavenly signs or symbols.

Opening your eyes

Inner sight is receiving messages from heaven in the form of colours, symbols, lights, dreams or images that you can see with your inner eyes, or in your mind. You don't think you have this ability? Of course you do.

Close your eyes, think of someone you love or care about who isn't with you right now and picture them in your imagination. An image of them will appear, almost like on a movie screen inside your head, and you will probably see them doing something in your inner vision. Now, think about a time in your life when you've pictured in your mind something happening. It doesn't have to be anything dramatic. Perhaps you were on your way to work and you saw yourself at your desk completing a task, or perhaps you needed to discuss something with your partner or a friend and you visualised the conversation unfolding in your head. If you have experienced something similar then you are already seeing clearly. The next step is to start receiving divine inspiration through your inner vision.

Opening your spiritual eyes is something that should feel natural and easy. It should not feel like hard work because you are tapping into your innate ability to think, dream and imagine in pictures rather than words. Hopefully, the following guidelines will nudge you in the right direction.

See a rainbow

Find somewhere you can safely close your eyes and try this exercise. Visualise in your mind the different colours of the rainbow. Start with red, then move to orange and so on. See them floating in front of you like a screen in your mind. When you feel comfortable doing that, try picturing in your mind some still objects like your mobile phone or favourite mug. Don't worry if the images shift and wobble at first because they always will. You could also try seeing the faces of friends and family, and then have a go at things that move. Start with nature and watch a tree sway in the wind or leaves falling to the ground in your mind. Take your time with moving images as they are harder to visualise than still ones, but if you keep practising you will find that greater clarity emerges.

Picture perfect

Young children love books with pictures, experiencing these pictures through their imagination. The pictures become real to them. They are absorbed by them. When was the last time you lost yourself in a picture? If it was years ago, may I suggest that you track down a photo, poster or painting that speaks to your heart and spend time really looking at every detail? Let the image inspire feelings in you. See yourself stepping inside the picture. Let the picture work its magic on you.

Sky high

Cloud watching is one of life's neglected pleasures. Clouds are truly magical and can take on so many shapes and forms, and observing them can be the most relaxing and lovely thing. Don't stare directly at the sun ¬ as that is bad news for your eyes. Lie down in the grass if you can (but standing up is fine too) and gaze at the clouds above. I say gaze because I don't think you should stare. Gazing is less focused and intense. Watch the clouds as they gradually shape-shift. What do you see? Are there any symbolic messages there for you?

Dreams

Dreaming is a wonderful way for heaven to show itself in images. It is such a huge topic, though, that I will deal with it separately a little later.

These visualisation exercises will help you to see heaven more clearly inside your mind. You might not make much progress at first but be patient and the images will eventually come. You may even be able to project the images outward and see flickers of light or coloured mists, but it doesn't really matter whether what you see is external or internal. What matters is that you are starting to think visually, and developing your visual ability will help you start to notice signs from heaven that manifest in physical things.

Heavenly signs

Heaven can also reveal itself to you in the material world. These aren't visions of the kind mentioned earlier, but everyday objects or events that can have deeply symbolic and spiritual significance. Often it is the timing of these signs that is the most striking thing, as they often seem to offer comfort, hope or a sense of purpose when most needed. Here are some of the most commonly reported signs but there are countless others because what is symbolic or significant to each person is unique.

Clouds

Cloud formations can be truly mesmerising, and I wanted to mention clouds again here because I have read many stories sent to me by people who have seen signs such as cloud-shaped faces that remind them of departed loved ones. Others have told me about clouds that look like wings or feathers or angels and offer the observer a deep sense of calm, comfort and peace.

Rainbows

Beautiful and inspiring, rainbows never fail to take my breath away. They fill me with a sense of awe and anything able to do that will bring you closer to heaven. I have had deeply touching emails from people who have seen rainbows suddenly appear on the day of a funeral of a loved one and the comfort they bring is indescribable.

Butterflies

Like rainbows, many of the stories I receive about butterflies are associated with funerals or the loss of a loved one. Recently, I had a wonderful email sent to me by an undertaker who is convinced that butterflies are messengers from heaven simply because he sees so many of them during the course of his work. Others tell me how the sighting of a butterfly close to the death of a loved one can offer the most incredible comfort.

Birds

In much the same way as butterflies, many people have found that unusually tame wild birds, or birds spotted at unusual times of the year, can feel like comforting signs from departed loved ones to let those they left behind know they are at peace on the other side.

Coins

Like feathers, coins can also appear in unlikely places at exactly the right time to offer much-needed guidance and reassurance that heaven is ever present. Sometimes the date on the coin can have personal significance so do take a moment to check it.

Flowers

Flowers are another sign that can offer a visual reminder of the presence of heaven, particularly ones that have personal significance for the observer. It doesn't matter how they come across the flowers – perhaps they are a gift or spotted in a park – it is the timing of the sighting that matters. Flowers that stay in bloom far longer than normal are another reassuring sign that there is no death.

Feathers

Feathers are perhaps the most commonly reported sign of the presence of spirit. I get so many lovely stories about how a tiny white feather has given someone a boost at exactly the right time. Typically, the feather is tiny and white and will appear in the most unlikely place when you are most in need of reassurance or to indicate that a departed loved one is close by. If this happens to you, keep your feather and carry it around with you for a while to remind you that the afterlife is real.

Numbers

Seeing the same numbers repeated in phone numbers, addresses, car number plates and so on can be intriguing visual signs from heaven. A lot of people find that they always seem to look at their watch when it is 11.11 and they have no idea why. As well as the number 11, sightings of the number 7 are also common. Numerology is a fascinating subject and I wish I could write a book on it one day, but for now all I want to say is that it doesn't really matter what the recurring number is; what matters is the message the number sends you. Does seeing it repeatedly fill you with a sense of awe? If it does, it is most definitely a message from above.

Photos

One of the things I love most about my job is receiving amazing photographs from people who believe they have captured spiritual energy on film, usually as an orb of unexplained white or brilliantly coloured light that doesn't appear to have any known source. Sometimes the hazy form of a face of an angel or departed loved one can be detected in the orb. When people send me their stunning pictures they often ask if they should get them tested and my answer is always the same. Yes, you could of course get them tested. Research shows that although the great majority of orb photos can be explained logically, a small percentage – around 5 per cent, I think – can't. So your orb photo could be the real deal, but I really don't think it's worth your while sending your photo for analysis. What really matters here are the feelings you experience when you look at your orb photo. If they fill you with a sense of awe, hope, possibility and wonder then they are in my mind true signs from heaven.

Signs

Clocks stopping, lost objects found, lights flickering and other unexpected visual experiences that give you pause for thought or a sense of being watched can also be signs from the other side reminding you that there is so much more to this world than meets the eye. (You may want to glance again at the stories in chapter 3, as some commonly reported signs are included there.)

Right time, right place

It's not so much the actual visual sign that inspires awe – although some of them like rainbows, stars and sunsets cannot fail to convince you heaven exists – it is the timing of their appearance. On many occasions a sign appears when a person desperately needs guidance or reassurance, perhaps following the death of a loved one or at a crucial turning point in their life. The perfect timing of the sign is often put down to coincidence, but when it happens it often feels so much more than that. It feels like heaven is reaching out.

If you close your mind to the possibility of heaven then co-incidence is mere chance, but if you open your mind it is a miracle that can inspire, transform and save lives. Mystic James Redfield in his bestseller *The Celestine Prophecy* suggested that paying attention to the coincidences in our lives is the first step towards spiritual growth and he could well be on to something. Even certain scientists are fast coming to the conclusion that the universe is self-driven and has a purpose because if it was totally random chaos would rule. Think about your own life and all the amazing coincidences that have brought you to where you are today. From all the research I've done it is clear that heaven can sometimes reveal itself through remarkable coincidences and the more you notice them and are grateful to them, the more you will encounter them.

The intriguing movie *Sliding Doors* with Gwyneth Paltrow illustrates brilliantly how something as seemingly inconsequential as missing a train can transform a life forever. Try to think of coincidences as signposts on your road to heaven, pointing you in the right direction or offering you reassurance that you are heading in the right direction. For example, you may find yourself in exactly the right place at the right time, or you may 'randomly' bump into someone who can help you in some way. Whenever you find yourself thinking 'What are the odds of that happening?', I want you from now on to think of it as a message from heaven. Pay attention to it.

Roadblocks

If you've given it a few days and feel disappointed that you aren't seeing clearly, the chances are you are trying a bit too hard. Remember, straining to make things happen comes from a place of self-doubt which can shut your spiritual eyes and prevent you from reconnecting with your heavenly birthright. As I've said many times, you do not need to have the so-called gift or be a psychic or a medium to see heaven – every one of us can see heaven. It also goes without saying that a positive attitude helps. And please try not to worry – nothing frightening is going to happen. If you have a loving heart there is never anything to fear; and if departed loved ones appear in your visions there will always be a glow of joy about them because they are in spirit and spirit is bliss.

Don't overthink or question every image you see, and expect the unexpected. When it comes to finding heaven you rarely get what you anticipate because that would make things too easy for you. Finding heaven is all about experiencing, growing and challenging yourself, and taking the harder path rather than the well-travelled one. You will only grow up to heaven through challenges and difficulties, as well as facing up to some uncomfortable truths about yourself. However spiritually advanced you become, you will never be perfect because human perfection does not exist. We all have flaws, doubts, insecurities and weaknesses, but what we can do is become aware of them, understand and work with them so that they don't limit our potential.

And while we are on the subject of roadblocks: a major obstacle to spiritual development can be people who drain your energy. I think you know the kind of person I'm talking about here – someone who drains you emotionally and doesn't have your best interests at heart, only their own. Avoid these people even if your instinct is to help them, because being kind and damaging yourself in the process is toxic for your spiritual growth and theirs. If you can't avoid these people for work or family reasons, draw up some clear boundaries and when you interact with them protect yourself. You can do this in your mind by visualising a bubble around yourself that is impossible to break through, or you could try using protective crystals like quartz or turquoise. Whatever you do, make sure to protect yourself and don't let them drain your energy.

And if the person or group of people who undermine you belong to the past, visualise a thread that connects you to them and your past and then in your mind's eye see that thread being cut by a huge pair of scissors. You could also write it down on a sheet of paper and then, as you rip the page to pieces – or hit the delete button if using a PC – tell yourself that you are free now. Because you are.

Touching the silence

If you are planning to do any of the exercises in this book, please don't forget that the most important thing is that they feel easy and natural. That is why I have kept talk of techniques or rituals to a minimum. I don't want to complicate what should be very simple. All you need to do is open your mind and heart and the rest should just follow naturally.

For this reason I don't typically recommend rules, products and techniques. I like to give talks in bookshops, but I don't do workshops or charge a fee for consultations or guided meditations and so on, and I don't call myself an expert on heaven because all this runs counter to what I believe. Heaven is not of this world and it cannot be summoned by candles, crystals, chants, oils or other material things. All these things can do is help you to relax and there is nothing wrong with that, as a relaxed frame of mind is conducive to spiritual development. But there are countless different ways to relax that don't cost a thing or involve detailed instructions to follow or understand. Here are a few simple yet effective exercises:

- Try walking tall. Most of us tend to look at our feet as we walk or hunch our shoulders, but try instead to pull your shoulders back and lift your head up so that you can see the clouds rather than the floor. I promise it will make a significant difference. And while you are walking tall you may also want to try some deeper breathing – from your stomach and not your lungs, as this can increase feelings of clarity and calm.

- Just tell yourself over and over again that you can feel, think, hear and see heaven. Even if you don't believe it or quite trust it, keep saying it to yourself. In time your ability to sense, hear, see and be inspired by heaven will grow.

- Every night before you go to sleep ask heaven to speak to you, and then the next day when you wake ask heaven to reveal itself to you during the day. If you continue doing this and keep your mind and heart open, miracles can happen. Everybody is crazily busy these days and a few minutes of reflection can work wonders. Remember, wherever there is peace, grace and silence, heaven is never far away.

You can also enter the silence in other ways, and you don't always need absolute silence. Listening to beautiful music for five or more minutes every day is highly recommended, as is singing, listening to birdsong, playing an instrument, writing, taking a relaxing bath, reading an inspirational book (like this one ☺), painting, drawing, gardening, walking by the sea, running on the sand, riding a horse or playing with your dog or cat. Thinking about the people you love and what you have to be grateful for but perhaps take for granted can also boost your wellbeing.

Find your own way to still your mind and touch the silence within. Whenever you do something you love that takes you to a place of peace and joy, it becomes easier for heaven to reveal itself to you. Touching the silence within or making contact with your true self is probably the only spiritual 'exercise' I wholeheartedly recommend because it costs nothing and you can do it anytime, anywhere. Get into the habit of finding ways to still your mind and invite heaven into your life. Talk to, think about, sense, see and dream about heaven as much as you can. The more your search for heaven becomes a way of life, the more you will notice it and be able to follow the guidance being offered to you.

If you still think you can't find heaven, keep asking heaven to show itself to you. The more you ask, the more you will receive. The more you see heaven inside and all around you, the more you play your part in creating a beautiful world. Viewed in this light, a better world might just begin with your heart.

Working with your dreams

And while we are on the subject of creating beauty – let's turn our attention now to the exquisite otherworld reality of dreams. As we are typically asleep and not awake when we dream, dreams do not really fall into the same category as visual representations of heaven on earth. They deserve a section of their own.

For many people, myself included, dreams are the first point of contact with the world of spirit, probably because they are so gentle and subtle. However, it is because of these gentle qualities that the great majority of us don't pay enough attention to our dreams and the important spiritual guidance they can provide. They are truly are a gift from the world of spirit, offering us invaluable advice on the way to heaven. When we are asleep our conscious mind is no longer in the driving seat and the unconscious mind takes over. The unconscious mind, remember, is where true creativity, magic and spiritual growth and transformation happen.

In dreams things often feel real, but then you wake up and are unable to make sense of what you've experienced. I have devoted many years of my life to encouraging people to work with their dreams because they are a treasure trove of insight and have the power to heal, guide and enlighten us. They are also a medium for the world of spirit to communicate with us.

There are two problems when working with dreams – remembering them and interpreting them. Fortunately, the first problem, forgetting your dreams, is easily solved. You just need to get into the habit of writing them down the instant you wake up. Don't get up or brush your teeth or do anything first, or the memory will vanish as your conscious mind takes control again. It might also help to tell yourself before you go to sleep that you will remember your dreams. Don't tell yourself not to forget as the mind works better with positives. It really is much easier to remember your dreams than you think. Just get into the habit of recalling them and writing them down – the more attention you pay to your dreaming mind, the more it will reward you.

And if you are one of those people who say you don't dream, you are wrong. Estimates suggest we dream many times every night and have over one hundred thousand dreams in a lifetime. Everyone dreams. You just haven't got into the habit of remembering them. Keeping a dream journal might help. I've kept one for decades and it can be fascinating to look back and see how my dreams have offered fantastic insights into my spiritual growth. I've noticed, too, that dreams tend to be like the pieces of a jigsaw – sometimes they only make sense when viewed in a series of dreams over several weeks or even years.

The second problem is understanding and interpreting your dreams. They rarely make sense but there is a reason for this. Your dreaming mind speaks a different language – the language of symbols. Your thoughts and feelings are turned into images or pictures. These images have typically been selected from people and things in your waking life, triggering memories or associations that connect with your past or present situations. They may appear nonsensical but the opposite is the case. Dreams are not meant to be interpreted literally and you need to think hard about what each dream image or scenario means to you. That's why I don't typically recommend standard interpretations for dreams because although certain symbols – for example, a cross suggests religion – are fairly universal, almost everything else is deeply personal. For one person a cat may be a reassuring sign, but for someone who doesn't like cats there will be a completely different response. The best dream interpretation book, therefore, is the one written by you.

Another important thing to remember about dreams is that they are very egocentric. Your dreams are all about one person – *you*. Everything in your dream – every symbol, image and scenario – represents an aspect of yourself or your feelings towards yourself or someone or something else. Your task is to understand what that aspect is. For example, if a loved one dies in your dream this does not mean their life is at risk; it means that your relationship with that person is going through a period of change. If you have an affair with someone in your dream, like your neighbour or your boss, it does not mean you are sexually attracted to them in real life; it might mean that you need to incorporate them into your life or learn from certain aspects of their personality.

These days I think of my dreams as my internal therapist. When I'm asleep my unconscious can get to work making connections and finding solutions that will help me in my daily life. If ever I have an issue that worries me or an important decision to make, I always follow the age-old advice to sleep on it because I know when I'm sleeping and dreaming heaven is communicating with me through my unconscious. Almost always I wake up the next morning with a fresh perspective.

The vast majority of dreams are not prophetic but symbolic. As mentioned above, such dreams are wonderful gifts from heaven because they enable the dreamer to examine themselves at a deeper level and, by so doing, nurture spiritual growth. They bring to attention feelings, issues or situations in everyday life that can hinder psychological and spiritual growth and also reveal hidden strengths and talents. And if your dreams are particularly racy, with all sorts of bizarre scenarios or passionate situations, there is nothing to worry about. Your dreaming mind is simply giving your curiosity a chance to express itself safely without you or anyone you care about getting hurt.

So, think of your dreams as your inner self trying to help you understand yourself and your life better. Your job is to decode the meaning of the symbols it sends you. However, a very tiny percentage of your dreams will not be symbolic but a direct communication from heaven. I call them night visions because in these dreams departed loved ones or spiritual beings may actually reveal themselves or aspects of the world of spirit. Night visions are so clear, direct and vivid there is no mistaking their meaning. The only option is to take them literally.

You may only ever have one of these kinds of dream in your life, or you may have several, but you will know when you've had a night vision because, unlike most dreams which are easily forgotten on waking unless you make a conscious effort to remember them, these can be remembered in vivid detail on waking and for days, weeks, months, years, even decades afterwards. You also have absolutely no doubt that your night vision was more than just a dream.

More than just a dream

Night visions are often the safest and gentlest way for spirits of departed loved ones to reassure us of their constant presence in our lives, because in sleep our hearts and minds are wide open to heaven. In our daily lives stress, fear and tension often shut our eyes, minds and hearts to such magical possibility.

If you still aren't sure whether you've had a dream or a night vision one of the defining characteristics, alongside being able to remember it instantly on waking, is that it will seem as real as your waking life. You'll wake up in the morning thinking it actually happened because there was a sense of reality you could touch and sense. It may actually take a few moments for you to realise that it was a dream.

Many people who write to me about dreams of those they've lost are absolutely convinced they were visited by the spirit of a loved one and it brings them a tremendous sense of relief and comfort. I have had a night vision myself of my departed mother and I know it was more than just a dream. I know it was real. It is easy to argue that such dreams are an attempt by our minds to offer relief from the pain of grief, but I disagree completely because there are a number of distinguishing features that set these kinds of dreams apart.

Firstly, the spirit of a departed loved one will appear in a realistic setting, not a fantasy one. So, perhaps in your house or garden or in your bedroom. Second, there is an absence of storyline in the dream; the loved one will simply be there talking. This is unusual as most dreams consist of more than just one conversation or monologue. The dreamer will have no idea they are dreaming – what they are experiencing will feel like a reality to them. In addition, the loved one's mannerisms and personality will be instantly recognised, leaving the dreamer with no doubt in their mind when they wake that the loved one was there. Sometimes this extreme reality can be heartbreaking. I remember waking after a night vision of my mum and lying in bed for a few moments, waiting for her to knock on my door as she used to do when I was a child and ask me if I wanted a cup of tea!

Finally, night visions are incredibly comforting. As I know from bitter experience, when you are devoured by grief you are in the midst of a whirlwind of emotions. Feeling comfort of any sort is difficult to imagine, so when you wake with an unexpected sense of reassurance it really can feel like a gift from heaven. Taking all the above into consideration, night visions are not wishful thinking or a normal part of the grieving process. They can bridge the gap between this life and the next and bring messages of love, hope and comfort to the dreamer.

Not only can night visions bridge the gap between heaven and earth, they can also blur the boundaries between past, present, future and space and time itself. These are visions that can offer glimpses of potential futures and they are called precognitive dreams. You may be wondering at this point how you can tell the difference between a symbolic dream and a precognitive dream. For example, should a dream about a plane crashing be interpreted as lack of self-confidence or that an actual plane is going to crash? Fortunately, precognitive dreams have one defining characteristic that distinguishes them from other dreams: they make perfect sense. They have a storyline with a clear beginning, middle and end. Symbolic dreams, on the other hand, tend to jump around all over the place in a series of unconnected, surreal, random images – rather like a music video.

When the world was in shock and mourning after the 9/11 tragedy, a number of people came forward claiming to have had surprisingly accurate precognitive dreams of towers and planes, but exact predictions of this sort are extremely rare. It is far more common for your dreaming mind to offer you glimpses of potential futures, so that you can experiment with or preview outcomes if a certain path in life is followed. I think the purpose of such dreams is to help us make better choices for our spiritual growth, because if we feel uncomfortable with a projected outcome we can make changes. In short, such dreams remind us of the power we always have to change our futures for the better with the choices we make in the present.

Taking control

A running theme in this book has been awakening your sense of self – becoming rather than being and belonging – and dreams offer you a fantastic opportunity to examine who you really are and what truly matters to you in this life and the next. The world you visit in your dreams is a world created by your unconscious mind and your unconscious mind is your link to heaven, so explore that world, take risks, go and discover new horizons, be everything you want to be. Anything is possible when you are dreaming, so make those possibilities as magical and as infinite as you can.

You may be wondering why I'm talking here about your dreams as if they were something you can control. Most of us think of dreams as something that happens to us when we fall asleep but this isn't always the case. It is perfectly possible to create your own dream reality. It isn't easy but it is possible.

Imagine a virtual world created by you where you could be anyone or do anything you wanted. Imagine a world where you could discover the answers you have been longing for and where there is no boundary between this life and the next. Imagine a world without limitations. Imagine you could visit that world every night and it would give you all the answers, healing, hope and comfort you needed. Sounds a bit like heaven, doesn't it?

Taking control of your dreams is no easier than taking control of your daily life, so don't expect it to be simple – but this doesn't mean you shouldn't try. With practice you can awaken your sense of self in your dreams. Before you go to bed every night think about where you want to go in your dreams – rehearse scenarios you would like to encounter in your mind. Then in your visualisation every time you encounter something you recognise from your waking life – for example, checking your watch, getting dressed or using your phone – tell yourself that you are dreaming or imagining. Keep rehearsing your dream like this until you fall asleep. Hopefully something of what you imagined will feature in your dream and your unconscious will be aware that you are dreaming. Once you become aware that you are dreaming the rest is up to you. It is time for you to fly . . .

Waking up in your dream is a thrilling and empowering experience and I highly recommend it. I have gone on the most fantastic adventures in this way, but it happens only rarely and usually when my sleep pattern is disrupted in some way. For example, if I wake up very early in the morning and then go back to sleep again I'm highly conscious of my dreams. It seems that when sleep is disrupted we are more likely to enter REM sleep – the stage where dreaming occurs. I don't advise doing this if you need to go to work the next day, or will be operating machinery or driving or doing anything that requires high levels of concentration, but you could try setting your alarm for 5am, getting up for an hour or so and then going back to sleep at around 6am.

Please don't worry if you find it impossible to know when you are dreaming. It does require a lot of time and practice to master the technique and you may even prefer not to do it, as there is also something thrilling about not knowing you are dreaming. I love those moments when I wake up in the morning convinced I've been selected to fly to Mars or have won an Olympic gymnastics gold medal. My unconscious is showing me in the only way it can that in the world of spirit I am amazing in every way, there are no limits to what I can do. It is urging me to bring that self-confidence and sense of excitement and adventure into my daily life. In much the same way, when I have dreams that alarm me in some way – for example, I am on a sinking ship or a plane that crashes – I wake up feeling a tremendous burst of gratitude that everything is okay and it was only a dream. Again, in its own unique way my unconscious is trying to remind me that things can always be worse and I need to be grateful for all that is good in my life.

Paradise

Hopefully, reading this chapter will have shown you that there are a number of amazing ways to find heaven on earth. Paradise is not a faraway place you only get to experience when you are dead. It can be discovered whenever you catch glimpses of magic in this life. As we've seen, this may manifest in a stunning coincidence, an astonishing dream or a remarkable flash of intuition or a bubble of joy that explodes inside you for no reason. Or it could reveal itself in those extraordinary but ordinary moments that take your breath away.

You don't think you've had those moments?

Think about all the magical moments in your life – falling in love, a new job, a success, becoming a parent, owning a pet, the unexpected kindness of a stranger. In that moment how did you feel?

Think about moments when the wonder and beauty of nature have left you speechless – a glorious sunset, a spectacular landscape, a stunning rainbow. In those moments how did you feel about the world you live in?

Think about moments when you step outside time – you may be completely absorbed in an activity or task, reading a book, listening to music, painting, writing, walking, running, daydreaming or doing nothing at all, but in those moments you feel completely in love and at peace with yourself and the beauty of now.

In those moments heaven was breaking through into your life. At the time you may not have realised it because the experience was so fleeting and hard to define, but hopefully the information in this chapter will have shown you that you can extend that experience with a shift in attitude. Heaven is a change of mind and when you change your mind and open your heart to the possibility of bliss revealing itself to you, you can find it everywhere.

Heaven is not something you have to earn. It is not a place you go to if you have been a good person. Heaven is your birthright. Heaven is already here. It is within you. It is in your eyes, your ears, your mind, your body, your everyday life, your dreams and your heart. You are on earth to find heaven. Paradise is everywhere.

And when you start discovering heaven within and all around you, then you play your part in bringing heaven closer to earth. This is because every person who transforms from the inside out starts changing the world for the better because we are all part of the world. Your energy will spread to others, lighting the way and awakening their desire to find their heaven.

All about you

If what you've read so far in this book has given you pause for thought I could not be more delighted, because I know my words are speaking to the divine spark within you. And if what you read felt somehow familiar, I'm guessing you are sensitive and intuitive. You probably have a gift for helping others but your own life may sometimes feel like a struggle. You are drawn to all things spiritual but life's routines and responsibilities can sometimes weigh you down and suck the magic out of things. You feel things very deeply and are often lost in thought. Perhaps other people open up to you a lot, but you don't tend to open up to others and this can make you feel lonely at times. And maybe you have always had a strong sense of purpose but have yet to find what that purpose is.

I am truly glad you were drawn to this book and are holding it right now in your hands. This book was written for everyone but most especially it is dedicated to sensitive souls like you. I sincerely hope reading it will reassure you and comfort you. I hope it will ease some of the pain brought upon you over the years because of your sensitive nature. I hope it will heal the suffering caused by feeling different in your approach to life and not quite fitting into the round holes dictated by schools, organisations, religions and the expectations of others.

Nothing would give me more joy than to know that this book has helped open your mind to magical, heavenly possibilities within and around you. I hope what you have read will reassure you that your sensitivity is a powerful indicator of your yearning for a more spirit-centred life, and your interest in matters spiritual – which others may criticise as 'absent-mindedness' or 'away with the fairies' or 'head in the clouds' – isn't a weakness or character flaw but your greatest strength and what defines you. It is your map to finding heaven. And if you have, like myself, gone through terrible periods of self-doubt and depression because of your questioning and sensitive nature, I pray that this book will help you understand that feelings of despair aren't a sign of disillusionment but a healthy indicator of spiritual growth. You are giving up a part of your 'old self' and that process can be extremely painful, but spiritually mature people must constantly evolve, constantly reach for the stars.

Growth involves letting go of old, outdated ways of doing and thinking and this will inevitably cause distress, doubt and despair, but as long as you don't overindulge in negative emotions or use them as an excuse not to confront problems, they can be signs of spiritual awakening. If you were attracted to this book because you thought it might help you avoid all suffering, problems and uncertainty, then it is not the book for you. Avoiding problems and struggles and the suffering and pain associated with them takes us further away from heaven and is the cause of all that is diseased, stunted and rotten in this life. Problems give our lives meaning because they demand our courage, insight and compassion. Without problems we would not grow psychologically or spiritually. Pain can be our greatest teacher and many of the world's greatest prophets instinctively knew that and demonstrated in their earthly lives the need to embrace rather than dread pain. The greater the pain, the greater the freedom.

To evolve spirituality you have to question, struggle, suffer, doubt, fear and come to terms with the experience of loss and pain. There is no other way. Life is a mixture of joy and pain and although on rare occasions the gift of joy does seem to be given to us gratis, the vast majority of the time we only get to experience joy it we suffer through the pain first. To get to that joy we need to exercise self-control, take responsibility for our problems and stop blaming everyone and everything. and then work towards a solution with a loving heart.

You may be asking yourself at this point if all this struggling and hard work is worth it. Perhaps it might be better to live your life with your head looking at the ground rather than the clouds, to satisfy your physical needs and belong to a group of people who do all your thinking for you. But if you ask that question then you probably haven't experienced pure joy in your life or placed enough value on it.

The kind of joy I'm talking about here is not laughter that comes from your mouth but smiles that come from your heart. It is the otherworldly joy that brings tears to your eyes when you hug someone you love or watch a beautiful sunset or listen to beautiful music. It is the kind of joy that fills you with feelings of love, compassion and awe, and once you experience it you will know that evolving spiritually is the only thing that really matters in your life and gives it true meaning.

And, as we're on the subject of the meaning of life, perhaps more than anything I sincerely long for this book to remind you that you are here on this earth for a reason. You have an important purpose or destiny and that is to grow spiritually and find heaven from the inside out. Once you discover who you really are in this way you become an inspiration to others, revealing through your inner light and through everything you say and do, the presence of heaven on earth.

So, although there are many wonderful ways to discover heaven, it is important not to forget – as we all tend to do – that perhaps the fastest, simplest and most honest and pure and powerful way is to look in the mirror . . .

Ten steps to heaven
There's been a lot of ground covered in this chapter so here is a brief overview:

1. *Heaven can be found within. Only when you find it within you, can you see it around you.*
2. *The mind is not the place to look for happiness. Your heart is the home of bliss. Learn to live from your heart, not from your thoughts or ego.*
3. *Learn to relax and stay open-minded no matter what.*
4. *Step outside yourself. Watch yourself. Do not identify with the experiences you are observing.*

5. *You are not the thoughts in your head or the feelings in your heart. You are the listener and the experiencer.*

6. *Learn to control your thoughts and manage your feelings.*

7. *Know that there is life after death, but facing the fact that our physical bodies die will help you realise that all material things are temporary. Take refuge in the eternal not the ephemeral.*

8. *Savour the now and the everyday details of your life. Every moment is precious and heaven can be found in the ordinary, small stuff as well as the sublime. Don't allow painful experiences from the past to influence the present. The past has gone. All that exists, the only reality, is right now.*

9. *If you want a life full of joy and love you must find joy and happiness within yourself first.*

10. *Bliss is within.*

CHAPTER FIVE

Lighting the way

There is only one path to Heaven. On Earth, we call it Love.
St Catherine of Siena

When you connect to heaven from the inside out you become a beacon and an inspiration to other people. You reveal heaven with your words, actions and presence. You light the way.

Others are irresistibly drawn to you because there is something joyful, astonishing and otherworldly about you, but also something deeply familiar because you remind them of the potential for bliss inside them that they have not yet released. Your inner light bypasses their thoughts, their reason and preoccupation with material things that don't really matter and makes a home in their hearts. In due course, when the time is right for them, that light awakens their hearts just as it has awakened yours. And then in turn they also become messengers of heaven, lighting up the world one heart, one person at a time.

Discovering heaven from within is a powerful way to transform not just yourself but the world around you. I'm aware all this sounds great in theory; in practice in your day-to-day life it can be so much harder. Although you may understand and even accept that encountering problems and experiencing suffering are crucial elements for your spiritual growth, at the time this doesn't always make these problems easier to deal with. Heaven can feel so very far away when, for example, someone you love cheats on you or you can't pay the bills or you suffer from poor health. So that's why I'm going to begin this chapter by discussing how it is possible to find heaven in your everyday life even when the odds feel stacked against you.

Heaven can't make decisions for you as that would make life too easy and, remember, an easy life is an unfulfilling, stunted life. It won't lead you to heaven. We need challenges to overcome and problems to solve to grow and mature spiritually. What heaven can do, though, is offer you guidance, pointers, signs and comfort when you need it the most. It can also inspire within you the courage and self-confidence you need to sort things out for yourself. Last, but by no means least, it can offer hope and a sense of boundless possibility by reminding you constantly that there is so much more to this life than meets the eye.

Love

The natural place to begin is with love because love is the beginning, the middle, the end, the forever in this life and the next.

There are many different levels of love, though, just as there are stages of faith and in this life our task is to learn from each stage. Young, passionate and physical love is an intoxicating first stage and many of us try to stay there forever, but this is neither possible nor healthy. You need that 'just-in-love' to deepen into something greater and more meaningful and it is when relationships can't make that transition that they flounder. This can be heartbreaking but it happens for a reason because your spirit is not being nourished in the relationship.

Passionate love maturing into spiritual, unconditional love is the ultimate aim but it is not something you can work for. It will happen when the time is right for you and you meet the right person. I get more letters about love than anything else, and so many people ask me if it is true that each one of us has a soulmate. I'm not sure I know the answer to that one, as you will have seen from the answer I gave to this question on page 190.

I think the desire for a soulmate is a sign of spiritual awakening. However, I also think that we have several soulmates, not just one, in the course of a lifetime. Each person we meet in our lives offers us a chance to learn about ourselves and make positive choices, and sooner or later we are going to meet someone who teaches us the meaning of love. Even people who break our hearts can teach us a great deal about what is lacking in our lives, because the idea of someone 'completing' us suggests that something was lacking before. Our spiritual challenge then if the relationship breaks down is to find ways to fill the void ourselves.

If you are floundering in the love and relationships stakes, there may be a few reasons why. First of all, many of us make the mistake of thinking that the only way to be totally fulfilled and happy is to be in a relationship or to find our one true love. This couldn't be further from the truth. You can be in a relationship and still feel dreadfully alone and unhappy, and you can be alone and feel fulfilled and blissful. The determining factor is the ability to love yourself first. Until you can fall in love with who you are, you can't experience fulfilling love with another person.

How can you possibly love and take care of someone else if you can't do it for yourself? So, my advice if you are longing for love is to start with yourself first – otherwise any relationship you enter into will be based around need and co-dependency and destined to bring disappointment in the long run. I've already given lots of advice in this book about learning to love yourself and I'm glad I've got the chance to touch on it again here, as it is absolutely crucial for happiness in all areas of your life.

If you take anything from this book I hope it will be the message that you are completely unique. Treat yourself as the amazing one-of-a-kind that you are. Go easy on yourself if you think you have flaws – remember, we learn from our mistakes more than from our successes and the purpose of our lives is to learn and grow. If you were perfect there would really be very little point to your existence! Take care of yourself and be the best that you can be. Encourage yourself to live life to the full and to laugh, as you would encourage someone you love. Don't look to a potential partner to give your life interest, magic and meaning. Look within and find that magic for yourself. Do things and seek out interests that fill you with passion and a sense of meaning. Make your heart sing and squeeze every moment of joy you can out of your life. If you can redirect your energy away from finding a potential partner to creating happiness and fulfilment in your life, I'm convinced love will find you. The best way to find love is not to search for it in another person, but to discover it within yourself by making your own life as interesting and as happy as you can.

Please don't think I'm talking about selfishness here, or a self-centred life. That would alienate other people. I'm talking about learning what interests you and what makes you feel fulfilled so that you can live your life with passion. You may well discover, as many people do, that they don't actually need a partner in order to feel happy as their love of friends, family and life is enough for them. Or perhaps you may find that being in a relationship is the best thing for you. If that is the case, think about the qualities you want in a partner and don't settle for anything less, as you are worth loving fully and deserve the best. Remember, though, that it doesn't really matter whether or not you are in a relationship; what matters when you make your life and love choices is the loving intention you have towards yourself and others.

Wellbeing

If your health is poor or you suffer from stress, anxiety and depression, or if you are experiencing a bout of illness, or find it hard to lose weight or have addiction problems, heaven can seem very far away. Mercifully, I've not suffered any serious physical complaint, but as you've seen from this book I've had my fair share of emotional illness and depression.

In my darkest hours I did often wonder if heaven was real, but somewhere or other the light always came shining through again and many people have written to me over the years with similar experiences. They are at their lowest ebb and then an insight, a coincidence, a dream or a burst of unexplained joy breaks through. Others have written to tell me how the kindness of other people has turned their lives around, or how the unconditional love of a pet made life worth living again.

I've also had many letters from people who believe heaven has intervened and saved their lives during times of poor physical health. Many of these miracle healings took place in hospitals and even the doctors involved can't explain why someone close to death pulled through, or a person with a life-threatening condition recovered against all the odds. In some cases miraculous intervention seems to be the only plausible explanation.

Although heaven can reveal itself during times of poor physical and emotional health this does not necessarily mean that all suffering will in every case be eased. It won't. I don't know why, but that is just the way things are in this life. Perhaps we will understand in the next life, but for now all we can do is open our hearts and minds to the idea that trusting in the existence of heaven can make any suffering we endure easier to bear.

Never forget that spiritual health, healing from the inside out rather than from the outside in, is the fastest way to find heaven. And when you do start to discover heaven from the inside out, you will encounter something wonderful too – a new-found sense of wellbeing and energy. Your spiritual health will make you 'glow'.

Money

It goes without saying that the best things in life are free and finding heaven is about spiritual wealth rather than financial wealth, but this doesn't mean that money is evil. Quite the opposite, in fact – money can be a force for good, if used wisely and compassionately. Being rich is not a barrier to finding heaven. You don't need to give away all your money and possessions to live a spiritual life. You only need to do that if these things are distracting you, giving you a false sense of superiority and stopping you being compassionate to others and valuing what truly matters in life.

Indeed, in the twenty-first century I think the path to heaven needs to include enough money. If you want to be happy and fulfilled, and to concentrate on your spiritual development, you need to be able to provide for yourself and your loved ones. Poverty is not a virtue and there is no point thinking that heaven will bless you with funds. It can happen, and I do get letters from people who have had surprise windfalls or found unexpected sources of cash when they begged heaven for help, but this is rare. In most instances, heaven will help by inspiring you to live within your means or to seek out new sources of income or to get organised with your bills and income.

It is possible for everyone to pull themselves out of penury, but the problem is that a lot of people have a mind-set conditioned to poverty. They tell themselves they cannot afford the things they need, but sometimes these people are poor because deep down they don't feel worthy of being financially solvent.

Also, a lot of people with a poverty mind-set are not very generous. Of course, you need to balance your generosity with common sense, but if you don't give to others you will see a world of destitution and want. Just as the best way to attract love into your life is to be loving, the best way to attract money into your life is to be giving, not necessarily of your wealth if you haven't got funds but of your time and energy. And if you do give money, the amount is irrelevant – what heaven notices is your loving intention.

And as well as managing your finances and giving appropriately to others, invest in your own spiritual development. If you are struggling financially, you have many spiritual lessons to learn about money. Don't just sit and wait for heaven to intervene. As I said earlier, it won't. Learn all you can about the importance of giving and receiving, saving and organising, spending and investing in your spiritual growth. If you think that money is rather dirty, try to change your mind-set and see it as a force for good and positive change and empowerment of yourself and others. You never know, that beggar in the street you just gave a few coins to could be an angel in disguise. And to digress a little: thinking of everyone you interact with in the course of your day as a potential angel in disguise would be a wonderful way to live.

Whatever you do, avoid the trap of thinking that because you are drawn to the spiritual you should not think about material concerns. The hippies tried that and it didn't really work out. You are a twenty-first-century spiritual warrior and your priority is finding heaven, but at the same time you need to learn how to handle money wisely and value it so that you can actually concentrate on your spiritual development. Heaven isn't going to do that for you because understanding money and abundance and the importance of giving and receiving could be a crucial life lesson for you on your spiritual journey.

Career

Perhaps you are one of those fortunate people and have always had a clear sense of what you wanted to do with your life. You have found ways to make that happen, and you get a great deal of satisfaction and fulfilment from your work. If this is you, heaven is speaking to you through your focus, dedication, discipline and determination to do what you feel is right for you. If, however, you have never really had a career goal in mind, or have always felt unfulfilled by your career choices, then this is positive too. Heaven is urging you to keep experimenting and experiencing career-wise because every path you go down, even if it is ultimately not successful, is an opportunity for learning and for spiritual growth. As far as heaven is concerned, there is no such thing as failure because sometimes we learn and grow the most from our shortcomings. Success can make us complacent and complacency is an enemy of spiritual growth.

If you are searching for inspiration regarding your career, keep looking around and within you for signs and messages from heaven. You may find that a dream offers you guidance, or a coincidence or a chance meeting points you in the right direction. I may be wrong but I think everything that happens to us does so for a reason, even apparently trivial things like unintentionally heading in the wrong direction or missing a train. I have read many stories sent to me by people who have caught the wrong train and ended up meeting the love of their life. Whether or not it is true that nothing is totally random in this life, I do know that feeling gratitude and respect for every moment – even the most inconsequential because it could potentially save or change your life – is a wonderful way to live. Gratitude for moments of joy draws heaven closer to you like a magnet. The more you are able to focus on the beauty of right now, on the potential offered by the present, the more likely it is that your future will be magical.

Bear in mind that your choice of career or work, even if it involves devoting yourself to the care of your family, children or loved ones, is your purpose in life. Most of us spend the majority of our lives working, and that adds up to a lot of time, so it is important for your emotional and spiritual growth that you make the right life choices. Your purpose is different from your desire because desire serves only you, whereas your purpose serves both yourself and others. There is also great spiritual energy associated with your purpose. It's great when your desires and purpose in life align but they don't always, and if you try to pursue your desires ahead of your purpose you will feel unhappy and unfulfilled. However, when you follow your purpose you'll know you are on the right path because you will feel energised and excited by what you do. If you don't feel that about your work then you haven't found your purpose . . . yet.

Discovering your purpose in life is a key to great spiritual growth. Identifying your purpose can be more of a challenge for some than others, but please don't worry if you don't feel you have found yours. You need to trust that you will be led to your purpose and that everything you have done previously has given you experience, insight and understanding that you can draw upon one day. You may not discover your purpose until late in life. I had one incredibly moving letter from a widow who said her husband discovered his purpose a week before he died at the age of eighty-two. He had always felt disappointed with himself because he didn't become the lawyer his parents hoped he would be. Instead, he followed his passion to write and ended up composing inspirational or funny messages for a greeting card company. He loved his job but because of his parents' expectations he always felt like a disappointment. It wasn't until the very end of his life that he realised making people smile had been more than enough. It had been his purpose in life and he continued to make people smile until the day he died with his offbeat humour and light-hearted approach to life.

Within your heart is the desire to find your true purpose in life, and one way to help you achieve that sooner rather than later is to be true to yourself and do what you love. If you hate what you do or feel stuck because you need the money and don't feel you can make a change, trust in yourself to take control of your life. Make finding your purpose in life your top priority. And a sure-fire way to start the search for your purpose is to do what you love, even if that means earning less than you hoped or disappointing the expectations of others. Do what you love to do and if you don't know what you love to do, experiment until you find it – because find it you will.

And don't think that your purpose has to be global or grand. Heaven reveals itself not just in the big things but also in the smallest and sometimes most trivial things. So whether you are waiting tables or signing international peace treaties, what matters spiritually is how your work, your role in life, makes you feel, especially if in the course of your working day you get the chance to give other people a lift, too – something as simple as a smile or a 'thank you' or a 'how are you?'. You will know when you've found your purpose because it will fill your life with joy, meaning and passion and benefit not just you but others as well. This may involve making changes, and you will need patience and discipline to implement those changes, but the important thing is that you are taking control and thinking about who you are and what direction you want your life to head in. You are finding your true path. It will be exciting.

Smile

Once you start looking within and taking control of your life your spiritual journey is well under way. It is an exciting time because you will start finding all sorts of ways to connect with the piece of heaven that lives within you. Your dreams may become more intense and vivid and you will find yourself drawn, through your thoughts and feelings, to people, places, events and ideas that will comfort you and point you in the right direction.

And a certain sign that heaven is calling your name is that you will feel things more deeply. This may mean that you cry more easily and hurt more deeply. There may well be days when you feel quite low, but if that happens keep reminding yourself that you are not your feelings. Feelings are transitory. They will pass and in time you will feel better. However, an added bonus of feeling more deeply and living more spontaneously is that you will also smile more readily. You will find so many reasons to smile. As you draw closer to heaven, laughter and joy will fill your heart.

One of the most frustrating things about writing spiritual books is that everybody takes heaven so seriously. It's the same with most religions. There is no laughter. I guess this is under-standable, as death is not a laughing matter and neither is the search for the meaning of life, but humour can be a wonderful tool for spiritual and personal growth. Yes, life can be hard and serious but it can also have some very funny moments. Think back on your life, about happy times and how memorable they were. Finding heaven takes self-discipline and serious thought but there is no reason why you can't smile on your journey. Many of us don't have a problem thinking of heaven guiding, healing, comforting and inspiring us in our daily lives, so is it so hard to believe that heaven wants us to laugh more, too? Laughter can be very healing.

Children

And, talking of laughter, it is time to mention children, as laugh-ter comes naturally to them. They laugh four or five times more a day than adults do. Trust in heaven also comes naturally to them because they have the innocence and open-mindedness to see magic in everyone and everything.

It is easy to dismiss as imagination the ability of children to let go of the expectations of others and the need to conform to rules and logic, but it is this ability that draws heaven closer to them. We can learn a lot from children. They don't question what they see and, if they do catch a glimpse of heaven, they trust that what they've seen is real. Ashley had absolutely no doubt what she saw was real. Here is her story sent by her mother, Michelle:

Sounds strange?

This may sound strange 'cause it still sounds strange to me but I'd just put my daughter Ashley, who is nearly two, into her highchair. Nothing strange there, just that I'd left the chair pulled out from the table because I didn't want her to start grabbing her meal which was laid out on the table. I turned away to get her juice and some wet wipes and when I turned round she was pushed in and already eating. When I asked her who pushed her in she said, 'Oma.' I nearly dropped the juice because I always used to call my grandmother Oma (I'm Dutch Indonesian and Oma is the word for grandma I used when I was growing up) and as far as I can remember I had never spoken of her to Ashley. She died when I was about ten years old. I do remember her, though, and my mum always used to say to me that the first time I had solid food it was my grandmother who fed me.

Jessica, like Michelle, also found her baby's behaviour inexplicable.

Pictures

I always try to rule out any logical explanation first. I have a balance between the scientific and the unexplained. My daughter is fourteen months and as soon as she was old enough to babble she would talk to pictures of my father, whom she has never met. I didn't think there was anything unusual about this. Then a month or so ago she said she saw an angel. I asked her what the angel was doing and she said juggling. Then I asked what her angel looked like and she pointed to a picture of my father. My eyes filled with joy as, although my father had been in the army and died before I was born, my mother had told me once that he used to be a brilliant juggler. I haven't talked about him to my daughter yet and my mother certainly hadn't as she lived abroad and the last time she saw my daughter was eight months ago, but I'm so happy my daughter is getting to know him and being entertained by his juggling.

It is unfortunate that we often react with suspicion and disbelief when children talk to us about the magic they can see. They learn that it is better not to say anything at all and this is incredibly sad. We should be encouraging children to treasure their innate receptivity to the world of magic and enchantment. The world children are born into today is an unsettling and often cruel and unfair one, and encouraging them to protect and value the innocent child inside them that trusts in magic, goodness and joy will help them avoid soul-destroying 'grown-up' pessimism and fear.

The term 'inner child' is a clichéd one but like many clichés it resonates with the truth. The inner child is the child you once were, the child that longs to be nurtured, guided, comforted and loved. This child resides within you no matter how old you are, and it is the part of you that is sensitive, creative, passionate and spontaneous, but it is also the part of you most in need of love and comfort and guidance. Many of us lose touch with our inner child as we grow up but it stays with us all our lives. We are all children at heart, innocent and trusting, and it is through our inner child that heaven will first reveal itself.

As we've seen, heaven lives inside each one of us, waiting to be discovered, and one way to unlock it is through your inner child. In this way, with trust, love and a spontaneous, loving heart and mind, anyone whatever their age can see, hear or sense the closeness of heaven. A uniting theme among all the stories people have sent me over the years about their interactions with heaven is their ability to see the world through the eyes of a child, whether they are old or young in years. Seeing the world in this way does not mean being naive, ignorant or gullible, but it does mean having an open mind and the ability to feel things deeply and express them spontaneously. It is this openness, trust and spontaneity that will open the doors to heaven and let laughter, love and magic flow in.

Animals

Just as children can show us the way to heaven by teaching us important spiritual lessons about being open to the magic within and all around us, animals too can guide us on our spiritual journey by teaching us about the importance of unconditional love, empathy and healing.

If you aren't an animal lover you can skip this section, but you might just want to open your mind to the joy, comfort and hope that pets can bring into the lives of their owners by reading these next two stories, the first sent by Catharine and the second by Tracey.

Toby

A while ago now I lost my beautiful Border collie Toby. He was poorly and sadly we had to have him put to sleep. He had the most kind, loving nature and was so special to us all. I grieved for him so much. He used to sleep on the end of the bed at times, until he injured his back leg and could no longer jump up.

One morning after he died — it was still dark and we were still in bed — I felt a 'thump' on the end of the bed and movement as if something was moving up the bed towards me. Then I felt his fur and smelt his familiar 'teddy bear' smell. I put my arms around him and cried, saying his name, and my head was buried in his neck. I was aware he had his collar on. My husband heard me crying and woke up; as he did so, Toby was gone. It was such an emotional feeling and so real. I wrote about it in my diary. I know my dear husband was sceptical about it but I know it was not just a dream.

I now have a new Border collie called Jack. He was born 18 September. Toby died 18 August. Coincidence?

Smudge

One thing you may be interested in is that two weeks after my lovely cat Smudge was killed by a car my husband saw him sitting in the hall watching us eat our dinner. He said it was so real he was about to get up to open the door for him! My husband is not easily convinced about such things but was absolutely sure about this.

The language of heaven isn't just articulated by pets, but by all living creatures on the planet. I've been flooded with stories about heaven communicating messages of love and reassurance to people through butterflies, birds, insects and a huge variety of wild animals. Love is the defining force in the universe and it doesn't matter if that love is for human or animal, it can't be destroyed by death. As I was writing this chapter, the touching video of a cancer patient's dying wish to see her horse was doing the rounds online. A few hours after staff at Wigan hospital wheeled 77-year-old Sheila Marsh outside so that her horse could nuzzle her cheek one last time, she died. I defy anyone reading this book to watch that video without noticing their heart.

I've also had a number of stories about the spirits of pets or animals continuing to visit their owners from the afterlife. Like stories about children and heaven, accounts of animals and the afterlife deserve a book of their own and there simply isn't room here. I just hope, though, that by touching briefly on the subject I have at the very least opened your mind to the idea that animals can offer endless love and comfort in both this life and the next.

Other people

Heaven can also talk to you through the words and actions of other people!

As you saw in the stories in chapter 3, sometimes these people may be strangers who seem to arrive miraculously at just the right time to save or guide a person in need of help or comfort. Intriguingly, some of these stories end with the stranger mysteriously vanishing afterwards, leaving the person involved to wonder if they were truly heaven sent. In other cases, the Good Samaritan is most definitely human but acting with extraordinary courage, compassion and kindness.

However such stories are explained, what they show is that heaven is out there in the guise of our fellow human beings and the selfless actions of strangers. They also show that heaven can exist within everyone, including yourself. Elaine sent me this story and I'm grateful to her as it illustrates my point perfectly.

Sunday

I've just remembered an uncanny meeting I had with a stranger one Sunday morning last year. I had just crossed over the road where I live when a young woman stopped me in the street to ask where she could get hold of a copy of the local free paper. She looked tired and quite stressed out. The free papers can be found in the library, but as it was Sunday the library was shut. I offered to let her have my paper but then I remembered I'd thrown my paper out. For some reason I felt compelled to ask her why she was looking for the local paper. She explained she was living with her mum about half a mile away and was looking for somewhere to rent. She had moved away from another area to escape an abusive partner. As we chatted I discovered she was a nurse and due to moving away she had had to leave her job.

Suddenly I remembered something as I chatted to this woman. Just a few weeks earlier I had attended a conference. One of the guest speakers at the conference was from the Cavell Trust, an organisation that was set up to help nurses in times of need and distress. I urged this woman to get in touch with the Cavell Trust as soon as possible. She had heard of the trust but it hadn't occurred to her to approach them. She thanked me for the information and went away looking as if some of the heavy burden on her shoulders had been lifted. I felt somehow as though my path had crossed with this woman in order for me to pass on this information to help and guide her.

We can all be heavenly helpers in disguise. By this I don't necessarily mean intervening to save a life and putting your own at risk in the process, and it isn't possible for all of us to give our energy and money to charity. What I am talking about here is making a difference in the lives of others by making them smile or feel good about life. It does not have to be a grand gesture. Something as simple as holding open a door or paying a compliment or giving up your seat or saying 'thank you' and smiling to the sales person who put your shopping through the tills. The simplest gestures of gratitude, respect and joy can truly make another person's day.

If you don't believe me, try it for a day. Be as joyful, considerate, kind and interested in the wellbeing of others as you can, and then let me know how it made you feel at the end of the day. I guarantee that it will make a difference both to the people you interacted with, and to you too. You will feel a warmth and a glow from within. Reaching out to help or boost others is a truly heavenly thing to do.

Another amazing facet of discovering heaven from the inside out is that it not only changes how you feel about yourself, but also how you feel about other people. You will experience a new-found respect for others, especially those who have or are living through great hardship or suffering, or those who demonstrate extraordinary courage and compassion, because you will wonder if you would be able to cope in similar circumstances. Sometimes I don't think I could cope at all, but when I ask people how they've managed they tell me that somehow they uncovered the resources, strength and power within them to get by. It isn't easy but they have found a way to cope. They have discovered heaven within them.

The deeper I go within myself, the more I find myself in awe of other people. I know how complex my thoughts and feelings are and how many mysteries are hidden inside me; and I know that complexities, insights, talents lie deep beneath the surface of other people too, however hard they try to pretend that it's not so. Every one of us is completely unique and sensationally mysterious, and there is always something fascinating we can learn from each other. In the past I used to judge people very much on appearances, but I never do that now because I know that what I'm seeing is just the tip of an iceberg. There is so much more hidden beneath, in the depths of their being.

If you don't feel connected or empathetic towards others and want to shut yourself away physically and emotionally, this is a sign that you are not quite ready to begin your journey to heaven. When you are on your spiritual path other people will fascinate and inspire you. You may need plenty of peace and solitude but when you are in the company of others your heart will feel more open towards them. This is especially the case if you know that they, like you, have been through great pain or suffering. Instead of making you feel bitter, you will feel compassionate. You will want to show others that you understand what they are going through because you have been there too. You will want them to feel reassured and comforted. You will want to tell them that they are not alone.

This is heaven speaking to others through you.

You

Perhaps at this point you are still thinking to yourself: why hasn't something like this ever happened to me? Why can't I have such a life-enhancing experience?

As you read on, I'd like to ask you to hold this thought in your head – and I'm gently warning you, it's an incredibly powerful thought that may trigger all sorts of astonishing experiences: perhaps I already have.

Dig deep into your heart and perhaps you will find an echo of something that you might have missed before. Perhaps this something came in a dream, in the wise words of someone else, or in a surge of hope, love, elation or a sense of deep and true knowing in the depths of despair? Perhaps it came but you didn't recognise it at the time. Perhaps it is with you now as you read this book.

And perhaps by remembering and reconnecting with it here and now, or anticipating it in your future, it can transform into one of the defining moments of your lifetime – the first of many defining moments in your past, present and future, when 'something' becomes everything.

I hope this section will have shown you that it is possible to find heaven in all aspects of your life; even in the so-called mundane and ordinary there is always more than meets the eye. I also hope that, along with the rest of the book, it will have encouraged you to look within your heart for your inspiration. If you can take control of your life in this way your spiritual awakening has most definitely begun. There is no going back now. You are already walking on your own path to heaven. Your intuition will become more finely tuned, guiding you to people, places, words, ideas and other wonderful things that can nurture and motivate you. Your life will become a magical voyage of discovery.

Expect the unexpected in the days ahead.

Working with spirit

Once you truly begin discovering heaven from the inside out in your everyday life, the boundaries between this life and the next may start to fade. You may even notice heaven revealing itself to you from the outside in. The experience differs in intensity and frequency from person to person. For some, heaven will be glimpsed in everyone and everything. Others will discover it in moments of reflection or in subtle signs and coincidences, while others may discover it through a deep connection with the spirits of departed loved ones.

So far I have deliberately tried to avoid using familiar words like clairvoyant or psychic or medium, because such terms make it seem as if only a gifted elite with special powers to read minds, see spirits or glimpse the future can connect with the other side. This isn't the case at all. Everyone, whether they consider themselves psychic or not, can connect with the afterlife. It is just a matter of seeing the light in your own unique way. In other words, opening your mind and heart to the possibility that this life is not all that there is. You don't need to be psychic or clairvoyant to do that, and you don't really need to visit a medium either.

I know there are extraordinarily empathetic and sensitive psychics out there who may be able to tune into vibrations from the other side and bring comforting messages of reassurance if you are grieving the loss of a loved one. Sometimes the words of a gifted medium have quite literally saved and transformed lives. However, there are also those who can use simple people-reading skills and wish fulfilment to deceive. If you've ever read Derren Brown's book, *Tricks of the Mind*, you will have noted that one chapter is devoted to the technique of cold reading: it shows how a group of people were all convinced that exactly the same reading applied to them because, as human beings, we all share common traits and needs! So, as far as mediums are concerned, be careful; it's best only to go if you have a personal recommendation from someone you trust. The jury is out for me, as I've never had a convincing reading from a medium, but I will keep an open mind. However, I am inclined to think, after all the research I've done over the years, that the messages from departed loved ones that you notice and discover for yourself rather than seek out via a third party are the most powerful.

And departed loved ones can and do send us messages all the time. We just need to learn to notice and understand them. After death the physical body decays but the spark of life, the energy, light and spirit inside us, doesn't. It lives on and can interact with us in the physical world. Sometimes spirits can appear in full-blown visions, looking very much as they did when they were alive, or they can appear in dreams or in our thoughts and feelings, or they may reveal themselves to us through sounds, scents, signs and coincidences. If you are struggling to accept that all this can happen, remember what scientists tell us: that the universe we live in consists of strings of energy. Everything consists of energy and the way this energy vibrates determines how it manifests in this world. So, if our bodies and minds are energy, surely when we die the energy of our thoughts and feelings could survive in another dimension?

I've lost count of the number of stories I've received from people who are convinced they have been visited by the spirit of a departed loved one, and in every case the experience has been comforting, uplifting and inspiring. Heaven knows only love and joy, so if you have had an experience that is unsettling it is not heaven reaching out to you but the result of fear, stress and tension overstimulating your mind.

In most cases spirits of departed loved ones simply want us to know that they are at peace. They want to tell us that this life is not all there is and one day we will see them again in heaven. They want to remind us that we are never alone and they have not died but are alive within us. In some instances, a spirit may appear in order to say goodbye if a loved one wasn't there with them when they died. This happened to me and the feeling of relief and comfort the experience offered was out of this world. I wasn't there when my mother died and this made me feel unbearably sad and guilty, but when my mum reached out to me in my dreams I found the comfort I'd longed for. She loved me and chose to die without my spirit willing her to stay. I got the sense from her that it was less painful for her and for me this way.

Spirit signs

As mentioned previously, dreams are one of the most common ways for departed loved ones to reach out to us because they are gentle and least likely to cause alarm. Just ask your loved one to appear in your dreams and to help you remember your dream afterwards. A night vision will be very peaceful. If you have a dream that causes you alarm this is not heaven but stress and anxiety talking to you.

Although dream visitations are common they are not the only way spirits can manifest their presence. Those who are extremely sensitive may receive a vision when they are fully awake, but this is extremely rare and not always helpful. In the spirit world, making up your mind for yourself because you trust rather than because you have definite proof is far more beneficial to your spiritual growth. Therefore, if you can't actually see or feel spirit you are far more likely to notice the energy of departed loved ones through subtle signs and coincidences. The most commonly reported ones I have listed below:

- Time stopping: watches or clocks may stop for no reason in particular.
- Electricity: there may be problems with TVs, computers, mobile phones or electrical appliances stopping and starting for no reason. Lights may also flicker or burn out.
- Random thoughts: pay attention to thoughts that just pop suddenly into your head. It could be a message because in the world of spirit, departed loved ones don't have audible voices. Instead, they communicate telepathically through your thoughts. How will you know if it's your own thought or a communication from the other side? If you are thinking of something and it triggers thoughts of your loved one, then this is your thought; but if your loved one just popped into your head randomly for no reason, then it may well be them communicating their love to you.
- Ringing in the ear or tingling sensation in the body: as spirit is a different, higher energy frequency from everyday life, if you hear a high-pitched gentle tone in your ear, or feel a tingling sensation in your body, it could be a spirit trying to connect with you.
- Flowers: staying in bloom longer than usual.
- Animals: a bird, insect or animal that is connected to a

person who has died may grab your attention. Or the animal will do something unexpected.

- Scent: the unexpected scent of vanilla or a flower or a familiar scent associated with someone who has passed over, such as their perfume, when there is no source for it.
- Numbers: repeating numbers, typically 1111, 2222, 3333, 7777, or numbers significant in some way, such as birthdays, anniversaries, may appear on watches, clocks, iPads and billboards.
- Phone calls: I have read amazing stories where people have told me they have actually spoken to a departed loved one on the phone. Others have told me about receiving unexplained texts or calls from the departed person's phone but when they answer there is no one there.
- Feathers: the unexpected appearance of white feathers at meaningful moments is another medium for the departed to reach out and offer reassurance.
- Coins: in the same way as for feathers, you may notice pennies or other coins in unusual places.
- Noise: reports of footsteps, knocking, ringing or scratching may also occur but none of these sounds will cause alarm.
- Turn around: you may get a feeling that you are being watched, but when you turn around there is nobody there. Sometimes people write to me about seeing shadows with no source.
- Breath of fresh air: you may feel as if someone invisible is gently breathing on you, or you may feel a gust of fresh air with no explainable origin.

- Kisses: sometimes people write to me about the sensation of a gentle kiss on the cheek or an invisible hug, or someone you can't see holding your hand. All offer incredible feelings of comfort and reassurance.

- Music: songs that were associated in some way with the person who has died may be heard on the radio or in a shopping centre on repeated occasions. Or you will hear a song playing with exactly the right words.

- Heart and mind: every time you think about a departed loved one or remember them with feelings of joy in your heart, they are never far away but close by you in spirit.

- Bliss: also, if you feel a moment of unexpected bliss and you don't know why, a loved one in spirit is reaching out to you or may even be standing close beside you. Treasure that connection. Don't question it.

These are just a few of the many different ways that departed loved ones can call out to you, and if your definition of heaven is to be reunited with departed loved ones all you need to do is start noticing them. You don't actually need to look for signs – they will come to you. Remember, the most spiritually empowering way for heaven to reveal itself is through your thoughts, feelings, dreams and other subtle signs. Don't stress if you don't think you have received any of these signs; in the days ahead just think about those you have loved and lost and ask them to gently let you know they are alive. Tell them you would like to meet them in your dreams and to help you remember that dream when you wake up. Don't rush things. Be patient and you will in time get the signs you long for. Those who have crossed over really are alive and they want you to know that.

I am so happy that I have been given the privilege and honour to write a book published by a mainstream publisher about the very real possibility of life after death. It is a sign that more people are opening their minds and their hearts to the idea that death is not the end. This is exciting because the more people change their ideas about death, the more likely it is for heaven to reveal itself through the spirits of departed loved ones. And if you don't think you have had any sign of 'life' yet from the other side, the fact that you are reading this book suggests that you may be closer than you think to glimpsing heaven. You may be ready to make contact.

Before that, though, if you haven't already, you will need to take the hardest and most difficult journey of all – the journey through grief

The hardest road of all

A major theme in this book is one of journeying – finding your path to heaven – so I'm now going to discuss perhaps the toughest journey any of us ever take in this lifetime: the loss of a loved one.

Losing someone you love is beyond devastating. The pain is intense. It will feel as if your whole world has stopped and you have no idea how you are going to get through the next hour, let alone the rest of your life. You may wonder how on earth you will be able to survive this. You may be full of regret for not telling that person how much you cared about them when they were alive. However much you trust in heaven and are convinced in the existence of an afterlife, the fact that you can't physically hug them any more hurts intensely.

If you are missing someone you loved deeply, I wish I could say something now to help ease the pain of separation but I can't. All I can say is that loved ones stay alive in our hearts and in time the pain will pass and you will be able to enter into a new relationship with them in spirit. Before that can happen, though, there needs to be an acceptance of their passing. In other words, you need to journey through the pain of grief and come to terms with the physical loss.

I get so many emails, messages and letters from people who are desperate to receive a sign of life from a departed loved one, but all they get is silence. Sometimes a loved one has recently departed and sometimes the death occurred years ago, but either way the pain, confusion and longing for a sign, any sign that will offer comfort, are overwhelming. Sometimes people will ask me if there is a set period of time after death before a sign can be received. Others ask why their loved ones aren't communicating with them.

My heart goes out to everyone who has felt abandoned and alone after the death of a loved one. As I said earlier in the book, when my mother died I felt that I should receive a sign but I got absolutely nothing and the silence tore me apart. I only started to make contact with my mother when something very important happened: I fully experienced my grief.

The world of spirit cannot make contact until you are in the right frame of mind and come to terms with physical loss. To do that you need to mourn, to cry and to grieve. After my mother died, I was so confident that she would send me signs from the afterlife that I didn't grieve. I felt that crying was like a betrayal of my belief in the afterlife. What I needed to understand was that if I didn't grieve fully, emotional wounds would remain unhealed and my spiritual journey would not progress.

Grieving for someone you love does not mean you have no confidence in the existence of an afterlife; it just means you are human and missing physical contact. Before you can reunite in spirit you must mourn this loss, and I often compare it to the darkness before the dawn or the pain of labour before a new birth.

Grief can be very frightening because it unleashes feelings that you never thought you had. You will experience a maelstrom of confusing emotions – not just sadness but also anger at being left alone or at the universe for taking someone you loved; guilt for not saying or doing all you wanted before the loved one died; helplessness because there is no going back and changing things; and panic as you don't know how to live life any more. As frightening as these feelings are, remember what you learned in chapter 3: feelings are not good or bad, they are just feelings. It is what you do with your feelings that make them positive or negative. Alongside this you may also experience fatigue, insomnia, stomach upsets and a variety of aches and pains. It is impossible to say how long your journey through grief will last as everybody is different. You have to give yourself the amount of time you need; there are no short cuts and you certainly won't be able simply to get better overnight. Healing a broken heart takes time – and sometimes a lot of time.

The pain of grief can be terrible and sometimes we try to avoid it, deny it or even make light of it, but that is the worst thing you can do. Denying how you feel will not make the pain go away. Sooner or later the emotions will come out. Remember, it is fine to cry and it is fine to feel angry or the need to scream. You aren't losing it. You are reacting to the loss of someone very important to you.

Seeing a counsellor or GP is recommended if you can't open up to family or friends about how you feel. It is very important not to shut yourself off from others when you are grieving. If you had a physical wound you would seek help from a doctor. It is the same with emotional wounds. Let others take care of you, be there for you. And be there for yourself, too. Try as far as possible to eat healthily, exercise gently and get enough sleep. It will help.

If you don't want to take care of yourself because you feel guilty that you are still alive and the person you loved isn't, then let me remind you what I stated earlier. There is nobody else like you on this planet and heaven wants your energy for now to remain on earth. There is still a destiny for you to fulfil and perhaps part of that destiny is to learn to become yourself again. When you love someone you give a part of yourself away to them and this is one of the most inspiring things about love as long as you don't give too much and lose your sense of self in someone else. If too much of your happiness and self-worth is linked to another person this isn't love, this is need. Real love has a spiritual dimension and is the kind of powerful and healing love that can set a spirit free. So when a loved one dies, the gift they give to you is the chance to reclaim the creativity, love and passion you gave away to them. That's why in time, when you have moved through and beyond grief, you will find a strength, purpose and passion within you that you didn't know you had. This will be you rediscovering your true and whole self in spirit and nothing in this life is more healing, reassuring and wonderful than that.

At some point you will emerge from the confusion and tears and feel ready to join life again. Making contact once more with the world around you can give you a sense of purpose. You may feel scared and alone at first, but never forget that heaven is always with you. I have lost people I thought I couldn't live without but, trust me, the pain will eventually fade. I'm not going to lie – it won't completely go away but it will lessen and you will find love, peace, comfort and joy again. You will also enter into a new relationship with your loved one in spirit and you will come to a place where you can remember them without your heart ripping into pieces. You will come to a place where memories are gentle and sweet.

I'm not talking about forgetting or life returning to normal. You can never forget someone you truly loved and things can't ever go back to how they were because loss changes you forever. What you can do, though, once you've journeyed through grief, is take control and decide if you want to live your life in bitterness and sorrow or with an attitude of gratitude and joy for the time you shared together. It is clear what life choice your departed loved one in spirit would like you to take. Think about it – what better way is there to honour the memory of someone you loved than to remember them with feelings of joy?

Waking up

You may not want to hear this now if you are mourning the loss of a loved one but the journey through grief can help you find your path to heaven. If you fully experience your loss, it can open your heart to the world of spirit. After my mother died I went through all the confusing and painful feelings of grief – from denial to bargaining to anger to despair and finally acceptance – but at the end of my long journey the feeling that eventually silenced all the rest was love. I just knew that the love I had for my mother and the love she had for me was still very much alive. That love had conquered death.

The shock of my mother's death opened a spiritual door for me. My life transformed forever. I still had and have a lot to learn, but today I look back at her death and it was a turning point spiritually for me – the moment light started to creep in. There are some rare individuals who seem to be born with a strong connection to heaven and the ability to see spirit but I'm not one of them. I think there are many people out there like me who have been brought closer to the light through suffering, loss and difficulty.

Perhaps you are mourning the loss of a loved one. Perhaps you are experiencing a personal crisis, such as a job loss, relationship ending or divorce. Perhaps you are going through an emotional crisis, such as depression or addiction. Or perhaps a physical crisis, such as a bout of illness, which has forced you to confront your mortality and re-evaluate what really matters in your life. Or perhaps it is something less distressing, like a stunning coincidence or a night vision, or a profound insight that just seemed to come out of nowhere. Or perhaps this book has served as a catalyst. Or perhaps you have simply come to a point in your life when you know deep down that this world is not all that there is.

The turning point or catalyst will be different for everyone but, whatever it is, the hallmark of spiritual growth is a re-evaluation of everything you thought you ever knew. At times this can feel deeply confusing and uncomfortable, but if you treat yourself and others with love, kindness and respect, and continue to open your mind and heart to the very real and very beautiful idea that heaven exists, you are on the right path – lighting up the way ahead for others to follow.

Heaven is calling your name.

Your true purpose now is to listen and let it guide you through this life and the next.

My gift to you

When grief is intense or times are hard or suffering seems insurmountable, we all need a boost occasionally. I hope this whole book will give you one big boost and be a constant source of guidance and inspiration on your spiritual path, but perhaps this final section will offer some extra guidance, inspiration and comfort.

Sometimes in my life I have stumbled across profound and thought-provoking quotes, and the divine insights they contain have clearly spoken to my heart or given me a much-needed comfort boost and shift in perspective on my spiritual quest. So, as my parting gift to you I decided to gather as many of them together as space would allow. Dip into them anytime you need reassurance that heaven is real and can be found right here and right now. You may also want to share them with someone you feel is in need of comfort or guidance.

Words, if chosen wisely and read with an open heart and mind, can truly change lives. I will let the heavenly wisdom that follows – loosely arranged according to certain themes touched on in this book – speak for itself. I hope something in here helps you find your path to heaven.

Finding heaven

The divine is not something high above us. It is in heaven, it is in earth, it is inside us.

Morihei Ueshiba

You cannot walk on a way made by others for you. You have to walk, and make your road by walking.

Osho

You cannot travel on the path until you become the path itself.

Buddha

Can you tell a plain man the road to heaven? Certainly, turn at once to the right, then go straight forward.

William Wilberforce

Of all the music that reached farthest into heaven, it is the beating of a loving heart.

Henry Ward Beecher

Aim at heaven and you will get earth thrown in. Aim at earth and you will get neither.

C.S. Lewis

The spiritual journey does not consist in arriving at a new destination where a person gains what he did not have, or becomes what he is not. It consists in the dissipation of one's own ignorance concerning one's self and life, and the gradual growth of that understanding, which begins the spiritual awakening. The finding of God is a coming to one's self.

Aldous Huxley

Heaven is under our feet as well as over our heads.

Henry Thoreau

The power of doubt

Never fear shadows – they always mean there is light shining somewhere.

Jonathan Santos

The truth is that our finest moments are most likely to occur when we are feeling deeply uncomfortable, unhappy or unfulfilled. For it is only in such moments, propelled by our discomfort, that we are likely to step out of our ruts and start searching for different ways or truer answers.

M. Scott Peck

Some plants grow quickly, some slowly, but the real miracle is that they grow. Within our growing is a miracle, too.

Karen Goldsmith

Belief is borrowed. Trust is yours . . . Doubt and go on doubting until you come to a point that you cannot doubt anymore. And you cannot doubt anymore when you have come to know something on your own.

Osho

What lies behind us and what lies before us are tiny matters compared to what lies within us.

Henry Haskins

People who are crazy enough to think they can change the world are the ones who do.

Steve Jobs

The man who removes a mountain begins by carrying away small stones.

Ron Goodman

When one door of happiness closes, another opens; but often we look so long at the closed door that we do not see the one which has been opened for us.

Helen Keller

Change your thoughts and you change your world.

Norman Vincent Peale

When everything seems to be going against you, remember that the airplane takes off against the wind, not with it.

Henry Ford

Everything you have ever wanted is on the other side of fear.

George Addair

When we finally know we are dying, and all other sentient beings are dying with us, we start to have a burning, almost heartbreaking sense of the fragility and preciousness of each moment and each being, and from this can grow a deep, clear, limitless compassion for all beings.

Sogyal Rinpoche, *The Tibetan Book of Living and Dying*

You can never cross the ocean until you have the courage to lose sight of the shore.

Columbus

When it is dark enough, you can see the stars.

Anon

The power of love

To love is to receive a glimpse of heaven.

Karen Sunde

Spread love wherever you go . . . let no one ever come to you without leaving happier.

Mother Teresa

The way is not in the sky . . . The way is in the heart.

Buddha

It isn't possible to love and part. You will wish that it was. You can transmute love, ignore it, muddle it, but you can never pull it out of you. I know by experience that the poets are right: love is eternal.

E.M. Forster

How wonderful it must be to speak the language of the angels, with no words for hate, a million words for love!

Eileen Elias Freeman

Every time you smile at someone it is an action of love, a gift to that person, a beautiful thing.

Mother Teresa

Love is real. Real is love.

John Lennon

It is only with the heart that one can see rightly: what is essential is invisible to the eye.

Antoine de Saint-Exupéry

The afterlife

Perhaps they are not stars, but rather openings in heaven where the love of our lost ones pours through and shines down upon us to let us know they are happy.

Eskimo quote

We have no evidence whatsoever that the soul perishes with the body.

Mahatma Gandhi

For death begins with life's first breath. And life begins at touch of death.

John Oxenham

Missing someone gets easier every day. Because, even though it is one day further from the last time you saw each other, it is one day closer to the next time you will.

Anon

Have you ever had a dream . . . that you were so sure was real? What if you were unable to wake from that dream, Neo? How would you know the difference between the dream world and the real world?

Morpheus, *The Matrix*

Everything science has taught me – and continues to teach me – strengthens my belief in the continuity of our spiritual existence after death. Nothing disappears without a trace.

Wernher von Braun

End? No, the journey doesn't end here. Death is just another path, one that we all must take. The grey rain-curtain of this world rolls back, and all turns to silver glass, and then you see it . . . White shores, and beyond, a far green country under a swift sunrise.

Gandalf, *The Lord of the Rings*

Death is not extinguishing the light; it is only putting out the lamp because the dawn has come.

Rabindranath Tagore

Heaven – the treasury of everlasting life.

William Shakespeare

Living beautifully

Remembering that I'll be dead soon is the most important tool I've ever encountered to help me make the big choices in life. Because almost everything – all external expectations, all pride, all fear of embarrassment or failure – these things just fall away in the face of death, leaving only what is truly important.

Steve Jobs

Thousands of candles can be lighted from a single candle, and the life of the candle will not be shortened. Happiness never decreases by being shared.

Buddha

Our lives begin to end the day we become silent about things that matter.

Anon

Every major religion has reference to inner guidance in its teachings.

Christine Comstock

There is a difference between knowing the path and walking it . . . I'm trying to free your mind . . . But I can only show you the door. You're the one that has to walk through it.

Morpheus, *The Matrix*

The moment is sacred. I am now ready, willing and able to embrace my inner child.

Louise Hay

Be assured that just as an hour is only part of a day, so life on Earth is only part of eternity.

C.L. Allen

Beauty is not in the face; beauty is a light in the heart.

Kahlil Gibran

The secret of genius is to carry the spirit of the child into old age, which means never losing your enthusiasm.

Aldous Huxley

I give myself permission to let go.

Louise Hay

At any moment, you have a choice that leads you closer to your spirit or further away from it.

Thich Nhat Hanh

The secret of health for both mind and body is not to mourn for the past, not to worry about the future, or not to anticipate troubles, but to live in the present moment wisely and earnestly.

Buddha

You never know when it is going to happen – when you will experience a moment that dramatically transforms your life. When you look back, often years later, you may see how a brief conversation or an insight you read in a book changed the entire course of your life.

Gay Hendricks

You will not be in heaven two seconds before you cry out, Why did I place so much importance on things that were temporary?

Rick Warren

It certainly seems like a good idea to talk about Heaven, meditate about Heaven and read about Heaven, because, after all, that's where we're going to spend eternity.

David Brandt Berg

The most beautiful thing we can experience is the mysterious. It is the source of all true art and all science. He to whom this emotion is a stranger, who can no longer pause to wonder and stand rapt in awe, is as good as dead: his eyes are closed.

Albert Einstein

Just as a candle cannot burn without fire . . . man cannot live without a spiritual life.

Buddha

As you awaken to your divine nature, you will begin to appreciate beauty in everything you see, touch and experience.

Wayne Dyer

If you want to awaken all of humanity, then awaken all of yourself. If you want to eliminate the suffering in the world, then eliminate all that is dark and negative in yourself. Truly, the greatest gift you have to give is that of your own self-transformation.

Lao-Tzu

You have reached your destination!

Within you lies the seed of heaven.

All along without realising it you have carried within you the questions and answers you need. Your entire journey through this life is an incredible voyage of spiritual self-discovery. In the immortal words of T.S. Eliot, you arrive where you began.

> *We shall not cease from exploration*
> *And the end of all our exploring*
> *Will be to arrive where we started*
> *And know the place for the first time.*

Your true self can never been found on the surface of life. Look deep inside yourself for the adorable, beautiful, joyful, innocent, compassionate, loving, spontaneous and most magical part of you. Love that part of you because it is a spark of heaven – just waiting to catch fire and set you alight. The trigger could be anything, it could be a word, a thought, an event, an action, a feeling, a sound, a text, a hug, a look, a miracle, a spirit, a vision or nothing at all but astonishing silence. There is no science to it but the potential is always there. Any day, any moment, heaven can erupt within you and you can be spiritually reborn.

That moment could even be now . . .

There really is nothing stopping you from finding heaven on earth right now or connecting with departed loved ones in spirit at any moment. Heaven has never been far away. It has been there all the time within you, sending you divine messages – you just haven't noticed or heard. But when you open your mind, heart, eyes and ears to the divine guidance, inspiration, comfort, love and joy that is your birthright, your destiny, heaven will be yours. You will be on your path and there will be no going back.

The fact that you have this book in your hands is a clear sign that heaven is seeking you out, whispering your name. Not you finding heaven, but heaven finding you! There are billions of books to choose from in today's overcrowded publishing market but you were drawn to this one. Why? Trust me, you are reading it for a reason. And that reason is to help you rediscover the abundance of love, truth and joy that exists within you so that your spirit can grow wings and soar with the music and magic of everything that is blissful and enchantingly beautiful in this life and the next.

So that you can say with complete conviction and total trust: 'Now I have found heaven.'

Calling all truth-seekers

Last, but by no means least, if at any point when reading this book you felt confused or have a story or insight you would like to share with a wider audience in my future books, or have a burning question you need answered or want to discuss further, please don't hesitate to get in touch with me.

You can contact me via my website www.theresacheung. co.uk and my email angeltalk710@aol.com. I would be honoured to hear from you and will answer every question or discuss any issue personally. Sometimes I get so many letters and emails that it may take a month or two before I reply, but I will do so as soon as I can. Alternatively, for a more immediate response, you may want to meet fellow truth-seekers via my Facebook page or keep right up to date by following me on Twitter. And if you prefer writing letters, you can contact me care of: Simon & Schuster, 1st Floor, 222 Gray's Inn Road, London WC1X 8HB.

Please don't feel alone in your quest for the truth. I truly welcome all your thoughts, questions and stories. Communicating with you is the thing I love most about writing books that explore the reality of heaven.

Final word

Dr Wernher von Braun, well known for his part in pioneering the US space program, said that he had 'essentially scientific' reasons for believing in life after death. He explained: 'Science has found that nothing can disappear without a trace. Nature does not know extinction. All it knows is transformation. If God applies the fundamental principle to the most minute and insignificant parts of the universe, doesn't it make sense to assume that He applies it to the masterpiece of His creation – the human soul? I think it does.'

Dr Wernher von Braun

The conclusion is always the same: love is the most powerful and still the most unknown energy in the world.

Pierre Teilhard de Chardin